A Timeless Faith

John Wesley for the 21st Century

A Timeless Faith

John Wesley for the 21st Century

Edited by Stephen Gibson

Evangel Publishing House
Nappanee, Indiana 46550

A Timeless Faith: John Wesley for the 21st Century

Requests for information should be addressed to:
Evangel Publishing House
2000 Evangel Way
P.O. Box 189
Nappanee, Indiana 46550
Phone: (800) 253-9315
Internet: www.evangelpublishing.com

Edited by Mark Garrett
Cover Design by Matthew R. Gable

ISBN-10: 1-928915-88-4
ISBN-13: 978-1-928915-88-1
Library of Congress Catalog Card Number: 2006927320

Printed in the United States of America

5 6 7 8 9 EP 8 7 6 5 4 3 2

Table of Contents

Preface

Grace, Faith, and Christian Experience

Christian Unity

Practical Issues

The Moral Law of God

Critique of Calvinism

Prefacc

Why a New English Edition?

Language evolves. Terms change in meaning or drop from use entirely, while new terms take their place. Because of this process, all writings gradually become more difficult to understand. Because of the extra effort necessary for a reader to understand older books, those books will be opened less and less frequently, until they are practically forgotten.

Many Christians who hold to the doctrinal distinctives of John Wesley have never read a page of his writings. His sermons are in danger of joining the collection of antiquated writings that only scholars read. The purpose of this volume is to call today's followers of Wesley to rediscover and reaffirm the scriptural, rational, and experiential basis of their theology as expressed by Wesley himself.

The selected writings include Wesley's views on essential doctrines, his distinctive views of Christian perfection, and practical consideration of such areas as the unity of all believers, fanaticism, and Christian standards of dress and behavior. Some sections show Wesley in debate with other Christian traditions, including Roman Catholicism and Calvinism.

These writings were edited for conciseness and readability. Archaic expressions were replaced with modern terms, and sentences or paragraphs that were not essential were deleted or shortened. Section headings were added in some places to make the flow of thought easier to follow. As much as possible, Wesley's style was preserved. In no case was a change made for the purpose of correcting Wesley's opinions or to make a statement express a meaning or emphasis other than he intended.

Introduction to John Wesley

John Wesley was born into the home of an Anglican pastor in 1703, but did not understand the doctrine of justification by faith or find personal assurance of justification until 1738, after he had graduated from Oxford and had preached for several years. He observed that Scripture describes a personal, conscious faith as the basis for personal assurance, but said he would not believe that it is for all Christians unless he could meet living witnesses. He soon met living witnesses among the Moravians, who emphasized that genuine religion is internal and heart-felt. Soon after this meeting, as Wesley was with a group of friends listening to a reading of Luther's preface to the book of Romans, he was enabled to put his faith in Christ alone for salvation. He said that his heart was "strangely warmed," and he was conscious that his sins were forgiven. From that day on, he understood and preached the gospel of justification by faith.

Wesley's pattern for life expressed his principle of total stewardship: "Do all the good you can, by all the means you can, in all the ways you can, in all the places you can, at all the times you can, to all the people you can, as long as ever you can." Besides graduating from Oxford with a Master's degree, Wesley learned at least seven languages and read approximately 100 books every year. He rode 250,000 miles on horseback, equivalent to riding around the world ten times. It has been estimated that he preached 40,000 times. He often preached outside to crowds of more than 10,000. He frequently preached three times a day, and refused to let weather conditions affect his schedule. At age 72 he wrote in his diary that his health was better than it had been at age 40. He said the improvement was due to always rising at 4:00, preaching at 5:00 ("the best exercise"), and traveling 4,500 miles per year. Among other international trips, Wesley visited Ireland 42 times and Scotland 22 times.

In the course of his ministry, Wesley was attacked many times by mobs, and was known to have had to swim across a pond to escape. However, he seemed to have a special ability to turn leaders of mobs in his favor and quell the resistance. He described special protection that God gave him at times, when bricks and other objects being thrown fell all around him without striking him.

Wesley was often criticized by the religious world for his doctrine of Christian perfection. Much of this criticism was based on misunderstanding. Wesley defined Christian perfection as love for God and man ruling all of one's motives, words, and actions. If he seemed unconventional in this doctrine, it was simply because he took it further than those who only nominally affirmed it. Wesley expected that the believer could, by grace received through faith, actually meet God's requirement of Christian perfection.

Much of Wesley's long-term effectiveness was due to his organization of the Methodists into small groups. He first began this practice while he served as a missionary in Georgia, then a British colony. When he returned to Oxford, he joined a group of faculty and students who met regularly to study, cooperate in ministry, and attempt to live scriptural Christianity. Members of this group were the first to be called "Methodists," when observers used this name to deride their strict methods of self-discipline. Throughout Wesley's ministry, every Methodist was a member of a local society. These societies were further divided into classes so that leaders could hold members accountable for their spirituality and behavior. Other special groups called bands were organized to help members who were seeking greater spirituality or more complete spiritual victory. The members of the classes and bands provided accountability and edification for one another that was not available through any other means.

Wesley has been called "The Father of the Religious Paperback," because he produced 5,000 various writings for common people. He said his purpose was to provide plain truth for plain people. He published a 50-volume set of writings from Pietists, Puritans, Anglicans, and church fathers, which he edited extensively. He also published a magazine called *The Arminian*.

Wesley used the profits from his writings to relieve poverty. He lived on 28 pounds a year and used all else for ministry. Much of his preaching of plain dress and frugal living was in the context of a country where many were suffering in poverty.

At Wesley's death in 1791, there were 79,000 Methodists in England and 40,000 in America.

There are modern movements who still hold to the distinctives of Wesley, but they are not necessarily the denominations that have the term *Methodist* in their name. Many of these now have little in common with Wesley. Wesley is represented today by an assortment of denominations, schools, and individual churches that still adhere to his doctrines and apply the same principles to standards of Christian living.

Wesley's Theological Roots

Like the Reformers, Wesley believed in the supreme authority of Scripture. Like Anglican thinkers such as Hooker, Wesley believed that reason, tradition, and experience together make a balanced approach to interpreting the Bible.

Like Roman Catholics, Wesley believed that the tradition of the early church fathers was a valuable aid to understanding the Bible. By early Eastern Christian writers, Wesley was influenced to see a process involved in reaching Christian perfection.

Wesley's theology resolved the Augustinian-Pelagian debate. Like Augustine and Calvin, he believed in the seriousness of inherited depravity and the utter helplessness of man to choose right apart from God's grace; but, in contrast, he believed that God's prevenient grace reaches every person, enabling free will and the desire to obey God. He said that if a person is lost, it is not because he has no grace but because he does not use the grace he has. Like Arminius, Wesley believed that the origin of sin is in the misuse of free will, permitted but not decreed by the sovereignty of God.

Wesley was interested in Christian mystics because of their emphasis on genuine religious experience and inward religion and holiness. However, he was concerned about their tendency to withdraw from the world, their criticism of any means of grace (ways in which believers may prepare themselves to receive God's grace), and their neglect of works of service to others. He called mysticism the rock on which he almost made shipwreck.

Pietism influenced Wesley strongly, especially through the Moravians. It was through them that he was led to believe in a divine assurance of personal salvation. He considered Herrnhut a model Christian community. Their influence may also be seen in his tolerance of differences and emphasis on unity arising from the basis of inward, genuine faith and commitment. However, he criticized their underemphasis of the sacraments and their view of completed holiness at justification, which practically excluded all expectation of growth.

Wesley never tried to be an original theologian. He insisted that anything essentially new in religion is essentially false. He sought always to speak as the Scripture speaks, and to apply his doctrines to real Christian experience. It is because of this carefulness that his work has lasting value, and his voice should be heard again in this generation.

1

Justification by Faith

"To him that worketh not, but believeth on Him that justifieth the ungodly, his faith is counted for righteousness."
Romans 4:5.

How a sinner may be justified before God is a question of importance to every man, for there can be no true peace or secure joy while we are enemies of God, either in time or in eternity. Yet how little has this important question been understood! What confused ideas many have had about it!

In order to do justice to the vast importance of the subject, I will try to show: first, what the basis of the doctrine of justification is; second, what justification is; third, who the justified are; and fourth, on what terms they are justified.

I. What Is the Basis of the Doctrine of Justification?

Man was made in the image of God, holy as He that created him is holy. As God is love, so man, living in love, lived in God, and God in him. He was pure, as God is pure, from every spot of sin. He knew no evil, but was inwardly and outwardly sinless. He "loved the Lord his God with all his heart, and with all his mind, and soul, and strength."

To this upright and perfect man, God gave a perfect law, to which He required perfect obedience. No allowance was made for falling short, for man was equal to the task.

To the law of love written in man's heart, God added a law: "Thou shalt not eat of the fruit of the tree in the midst of the garden;" connecting to it the penalty, "In the day that thou eatest thereof, thou shalt surely die."

This was the state of man in Paradise. By the free love of God, he was holy and happy: He knew, loved, and enjoyed God. He was to continue in this life of love forever, if he continued to obey God in all things; but, if he disobeyed, he was to forfeit all of it. "In that day," said God, "thou shalt surely die."

Man did disobey God. He ate of the tree which God had forbidden. In that day he was condemned by the righteous judgment of God. The penalty of which he was warned began to occur. The moment he tasted that fruit, he died. His soul died and was separated from God, without whom the soul has no life. Likewise his body became mortal, so that death took hold of it. And being dead in spirit, dead to God, dead in sin, he rushed on toward eternal death; to the destruction both of body and soul in the fire which is never to be quenched.

Therefore "by one man sin entered into the world, and death by sin. And so death passed upon all men," through him who was the father and representative of us all. Therefore, all are dead, dead to God, dead in sin, living in a mortal body soon to disintegrate, and under the penalty of eternal death. For as, "by one man's disobedience," all "were made sinners;" so, "judgment came upon all men to condemnation" (Romans 5:19, etc.).

We were in this state along with all of mankind, when "God so loved the world, that He gave His only begotten Son, that we might not perish, but have everlasting life." He was made Man, another Head of mankind, a second Representative of the whole human race. As such "He bore our griefs," "the Lord laying upon Him the iniquities of us all." He was "wounded for our transgressions, and bruised for our iniquities." "He made His soul an offering for sin:" He poured out His blood for sinners. He has redeemed me and all mankind; having made a full, perfect, and sufficient sacrifice and satisfaction for the sins of the whole world.

Because the Son of God has "tasted death for every man," God has now "reconciled the world to himself, not imputing to them their" former "trespasses." And so, "as by the offense of one, judgment came upon all men to condemnation, even so by the righteousness of one, the free gift came upon all men unto justification." So that, for the sake of His Son's suffering for us, God now guarantees, on only one condition (which He also enables us to meet), to cancel the punishment due for our sins, to reinstate us in His favor, and to restore our dead souls to spiritual life, giving us the assurance of eternal life.

This is the basis of the whole doctrine of justification. By the sin of the first Adam, who was not only the father, but also the representative of us all, we all fell from God's favor; as the Apostle expresses it, "judgment came upon all men to condemnation." Yet, by the sacrifice for sin made by the Second Adam, as the Representative of us all, God is so far reconciled to all the world, that He has given them a new covenant. And when its condition is fulfilled, "there is no more condemnation," but "we are justified freely by His grace, through the redemption that is in Jesus Christ."

II. What Is Justification?

It is evident that justification is not being made actually just and righteous. This is sanctification; which is to some extent the direct result of justification, but nevertheless a gift of God distinct from it. The one implies what God does for us through His Son; the other, what He works in us by His Spirit. Although some rare instances may be found where the term *justification* is used in a sense which includes sanctification, ordinarily the two terms are distinguished from one another in Scripture.

Least of all does justification imply that God is deceived in those whom He justifies; that He thinks them to be what they are not; or that He counts them to be otherwise than they actually are. It does not imply that God judges us contrary to reality; that He considers us to be better than we really are, or believes us to be righteous when we are unrighteous. Certainly not. The judgment of God is always according to truth. It can never be consistent with His unerring wisdom to think that I am innocent, to judge that I am righteous or holy, just because someone else is. In this way, he can no more confuse me with Christ than with David or Abraham. Let anyone, to whom God has given understanding, consider this without prejudice; and he will see that this idea of justification is not consistent with reason or Scripture.

The plain scriptural concept of justification is the forgiveness of sins. It is that act of God the Father by which, for the sake of the propitiation made by the blood of His Son, He "showeth forth His righteousness (or mercy) by the remission of the sins that are past." This is the natural explanation of it given by St. Paul throughout this whole epistle. He explains it himself, both in this chapter and in the one following. "Blessed are they," he says in the next verses, "whose iniquities are forgiven, and whose sins are covered: Blessed is the man to whom the Lord will not impute sin." To him that is justified or forgiven, God "will not impute sin" to his condemnation. All his past sins, in thought, word, and deed, are covered, are blotted out, and will no longer be remembered against him. God will not inflict on that sinner what he deserved to suffer, because the Son has suffered for him. From the time we are "reconciled to God," He loves, blesses, and watches over us, even as if we had never sinned.

III. Who Is Justified?

Then who are the ones that are justified? The Apostle tells us specifically, the ungodly. He justifies the ungodly alone. It is only sinners that need pardon: It is sin alone which can be forgiven. Forgiveness, then, refers to sin, and to nothing else. It is our iniquity which he "remembers no more."

This seems to be ignored by those who argue that a man must be holy before he can be justified. The idea is impossible, for where there is no love for God there is no holiness, and there is no love for God except that which comes from a sense of His love for us. It is not a saint but a sinner that is forgiven, even while considered a sinner. God does not justify those that are holy already, but unholy. On what condition He does this will be considered shortly. But whatever it is, it cannot be holiness. To assert this is to say that the Lamb of God takes away only those sins which were taken away already.

The sinner's heart is inevitably, essentially evil, until the love of God is poured out there. And while the tree is corrupt, so are the fruits; "for an evil tree cannot bring forth good fruit." If the objection is raised, "But a man, before he is justified, may feed the hungry, or clothe the naked; and these are good works;" the answer is easy: he may do these even before he is justified; and these are, in one sense, "good works;" they are beneficial to men. But they are not necessarily good in themselves, or good in the sight of God. All truly good works follow justification; and are good and "acceptable to God in Christ" because they come from a true and living faith.

Perhaps those who doubt this have not properly considered

the reason given here as to why no works done before justification can be truly good. The reasoning is this: no works are good, which are not done as God has commanded them: but no works done before justification are done as God has commanded them to be done: therefore, no works done before justification are good. The first proposition is obviously true; and the second, that no works done before justification are done as God has commanded them to be done, will appear equally obvious. We need only to consider that God has commanded that all our works be done in love, in that love to God which produces love to all mankind. But none of our works can be done in this love while the love of the Father is not in us; and this love cannot be in us until we receive the "Spirit of adoption, crying in our hearts, Abba, Father." If, therefore, God does not justify the ungodly, and him that (in this sense) "worketh not," then no person can be justified.

IV. On What Terms Is One Justified?

On what terms, then, is one justified? On one alone, which is faith. "He that believes is not condemned." "For the righteousness (or mercy) of God is by faith of Jesus Christ unto all and upon all them that believe: — Whom God has set forth for a propitiation, through faith in His blood; that He might be just, and" (consistently with His justice) "the Justifier of him that believes in Jesus:" "Therefore we conclude that a man is justified by faith without the works of the law;" without previous obedience to the moral law, which he could not perform until now. We know that St. Paul refers to the moral law here because he says, "Do we then make void the law through faith? God forbid: Yea, we establish the law." What law do we establish by faith? Not the ceremonial law of Moses. Instead, the great, unchangeable law of love, the holy love for God and our neighbor.

Faith, in general, is a divine, supernatural evidence or conviction "of things not seen," not discoverable by our bodily senses.

Justifying faith implies not only a divine conviction that "God was in Christ, reconciling the world unto himself;" but a sure confidence that Christ died for my sins, that He loved me, and gave himself for me. At whatever time a sinner believes in this way, God justifies that ungodly one. God, for the sake of His Son, pardons him who had in him, until then, no good thing. God had given him repentance before; but that repentance was neither more nor less than a deep sense of the lack of all good, and the presence of all evil. And whatever good he has or does from that hour when he first believes in God through Christ, faith brings. This is the fruit of faith. First the tree is good, and then the fruit is good also.

But we must be careful that we do not stop walking with God because of a wavering faith. Peter, coming to Christ on the water, was in danger of drowning because he failed to trust. So we, if we begin to doubt, may sink into the bottomless pit of hell-fire. Therefore, have a definite faith, not only that the death of Christ is available for all the world, but that He has made a full and sufficient sacrifice for you, a perfect cleansing of your sins, so that you may say that Christ loved you, and gave himself for you. This is to make Christ your own and to apply His merits to yourself.

By affirming that this faith is the condition of justification, I mean, first, that there is no justification without it. "He that believeth not is condemned already;" and as long as he does not believe, that condemnation cannot be removed, but "the wrath of God abides on him." Just as "there is no other name given under heaven," other than Jesus, no other merit by which a condemned sinner can ever be saved from the guilt of sin; so also there is no other way of obtaining a share in His merit than by faith in His name. Whatever virtues (so called) a man may have, whatever good works (so called) he may do, they are of no benefit; for he is still a child of wrath until he believes in Jesus.

Faith, therefore, is the only necessary condition. This is the second point to be observed; that the very moment God gives faith (for it is the gift of God) to the "ungodly" that "worketh not," that "faith is counted to him for righteousness." He has no righteousness at all before this, not even negative righteousness, or innocence. But "faith is imputed to him for righteousness," the very moment he believes. It is not that God thinks him to be what he is not. Rather, as "He made Christ to be sin for us," that is, treated Him as a sinner, punishing Him for our sins; so He counts us righteous, from the time we believe in Him: that is, He does not punish us for our sins; He treats us as though we were guiltless and righteous.

Surely any difficulty in accepting this doctrine, that "faith is the only condition of justification," must come from not understanding it. We mean this, that it is the only thing without which no one is justified; the only thing that is absolutely necessary for pardon. If a man has everything else without faith, he still cannot be justified; but, if he lacks everything else and yet has faith, he must be justified. Suppose that a sinner of any kind, in a full sense of his total ungodliness, of his utter inability to think, speak, or do good, and his absolute fitness for hell-fire; throws himself completely on the mercy of God in Christ (which he cannot do but by the grace of God). Who can doubt that he is forgiven in that moment? Who will say that any more is necessary before that sinner can be justified? Now, if there ever were one such instance (and have there not been millions?), it clearly follows that faith is, in the above sense, the only condition of justification.

It is not proper for poor, guilty, sinful worms, who receive whatever blessings they enjoy from grace, out of mere favor, to ask God the reasons for His conduct. It is not proper for us to call Him into question asking, "Why did You make faith the only condition of justification? Why did You decree, 'He that believeth, and he only, shall be saved'?" However, we may humbly imagine that one reason God set this condition of justification was to take pride from man. It was to a great extent because of man's temptation to pride, when the tempter said, "Ye shall be as gods," that Adam fell, and brought sin and death into the world. It was an example of wisdom worthy of God, to set a condition of reconciliation for Adam and his descendants which would effectively humble them. Such is faith. For he that comes to God by this faith must come as a mere sinner, inwardly and outwardly, self-destroyed and self-condemned, bringing nothing to God but ungodliness, offering nothing of his own but sin and misery. So it is that he can look to Jesus as the whole and only propitiation for his sins. Only in this way can he receive the "righteousness which is of God by faith."

You ungodly one, who hears or reads these words! You vile, helpless, miserable sinner! I charge you before God, the Judge of all, go straight to Him, with all your ungodliness. Be careful that you do not destroy your own soul by claiming any righteousness of your own. Go as completely ungodly, guilty, lost, destroyed, deserving and dropping into hell; and then you will find favor in His sight, and know that He justifies the ungodly. As such you will be brought to the blood of sprinkling, as a helpless, damned sinner. Look to Jesus! There is the Lamb of God, who takes away your sins! Claim no works, no righteousness of your own! That would be to deny the Lord that bought you. Claim only the blood, the ransom paid for your proud, stubborn, sinful soul. Who are you, that now sees and feels both your inward and outward ungodliness? You are the one! I challenge you to be a child of God by faith! You who feel you are perfectly fit for hell are perfectly fit to advance His glory; the glory of His free grace, justifying the ungodly and him that "worketh not." Come quickly! Believe in the Lord Jesus; and you, even you, will be reconciled.

2

The Great Privilege of Those That Are Born of God

"Whosoever is born of God doth not commit sin."
1 John 3:9.

Although justification and the new birth occur simultaneously, they are distinguished, as things of a completely different nature. God, in justifying us, does something for us; in giving birth to us again, He does a work in us. The one restores us to the favor of God, the other to the image of God. The one takes away the guilt, the other takes away the power of sin. So although they occur in the same moment, they are distinguishable.

Not understanding the difference between being justified and being born again has caused confusion for many, especially when they have tried to explain this great privilege of the children of God; when trying to explain how "whosoever is born of God does not commit sin."

In order to understand this, let us, first, consider the meaning of the expression, "Whosoever is born of God;" and second, consider in what sense he "does not commit sin."

First, let us consider the meaning of the expression, "Whosoever is born of God." In general, from the passages of Scripture where this expression, "the being born of God," occurs, we may learn that it does not imply baptism, or any outward change. Instead, it is a vast inward change, a change made in the soul by the work of the Holy Spirit, which results in our living in a very different manner than we did before. We are, it seems, in another world.

The reason for the expression is easy to understand. When we go through this great change, we may properly be said to be born again, because there is a close resemblance between the natural and the spiritual birth; so that to consider the circumstances of the natural birth is the easiest way to understand the spiritual.

The child's ignorance of the natural world that he lives in before his birth could be compared to the state of one not yet born again spiritually. Before the spiritual birth, although one is sustained by Him in whom all "live, and move, and have their being," he does not feel; he has no inward consciousness of God's presence. He does not perceive that divine breath of life, without which he cannot live a moment. God is continually calling to him, but he does not hear; his ears are shut. It is true that he may have some faint dawnings of life, some small beginnings of spiritual motion, yet he has no spiritual senses capable of discerning spiritual objects; consequently, he "discerns not the things of the Spirit of God; he cannot know them, because they are spiritually discerned."

Therefore he has hardly any knowledge of the invisible

world, just as he has hardly any interaction with it. Not that it is far off. No, the other world, as we usually call it, is not far from every one of us. It is above, and beneath, and on every side. But the natural man does not discern it; partly because he has no spiritual senses, by which he could discern the things of God, and partly because a veil hangs between that is so thick he does not know how to penetrate it.

But when he is born of God, born of the Spirit, his manner of existence is greatly changed! His whole soul is now conscious of God, and he can say, "Thou art about my bed, and about my path;" I feel You in all my ways. The Spirit or breath of God is breathed into the newborn soul; and the same breath which comes from God is returned to God. As it is continually received by faith, so it is continually returned by love, by prayer, and praise, and thanksgiving; for these make up the breath of every soul that is truly born of God. By this spiritual respiration, spiritual life is sustained and increased day by day, all the senses of the soul being awake, and capable of discerning spiritual good and evil.

"The eyes of his understanding" are now "open," and he "sees Him that is invisible." He sees "the exceeding greatness of His power" and of His love towards those who believe. He sees that God is merciful to him, a sinner, and that he is reconciled through the Son. He clearly perceives both the pardoning love of God, and His "great and precious promises." "God, who commanded the light to shine out of darkness, has shined in his heart," to enlighten him with "the knowledge of the glory of God in the face of Jesus Christ." All the darkness is gone, and he lives in the light of God's favor.

Having considered the meaning of the expression, "Whosoever is born of God," we now consider in what sense he "does not commit sin." As long as one who is born of God continually receives into his soul the breath of life from God, continually breathing it back in unceasing love, praise, and prayer, he not only does not commit sin while he keeps himself in this way, but as long as this "seed remains in him, he cannot sin."

By sin, I refer here to outward sin, according to the common use of the word: a voluntary transgression of the revealed, written law of God; of any commandment of God, known to be such at the time that it is transgressed. "Whoever is born of God," while he lives in faith and love, and in the spirit of prayer and thanksgiving, not only does not, but cannot, commit sin in this way. As long as he believes in God through Christ, and loves Him, and is pouring out his heart before Him, he cannot voluntarily transgress any command of God, either by saying or doing what he knows God has forbidden. That seed which remains in him, that loving, praying, thankful faith, compels him to avoid anything he knows to be offensive to God.

But here a difficulty arises, one that has appeared unsolvable to many, and has caused them to deny the clear statement of the Apostle, and give up the privilege of the children of God. The difficulty is that some of those who have been truly born of God (the Spirit of God having given us this testimony of them in His Word), did commit extreme, outward sin. They violated the clearly-stated, known laws of God, saying or doing what they knew He had forbidden.

I answer, what has been long observed is this: so long as "he that is born of God keepeth himself," (which he is able to do by the grace of God) "the wicked one touches him not:" But if he does not keep himself, if he does not stay in the faith, he may commit sin as any other man. Therefore, it is easy to understand how any child of God might waver in his own steadfastness, while the great truth of God, declared by the Apostle, remains uncontradicted. He did not "keep himself" by that grace of God which was sufficient for him. He fell step by step: first, into negative inward sin, by not "stirring up the gift of God which was in him," by not "watching unto prayer," by not "pressing on to the mark of the prize of his high calling;" then he fell into positive inward sin, by inclining to the wickedness in his heart, by yielding to some evil desire or attitude; next he lost his faith, his sight of a pardoning God, and, consequently, his love for God; and, being weak, he was then capable of committing even outward sin.

You see the definite progress from grace to sin. So it goes, from step to step:

(1) At first the divine seed of loving, conquering faith remains in him that is born of God. "He keeps himself," by the grace of God, and "cannot commit sin."
(2) A temptation arises; whether from the world, the flesh, or the devil, it does not matter.
(3) The Spirit of God warns him that sin is near, and directs him to watch in prayer.
(4) He turns his attention to the temptation, which now becomes pleasing to him.
(5) The Holy Spirit is grieved; his faith is weakened; and his love for God grows cold.
(6) The Spirit corrects him more sharply, saying, "This is the way; walk in it."
(7) He turns away from the painful voice of God, and listens to the pleasing voice of the tempter.
(8) Evil desire begins and spreads in his soul until faith and love vanish. He is then capable of committing outward sin, the power of the Lord having left him.

From the preceding considerations we may learn, first, to give a clear answer to a question which has perplexed many, "Does sin precede or follow the loss of faith? Does a child of God first commit sin, and, as a result, lose his faith? Or does he lose his faith first, before he can commit sin?"

I answer that some inward sin, at least some sin of omission, must precede the loss of faith. But the loss of faith must precede the committing of outward sin. The more any believer examines his own heart, the more he will be convinced of this. Faith working by love prevents both inward and outward sin from a soul watching in prayer; however, even then we are liable to temptation, especially when it pertains to the sin that previously defeated us. If the loving eye of the soul is focused on God, the temptation soon vanishes. If not, if we are (as in James 1:14) drawn out of God by our own desire, and caught by the bait of desired pleasures; then that desire, which is conceived in us, gives birth to sin; and, having destroyed our faith by that inward sin, we are then able to commit any outward sin.

We also see that the life of God in the soul of a believer implies the continual inspiration of God's Holy Spirit; God's breathing into the soul, and the soul's breathing back what it receives from God; a continual action of God on the soul, and a reaction of the soul toward God; an unceasing presence of God, the loving, pardoning God, shown to the heart, and perceived by faith; and an unceasing return of love, praise, and prayer, offering up all our thoughts, words, and works, all our body, soul, and spirit, to be a holy sacrifice, acceptable to God in Christ Jesus.

Therefore we can see the absolute necessity of this response of the soul, in order for divine life to continue there. For God does not continue to act on the soul unless the soul responds to Him. He first gives us the blessings of His goodness. He first loves us, and shows himself to us. But if we do not then love Him who first loved us; if we will not listen to His voice; if we turn our eyes away from Him, and will not give attention to the light He pours in on us; His Spirit will not always remain: He will gradually withdraw, and leave us to the darkness of our own hearts. He will not continue to breathe into our soul, unless our soul breathes toward Him again; unless our love and prayers and thanksgiving return to Him, a sacrifice with which He is pleased.

Finally, let us learn to follow the direction of the great Apostle, "Be not high-minded, but fear." "Let him that standeth take heed lest he fall." Even he who now stands firmly in the grace of God, in the faith that overcomes the world, may fall into inward sin, and "make shipwreck of his faith." How easily then will outward sin regain its rule over him! Therefore, man of God, always watch; that you may always hear the voice of God! Watch, that you may pray without ceasing, at all times, and in all places, pouring out your heart before Him! Then you will always believe, and always love, and never commit sin.

3

On Sin in Believers

"If any man be in Christ, he is a new creature."
2 Corinthians 5:17.

Is there any sin in those who are born of God, or are they completely delivered from it? This is a point of greatest importance to every serious Christian. I do not know that it was ever debated in the early Church, for all Christians were agreed on it. It seems that all ancient Christians who have left anything in writing declare with one voice that even believers, until they are "strong in the Lord and in the power of His might," must wrestle with an evil nature.

In this the Church of England copies the early church exactly; declaring in her Ninth Article, "Original sin is the corruption of the nature of every man, whereby man is in his own nature inclined to evil, so that the flesh lusteth contrary to the Spirit. And this infection of nature doth remain even in them that are regenerated; whereby the lust of the flesh is not subject to the law of God. And although there is no condemnation for them that believe, yet this lust hath of itself the nature of sin." The same testimony is given by all other churches; not only by the Greek and Roman Churches, but by every Reformed church in Europe, of any denomination. Indeed, some of these seem extreme, describing the corruption of heart in a believer in a way which implies that he is a slave to it, and leaving hardly any distinction between a believer and an unbeliever.

To avoid this extreme, many well-meaning men, particularly the followers of the late Count Zinzendorf, ran to the opposite; affirming that all true believers are not only saved from the dominion of sin, but also from the existence of inward and outward sin, so that it no longer remains in them. And from them, about twenty years ago, many of our countrymen accepted the same opinion that even the corruption of nature no longer exists in those who believe in Christ. It is true that when the Germans were debated, many of them gave up the point; allowing that sin did still remain, though not reign, in one that is born of God. But the English who had received it from them were not so easily persuaded to part with a favorite opinion. Even though most of them were convinced of its error, a few still hold it.

For the sake of those who truly fear God and desire to know the truth, it may be helpful to discuss this question calmly. In this discussion, I use as synonyms the words *regenerate, justified,* or *believers*; since, though they do not have exactly the same meaning (the first implying an inward, actual change, the second a relative one, and the third the means by which both are done), they all come to the same thing; since everyone that believes is both justified and born of God. By sin, I mean inward sin; any sinful temper, passion, or affection: such as pride, self-will, love of the world, in any kind or degree; such as lust, anger, the tendency to take offense; or any disposition which is contrary to the mind which was in Christ. The question is not concerning outward sin; whether a child of God commits sin or not. We all agree, "He that committeth sin is of the devil." We agree, "Whosoever is born of God doth not commit sin." Neither do we now discuss whether inward sin will always remain in the children of God or whether sin will continue in the soul as long as it is in the body. We consider simply this: is a justified man freed from all sin as soon as he is justified? Is there no sin remaining in his heart?

We acknowledge that the state of a justified person is inexpressibly glorious. He is born again, "not of blood, nor of the flesh, nor of the will of man, but of God." He is a child of God, a member of Christ, an heir of the kingdom of heaven. "The peace of God, which passeth all understanding, keepeth his heart and mind in Christ Jesus." His very body is a "temple of the Holy Spirit," and a "dwelling of God through the Spirit." He is "created new in Christ Jesus." He is washed; he is sanctified. His heart is purified by faith. He is cleansed "from the corruption that is in the world." "The love of God is shed abroad in his heart by the Holy Spirit which is given unto him." And as long as he "walks in love" (which he may always do), he worships God in spirit and in truth. He keeps the commandments of God and does those things that are pleasing in His sight; so as to "have a conscience void of offense, both toward God and toward men." He has power over both outward and inward sin from the moment he is justified.

Some say, "But was he not then freed from all sin, so that there is no sin in his heart?" I cannot believe it, because St. Paul says the opposite. He is speaking to believers, and describing the state of believers in general, when he says, "the flesh lusteth against the Spirit, and the Spirit against the flesh: These are contrary one to the other" (Galatians 5:17). The apostle here affirms that the flesh, the evil nature, opposes the Spirit, even in believers; that even in the regenerated there are two principles, "contrary one to the other." Again, when he writes to the believers at Corinth, to those who were sanctified in Christ Jesus (1 Corinthians 1:2), he says, "I, brethren, could not speak unto you, as unto spiritual, but as unto carnal, as unto babes in Christ. . . Ye are yet carnal: For whereas there is among you envying and strife, are ye not carnal?" (3:1–3). Now here the Apostle speaks to those who were unquestionably believers, as still being carnal, to some extent. He affirms that there was envying, which was causing fighting among them, and yet does not give the least indication that they had lost their faith. No, he clearly declares they had not; for then they would not have been babes in Christ. And (what is most remarkable of all) he speaks of being carnal and being babes in Christ as one and the same thing; clearly showing that every believer is to some extent carnal while still a babe in Christ. Indeed, almost all the exhortations of Scripture are based on this supposition; pointing at wrong tempers or practices in those who are acknowledged to be believers. They are continually urged to fight with and conquer these by the power of faith which is in them.

Again, when the Apostle calls believers to "cleanse themselves from all filthiness of flesh and spirit" (2 Corinthians 7:1), he clearly teaches that those believers were not yet cleansed from them. Will you answer, "He that keeps from every appearance of evil, in reality cleanses himself from all filthiness?" This is not true at all. For instance, when a man treats me hatefully I feel resentment, which is filthiness of spirit; yet I do not say a word. Here I "keep from every appearance of evil;" but this does not cleanse me from that filthiness of spirit, as I find to my sorrow. And just as this idea that "There is no sin in a believer, no carnal mind, no bent to backsliding," is contrary to the word of God, it is also contrary to the experience of His children. They continually feel a heart bent to backsliding: a natural tendency to evil; a tendency to leave God, and hold to the things of earth. Every day they are conscious of sin remaining in their hearts: pride, self will, unbelief. They are aware of sin clinging to all they say and do, even their best actions and holiest duties. Yet at the same time they "know that they are of God;" they cannot doubt it. They feel His Spirit clearly "witnessing with their spirit, that they are the children of God." They "rejoice in God through Christ Jesus, by whom they have now received the atonement." So they are equally sure, both that sin is in them, and that "Christ is in them the hope of glory."

"But can Christ be in the same heart where sin is?" Undoubtedly He can; otherwise it never could be saved. Where the sickness is, there is the Physician, doing His work, fighting until He drives sin out. Christ cannot reign where sin reigns; neither will He live where any sin is allowed. But He lives in the heart of every believer who is fighting against sin; even though the heart is not yet purified.

As observed before, the opposite doctrine, that there is no sin in believers, is quite new in the church. But whatever doctrine is new must be wrong; for the old religion is the only true one; and no doctrine can be right, unless it is the same "which was from the beginning." One more argument against this new, unscriptural doctrine may be drawn from the terrible results of it. One says, "I felt anger today." Must I reply, "Then you have no faith?" Another says, "I know what you advise is good, but my will is strongly opposed to it." Must I tell him, "Then you are an unbeliever, under the wrath and the curse of God?" What will be the natural result of this? If he believes what I say, his soul will not only be grieved and wounded, but perhaps completely destroyed; so much that he will "cast away" that "confidence which hath great recompense of reward." And having thrown away his shield, how will he "quench the fiery darts of the wicked one?" How will he overcome the world, since "this is the victory that overcometh the world, even our faith?" He stands defenseless among his enemies, open to all their attacks. So I cannot accept this statement, that there is no sin in a believer from the moment he is justified; first, because it is contrary to the whole theme of Scripture; second, because it is contrary to the experience of the children of God; third, because it is absolutely new, never heard of in the world until yesterday; and last, because it naturally brings the most deadly results.

However, to be fair, let us consider the arguments of those who try to support it. It is first from Scripture that they try to prove that there is no sin in a believer. They argue in this way: "The Scripture says that every believer is born of God, is clean, is holy, is sanctified, is pure in heart, has a new heart, is a temple of the Holy Spirit. Now, as 'that which is born of the flesh is flesh,' that is, altogether evil; so 'that which is born of the Spirit is spirit,' that is, altogether good. Surely a man cannot be clean, sanctified, holy, and at the same time unclean, unsanctified, unholy. He cannot be pure and impure, or have a new and an old heart at the same time. Neither can his soul be unholy while it is a temple of the Holy Spirit."

I have stated this reasoning as strongly as possible, so that its full weight may appear. Let us now examine it, part by part. First, "'That which is born of the Spirit is spirit,' that is, altogether good." I accept the text, but not the comment. For the text affirms only that every man who is "born of the Spirit," is a spiritual man. He is so: but he may be so, and still not be altogether spiritual. The Christians at Corinth were spiritual men, or else they were not Christians at all, and yet they were not entirely spiritual. They were still partly carnal. Second, "But a man cannot be clean, sanctified, holy, and at the same time unclean, unsanctified, unholy." Yes, he can. The Corinthians were. "Ye are washed," says the Apostle, "ye are sanctified;" that is, cleansed from "fornication, idolatry, drunkenness," and all other outward sin (1 Corinthians 6:9-11); and yet at the same time, in another sense of the word, they were unsanctified; they were not washed, not inwardly cleansed from envy, evil thinking, partiality. "But surely, they did not have a new heart and an old heart at the same time." It is most certain that they had, for at that time, their hearts were truly, but not entirely, renewed. "But could they be unholy while they were 'temples of the Holy Spirit?'" Yes, that they were temples of the Holy Spirit, is certain (1 Corinthians 6:19); and it is equally certain that they were, to some degree, carnal, that is, unholy.

There are also further objections to consider: "If any man be in Christ, he is a new creature. Old things are passed away; behold, all things are become new" (2 Corinthians 5:17). "Certainly a man cannot be a new creature and an old creature at once." I respond, yes, he may. He may be partly renewed, which was the case with those at Corinth. They were unquestionably "renewed in the spirit of their mind," or they could not have been so much as "babes in Christ;" yet they did not have the whole mind which was in Christ, for they envied one another. This whole argument, "If he is clean, he is clean;" "If he is holy, he is holy;" is really no more than playing with words. Frame the sentence logically, and it goes like this: "If he is holy at all, he is holy completely." That is unreasonable. Every babe in Christ is holy, only not completely so. Sin remains, though it does not reign. If you think it does not remain, at least in immature Christians, you certainly have not considered the extent of the law of God (even the law of love, laid down by St. Paul in the 13th chapter of Corinthians); that every *anomia*, failure to conform to, or deviation from, this law is sin. Now, is there no failure to conform to this in the heart or life of any believer?

Another objection is as follows: "But believers walk after the Spirit (Romans 8:1), and the Spirit of God lives in them; therefore, they are delivered from the guilt, the power, or, in one word, the 'being' of sin" In response, we observe that these are linked together as if they were one thing, but they are not. We agree that believers are delivered from the guilt and power of sin; but we deny that they are delivered from the being of it we. A man may have the Spirit of God living in him, and may "walk after the Spirit," though he still feels "the flesh lusting against the Spirit."

"But 'they that are Christ's have crucified the flesh, with its affections and lusts'" (Galatians 5:24). They have, but it still remains in them, and often struggles to break free from the cross. "But they have 'put off the old man with his deeds'" (Colossians 3:9). They have; and, in the sense described above, "old things are passed away; all things are become new." A hundred texts may be cited to the same effect; and they will all arrive at the same answer. "But, 'Christ gave himself for the Church, that it might be holy, and without blemish'" (Ephesians 5:25, 27). And so it will be in the end: but it has not yet been, from the beginning to this day.

"But from the very nature of things, can a man have pride in him, and not be proud; have anger, and still not be angry?" A man may have pride in him, he may think of himself in some respects higher than he should (and so be proud in those respects), and yet not be a proud man in his general character. He may have anger in him, even a tendency to become furiously angry, without giving way to it. "But can anger and pride be in that heart, where only meekness and humility are felt?" No, but some pride and anger may be in that heart where there is much humility and meekness.

"But sin cannot exist where it does not reign; for guilt and power are essential qualities of sin." Strange indeed! Sin cannot, in any kind or degree, exist where it does not reign? This contradicts all experience, all Scripture, all common sense. Resentment is sin; it is *anomia*, a failure to conform to the law of love. This has existed in me a thousand times. Yet it did not, and does not reign. "But guilt and power are essential qualities of sin; therefore, where one is, all must be." No. In the example just given, if the resentment I feel is not yielded to, even for a moment, there is no guilt at all, no condemnation from God. And in this case, it has no power. Though it "lusteth against the Spirit," it cannot conquer. Here, therefore, there is sin without either guilt or power.

"But if sin remains in a believer, he is a sinful man: if pride, for instance, then he is proud; if self-will, then he is self-willed; if unbelief, then he is an unbeliever; and, consequently, no believer at all. How does he differ then from unbelievers, from unregenerate men?" This is still a matter of playing with words. It means no more than, if there is sin, pride, or self-will in him, then there is sin, pride, or self-will. In that sense then he is proud or self-willed. But not in the same sense that unbelievers are; that is, governed by pride or self-will. In this he differs from unregenerate men. They obey sin; he does not. They "walk after the flesh;" he "walks after the Spirit."

"But this doctrine, that sin remains in a believer, that a man may be in the favor of God while he has sin in his heart, tends to encourage men to sin." Understand the doctrine right, and this will not happen. A man may be in God's favor though he feels sin; but not if he yields to it. Having sin does not forfeit the favor of God; giving in to sin does. Though the flesh in you "lust against the Spirit," you may still be a child of God; but if you "walk after the flesh," you are a child of the devil. Now this doctrine does not encourage us to obey sin, but to resist it with all our power.

To sum it all up, there are in every person, even after he is justified, two opposing principles, nature and grace, called by St. Paul the flesh and the Spirit. This agrees with the experience of the children of God. While they feel the witness of grace in themselves, they feel a will not entirely surrendered to the will of God. They know they are in Him and yet find a heart ready to leave Him, a tendency to do evil, and a reluctance to do that which is good. Although we are renewed, cleansed, purified, and sanctified the moment we truly believe in Christ, we are not completely renewed, cleansed, purified altogether at that time. The flesh, the evil nature, still remains (though subdued), and wars against the Spirit. So let us more earnestly "watch and pray" against the enemy within. Let us guard ourselves more carefully, and "put on the whole armor of God;" so that "we may be able to withstand in the evil day, and having done all, to stand."

4

The Repentance of Believers

"Repent ye, and believe the gospel."
Mark 1:15.

It is generally supposed that repentance and faith are only the gate of religion; that they are necessary only at the beginning of our Christian journey, when we are setting out on our way to the kingdom. And this may seem to be confirmed by the great Apostle, where, urging the Hebrew Christians to "go on to perfection," he teaches them to leave these "first principles of the doctrine of Christ;" "not laying again the foundation of repentance from dead works, and of faith towards God," which must at least mean that they should leave these, which at first consumed all their thoughts, in order to "press forward toward the prize of the high calling of God in Christ Jesus."

It is true that there are a repentance and a faith which are especially necessary at the beginning. This repentance is a conviction of our utter sinfulness, guiltiness, and helplessness; and comes before we receive the kingdom of God.

But there are also a repentance and a faith (taking the words in a sense not quite the same, nor yet entirely different), which are necessary *after* we have "believed the gospel," and in every stage of our Christian journey which follows. Otherwise, we cannot "run the race which is set before us." This repentance and faith are just as necessary for continuing and growing in grace, as the former faith and repentance were for entering into the kingdom of God.

But in what sense are we to repent and believe after we are justified? This is a question worth close attention.

The Sense in Which a Believer Is to Repent

Repentance frequently means an inward change of mind from sin to holiness. But we now speak of it in a very different sense, as a kind of self-knowledge, the knowing of ourselves to be sinners, even guilty, helpless sinners, even though we know we are children of God.

Indeed, when we first know that we are children of God, it is natural to think that we are no longer sinners, that all our sins are not only covered but destroyed. Since we do not feel any evil in our hearts, we easily imagine that none is there. Some well-meaning men have imagined this to be true not only at that time, but for always; having persuaded themselves that when they were justified they were entirely sanctified. They have established it as a general rule, ignoring Scripture, reason, and experience. They sincerely believe that all sin is destroyed when we are justified; and that there is no sin in the heart of a believer; but that it is completely clean from that moment. Although we readily acknowledge, "he that believeth is born of God," and "he that is born of God doth not commit sin;" we cannot agree that he does not feel it within. It does not reign, but it does remain. And a conviction of the sin which remains in our heart is one large part of the repentance we are now speaking of. For it is usually not long before the one who imagined all sin was gone feels that there is still *pride* in his heart. He is convinced that he has thought of himself too highly, and that he has accepted praise for something he had received, as though it were naturally his; and still he knows he is in the favor of God. "The Spirit" still "witnesses with" his "spirit, that he is a child of God."

Nor is it long before he feels *self-will* in his heart; a will contrary to the will of God. A will is an essential part of human nature. Our Lord had a will as a man; otherwise He would not have been a man. But His human will was invariably subject to the will of His Father. At all times, even in the deepest affliction, He could say, "Not as I will, but as Thou wilt." But this is not the case at all times, even with a true believer in Christ. He frequently finds his will more or less exalting itself against the will of God. He wills something because it is pleasing to his nature, which is not pleasing to God; and he is averse to something because it is painful to his nature, which is the will of God concerning him. If he continues in faith, he fights against this tendency; but this very conflict implies that it really exists, and that he is conscious of it.

Now self-will, as well as pride, is a kind of *idolatry*, and both are directly contrary to the love of God. The same observation may be made concerning the *love of the world*. Even true believers are liable to feel this in themselves; and every one of them does feel it, more or less, sooner or later, in one way or another. It is true, when he first "passes from death unto life," he desires nothing but God. He can truly say, "All my desire is unto Thee, and unto the remembrance of Thy name." "Whom have I in heaven but Thee, and there is none upon earth that I desire beside Thee!" But it is not always so. Eventually he will feel again either *the desire of the flesh, or the desire of the eye, or the pride of life.*

If he does not continually watch and pray, he may find *the desire of the flesh*, even *lust*, reviving and attacking him that he may fall, until he has barely any strength left. He may feel a strong tendency to "love the creature more than the Creator;" whether it is a child, a parent, a husband or wife, or a friend. He may feel, in a thousand different ways, a desire for earthly things or pleasures. To the same extent he will forget God, not seeking his happiness in Him, and, consequently, becoming a "lover of pleasure more than a lover of God."

If he does not keep himself every moment, he will again feel *the desire of the eye*; the desire of gratifying his imagination with something great, or beautiful, or uncommon. This desire assaults the soul in many ways, and often regarding the things of least significance, such as dress, or furniture; things never designed to satisfy the appetite of an immortal spirit. And yet, how natural is it for us, even after we have "tasted of the powers of the world to come," to sink again into these foolish, low desires for things that perish as we use them! How hard it is, even for those who know in whom they have believed, not to desire anything simply because it is new!

And how hard it is even for the children of God to fully conquer *the pride of life!* This is a desire for, and delight in, the praise that comes from men; and, always joined to it, is a proportionate *fear of dispraise*. Closely related to this is *evil shame*, or being ashamed of that in which we ought to glory. And this is seldom separate from the *fear of man*, which can easily entangle the soul. Now where is he, even among those that seem strong in faith, who does not find in himself a degree of all these evil tempers? So that even these are only partly "crucified to the world;" for the evil root still remains in their heart.

And do we not feel other tempers, which are as contrary to loving our neighbor as these are to loving God? Love for our neighbor "thinketh no evil." Do we never find any *jealousies*, any *evil speculations*, any groundless or unreasonable *suspicions*? He that is innocent in these respects, let him throw the first stone at his neighbor. Who does not sometimes feel other tempers or inward motions which he knows are contrary to brotherly love? If we find no *malice*, *hatred*, or *bitterness*, what about *envy* of those who enjoy something which we desire but cannot attain? Do we never find any degree of *resentment*, when we are injured or offended; especially by those whom we dearly loved, and worked the hardest to help? Does injustice or ingratitude never cause in us any desire for *revenge?* Any desire to return evil for evil, instead of "overcoming evil with good?" This also shows how much is still in our hearts which is contrary to loving our neighbor.

Covetousness of any kind or amount is certainly contrary to the love of God; whether the *love of money*, which is too frequently "the root of all evil;" or a desire of *having more*. And how few, even of the real children of God, are entirely free from both! One great man, Martin Luther, used to say he "never had any covetousness in him since he was born." But, even if it were true, I would say he was the only man (except Him that was God as well as man) who was born without it. I believe that there was never one born of God, that lived any length of time afterward, who did not feel more or less of it often, especially in the latter sense. We may consider it an undoubted truth that covetousness, along with pride, self-will, and anger, remains in the hearts even of them that are justified.

It is experiencing this that has inclined so many to interpret the latter part of the seventh chapter to the Romans, to speak not of those who are "under the law," that are convicted of sin, which is undoubtedly the meaning of the Apostle, but of those who are "under grace;" that are "justified freely through the redemption that is in Christ." And they are right to a point. There does remain, even in them that are justified, a mind which is to some degree carnal (so the Apostle tells the believers at Corinth, "Ye are carnal"); a heart bent to backsliding, always ready to "depart from the living God;" a tendency toward pride, self-will, anger, revenge, love of the world; and a root of bitterness, which, if the restraints were taken off for a moment, would instantly spring up. And a conviction of all this sin remaining in their hearts is the repentance which belongs to those who are justified.

But we should also be convinced, that just as sin remains in our hearts, it clings to all our *words* and *actions* as well. I fear that many of our words are more than mixed with sin; that they are entirely sinful; for this is all uncharitable conversation; all which does not arise from brotherly love; all which does not agree with that golden rule, "What ye would that others should do to you, even so do unto them." This includes all backbiting, all talebearing, all evil-speaking, that is, telling the faults of absent persons; for no one would want others to tell his faults when he is absent. Now how few are there, even among believers, who are innocent of this? And do they avoid unprofitable conversation? Yet all this is unquestionably sinful, and "grieves the Holy Spirit of God." And "for every idle word that men shall speak, they shall give an account in the day of judgment."

Suppose that they constantly guard their speech, so that all their "conversation may be in grace, seasoned with salt, and meet to minister grace to the hearers;" but do they not slide into useless discourse every day, in spite of all their caution? And even when they try to speak for God, are their words pure, free from unholy mixtures? Do they find nothing wrong in their motives? Do they speak only to please God, and not partly to please themselves? Is it to do the will of God alone, and not their own will also? When they are confronting sin, do they feel no anger or unkind temper toward the sinner? When they are instructing the ignorant, do they not find any pride, any self-preference? When they are comforting the afflicted, or encouraging one another to love and to good works, do they never perceive any inward self-commendation: "Now you have spoken well?" Or any vanity, a desire that others should esteem them highly? In some or all of these respects, how much sin clings to the best conversation even of believers! The conviction of this is another part of the repentance which belongs to them that are justified.

And how much sin, if their conscience is fully awake, may they find clinging to their actions also! Are there not many of these which, though they would not be condemned by the world, cannot be commended nor excused, if we judge by the Word of God? Are there not many of their actions which they know are not to the glory of God? Many times they did not even aim at this; their works were not undertaken with an eye toward God. And of those that were, are there not many in which their eye was not fixed on God alone; in which they were doing their own will at least as much as His; and seeking to please themselves as much as, if not more than, God? And while they are trying to do good to their neighbor, do they not feel wrong tempers of various kinds? Therefore, their so-called good actions are far from being strictly such, being polluted with such a mixture of evil. And is there not the same mixture in their works of piety? While they are hearing the word which is able to save their souls, do they not often find thoughts which make them afraid, should they lead to their condemnation, rather than their salvation? Is it not the same when they are trying to pray, whether in public or private? As a result, they are now more ashamed of their best duties than they once were of their worst sins.

How many sins of *omission* are they guilty of? We know the words of the Apostle: "To him that knoweth to do good, and doeth it not, to him it is sin." But are they not aware of a thousand instances in which they might have done good to enemies, to strangers, to their brothers, for either their bodies or their souls, and they did not do it? How many omissions have they been guilty of in their duty toward God! How many opportunities of taking communion, of hearing His Word, of public or private prayer, they have neglected! After all his labors for God,

Archbishop Usher, that holy man, had so great a reason to cry out, almost with his dying breath, "Lord, forgive me my sins of omission!"

But, besides these outward omissions, may they not find many *inward* defects in themselves? They do not have the love, the fear, the confidence they ought to have toward God. They do not have the love which is due every child of man; or even that which is due every child of God. They have no holy temper in the degree they should; they are defective in everything; and deeply aware of this they are ready to cry out, with M. De Renty, "I am a ground all overrun with thorns;" or, with Job, "I am vile: I abhor myself, and repent as in dust and ashes."

A conviction of their *guiltiness* is another part of that repentance which belongs to the children of God. But this is to be understood in a special sense. For it is certain, "there is no condemnation to them that are in Christ Jesus," that believe in Him, and in the power of that faith, "walk not after the flesh, but after the Spirit." However, they can no more bear the strict justice of God now, than before they believed. This pronounces them to be still worthy of death on all the preceding counts. And it would condemn them absolutely, if it were not for the atoning blood. Therefore they are thoroughly convinced that they still deserve punishment, even though it is turned aside from them. But most men either think they are condemned when they are not, or think they deserve to be acquitted. The truth lies somewhere in between. They still deserve, strictly speaking, only the damnation of hell. But what they deserve does not happen to them because they "have an advocate with the Father." His life, and death, and intercession still stand between them and condemnation.

A conviction of their *utter helplessness* is still another part of this repentance. By this I mean two things: first, that they are, in and of themselves, no more able now to think one good thought, to form one good desire, to speak one good word, or do one good work, than before they were justified. They still have no strength of their own; no power either to do good or resist evil; no ability to conquer, or even withstand the world, the devil, or their own evil nature. They can do all these things, but not by their own strength. They have power to overcome all these enemies; for "sin hath no more dominion over them:" But it is not from nature, it is the gift of God. Nor is it given all at once, as if they had some hidden supply, but rather from moment to moment.

Second, by this helplessness I mean an absolute inability to save ourselves from that guilt or deserved punishment of which we are still conscious; and an inability to remove, by all the grace we have (to say nothing of our natural powers), either the pride, self-will, love of the world, anger, and that general proneness to run from God, which we know, by experience, remains in the hearts even of those who are justified; or the evil which, in spite of all our efforts, clings to all our words and actions. Add to this an inability to avoid uncharitable and unprofitable conversation; and an inability to avoid sins of omission, or to make up for our countless defects; especially the lack of love both to God and man.

If any man is not convinced of this, if anyone believes that whoever is justified is able to remove these sins out of his heart and life, let him see for himself. Let him see if, by the grace he has already received, he can expel pride, self-will, or sin in general. Let him see if he can cleanse his words and actions from every hint of evil; if he can avoid all uncharitable and unprofitable conversation, along with all the sins of omission; and, last, if he can make up for the innumerable defects that he still finds in himself. Let him not be discouraged by one or two attempts, but repeat the trial again and again. The longer he tries, the more deeply he will be convinced of his utter helplessness in all these respects.

This is so evident that nearly all the children of God, despite their differences of opinion in other matters, generally agree in this; that although we may resist and conquer both outward and inward sin; although we may weaken our enemies day by day;

we cannot completely drive them out. By all the grace that is given at justification we cannot uproot them. Though we diligently watch and pray, we cannot fully cleanse either our hearts or our hands. We cannot, until it pleases our Lord to speak to our hearts again, to speak for the second time, "Be clean." Only then is the leprosy cleansed. Only then the evil root, the carnal mind, is destroyed; and sin no longer remains. But if there is no such second change, if there is no instantaneous deliverance after justification, if there is nothing but a gradual work of God (no one denies that there is at least a gradual work), then we must be content to remain full of sin until we die; and, if so, we must remain guilty until we die, continually deserving punishment. For it is impossible for the guilt, or the punishment we deserve, to be removed from us as long as this sin remains in our hearts and clings to our words and actions. According to strict justice, all we think, speak, and do only increases it.

The New Sense in Which a Believer Is to Believe

In this sense we are to repent after we are justified. And unless we do so, we can go no farther. For until we know of our disease, it cannot be cured. But, if we do repent in this way, then we are called to "believe the gospel."

And this too is to be understood in a special sense, different from that in which we believed for justification. Believe the good news of great salvation, which God has prepared for all people. Believe that He is "able to save unto the uttermost all that come unto God through Him." He is able to save you from all the sin that still remains in your heart and clings to your words and actions. He is able to save you from sins of omission and to make up for whatever is lacking in you. This is impossible with man, but with God-Man all things are possible. For what can be too hard for Him who has "all power in heaven and in earth?" Of course His power to do this is not a sufficient basis for our belief that He will do it, unless He has promised it first. But He has promised it over and over, and in the strongest terms. He has given us these "exceeding great and precious promises," both in the Old and the New Testament. We read in the law, in the most ancient part of the oracles of God, "The Lord thy God will circumcise thy heart, and the heart of thy seed, to love the Lord thy God, with all thy heart, and with all thy soul" (Deuteronomy 30:6). The Prophet writes, "Then will I sprinkle clean water upon you, and ye shall be clean: From all your filthiness and from all your idols will I cleanse you. And I will put My Spirit within you, and ye shall keep My judgments and do them. I will also save you from all your uncleannesses" (Ezekiel 36:25, etc.). Likewise in the New Testament, "Blessed be the Lord God of Israel, for He hath visited and redeemed His people, and hath raised up an horn of salvation for us, — to perform the oath which He swore to our father Abraham, That He would grant unto us, that we, being delivered out of the hands of our enemies, should serve Him without fear, in holiness and righteousness before Him all the days of our life" (Luke 1:68, etc.).

You have, therefore, good reason to believe that He is not only able, but willing to do this; to cleanse you from all your filthiness of flesh and spirit; to "save you from all your uncleannesses." This is the thing you now desire; this is the faith you now need, that the Great Physician is willing to make you clean. But is He willing to do this tomorrow or today? Let Him answer for himself: "Today, if ye will hear His voice, harden not your hearts." If you put it off until tomorrow, you harden your hearts; you refuse to hear His voice. Believe that He is willing to save you today. He is willing to save you *now*. "Behold, now is the accepted time." This very moment He says, "Be thou clean!" Simply believe, and you will immediately find that "all things are possible to him that believeth."

Continue to believe in Him that loved you, and gave himself for you; that took all your sins on himself and saves you from all condemnation by His blood which is applied continually. So it is that we continue in a justified state. And when we go on "from faith to faith," when we have faith to be cleansed from the sin that remains in us, to be saved from all our uncleannesses, we are likewise saved from all that guilt which we felt before. For by that faith in His life, death, and intercession for us, renewed from moment to moment, we are entirely clean, and now there is not only no condemnation for us, but also no such deserved punishment as was before, because the Lord is cleansing both our hearts and lives.

By the same faith we feel the power of Christ in us at every moment, only by which we are what we are; by which we are enabled to continue in spiritual life, and without which, in spite of all our present holiness, we should instantly become devils. Leaning on Christ, we receive help from Him to think, and speak, and do what is acceptable in His sight. And so He goes before those who believe, in all their doings, and moves them forward with His continual help; so that all their plans, conversations, and actions are begun, continued, and finished in Him. And so he cleanses the thoughts of their hearts, by the inspiration of His Holy Spirit, that they may love Him perfectly, and rightly magnify His holy name.

So it is, that in the children of God, repentance and faith exactly correspond to each other. By repentance we feel the sin remaining in our hearts and clinging to our words and actions. By faith we receive the power of God in Christ, purifying our hearts and cleansing our hands. By repentance we see that we still deserve punishment for all our tempers, words, and actions. By faith we are aware that our Advocate with the Father is continually pleading for us, continually turning aside all condemnation and punishment from us. By repentance we have the conviction that we cannot help ourselves. By faith we receive not only mercy, "but grace to help in time of need." Repentance rejects even the possibility of any other help. Faith accepts all the help we need from Him that has all power in heaven and earth. Repentance says, "Without Him I can do nothing." Faith says, "I can do all things through Christ strengthening me." Through Him I can not only overcome, but drive out, all the enemies of my soul. Through Him I can "love the Lord my God with all my heart, mind, soul, and strength;" and "walk in holiness and righteousness before Him all the days of my life."

Conclusion

From what has been said, we may easily learn the harmfulness of the opinion that we are fully sanctified when we are justified; that our hearts are cleansed from all sin at that time. It is true that we are delivered from the dominion of outward sin at that moment; the power of inward sin being broken, so that we no longer need to follow it. But it is not true that inward sin is totally destroyed then; that the root of pride, self-will, anger, and love of the world, is taken out of the heart; or that the carnal mind, and the heart prone to backsliding, are entirely uprooted. And to think wrongly about this is not, as some may think, simply a harmless mistake. It does immense harm: it blocks the way to any further change; for it is obvious, "they that are whole need not a physician, but they that are sick." If we think we are whole already, there is no room to seek further healing. Based on this assumption it is absurd to expect further deliverance from sin, whether gradual or instantaneous.

On the contrary, a deep conviction that we are not yet whole; that our hearts are not fully purified; that there is still a "carnal mind" in us which is still, in its nature, "enmity against God;" that a mass of sin remains in our hearts, weakened but not destroyed; shows the absolute necessity of a further change. We agree that we are born again at the moment of justification. In that instant we experience an inward change from "darkness into marvelous light," from the image of the brute and the devil, into the image of God, from the earthly, sensual, devilish mind, to the mind which was in Christ Jesus. But are we changed entirely? Are we transformed completely into the image of Him that created us? Far from it. We still retain a depth of sin, and it is the awareness of this which compels us to groan for full deliverance to Him that is mighty to save. So it is that those believers who are not convinced of the deep corruption of their hearts, or are only mentally convinced, care little about *entire sanctification.* They may hold the opinion that such a thing will occur, either at death, or at some unknown time before it. But they are not uneasy because they do not have it, and have no great hunger or thirst for it. They cannot until they know themselves better; until they repent in the sense described above, until God unveils the monster within, and shows them the real state of their souls. Only then, when they feel the burden, will they cry out for deliverance from it.

Second, we may learn from this that a deep conviction of our sinfulness, after we are accepted (which in one sense may be called guilt), is absolutely necessary in order for us to see the true value of the atoning blood; in order to feel that we need this as much after we are justified as we did before. Without this conviction we must consider the blood of the covenant something which we hardly need now, since all our past sins are removed. But if both our hearts and lives are unclean, there is a kind of guilt which we are experiencing every moment, which would continually expose us to fresh condemnation, except for the fact that He intercedes for us.

Third, we may see that a deep conviction of our utter helplessness, of our total inability to retain anything we have received, and to deliver ourselves from the world of sin remaining both in our hearts and lives, teaches us to live by faith in Christ, not only as our Priest, but as our King. By this we are brought to make Him a whole Christ, an entire Savior, and to set the crown firmly on His head. Then, His almighty grace having thrown down "every high thing which exalted itself against Him," every temper, thought, word, and action "is brought to the obedience of Christ."

5

Christian Perfection

Editor's Note: This section is a compilation of two sermons entitled "Christian Perfection" and "On Perfection." Since the second represents a logical continuation of the same theme, it has simply been attached to the first. Repetitions and unnecessary paragraphs have been deleted. Two paragraphs have been moved, and this change is noted in the text.

This essay is preceded by two paragraphs from Wesley's article, "Brief Thoughts on Christian Perfection."

"Not as though I had already attained, either were already perfect."
Philippians 3:12.

Controversy over the Term Perfection

There is hardly any expression in Scripture that has given more offense than the word *perfect*. Therefore, some advise us to stop using those expressions entirely. But are they not found in the oracles of God? If so, by what authority could any messenger of God set them aside, even if all men were offended by them?

We cannot discard these expressions, since they are the words of God and not of man. But we ought to explain them so that those who are sincere may not miss the mark of the prize of their high calling. And this is even more necessary because, in the verse that was quoted, the Apostle speaks of himself as not perfect. Yet, in the fifteenth verse, he speaks of himself, along with others, as perfect: "Let us," he says, "as many as be perfect, be thus minded."

The Sense in Which Christians Are Not Perfect

First, from experience and Scripture it appears that Christians are not perfect in knowledge. They are not so perfect as to be free from ignorance. They do know the general truths that God has revealed. They know, likewise (which the natural man does not understand, for these things are spiritually discerned), "what manner of love" it is, wherewith "the Father" has loved them, "that they should be called the sons of God." They know the mighty working of His Spirit in their hearts; and the wisdom of His providence which directs all their paths, and causes all things to work together for their good. Yes, they know what the Lord requires of them, and how to keep a clear conscience toward both God and man.

But there are countless things which they do not know. Concerning God himself, they cannot search Him out perfectly. I will not say that they cannot understand how "there are Three that bear record in heaven, the Father, the Son, and the Holy Spirit, and these Three are One;" or how the eternal Son of God "took upon himself the form of a servant;" but they cannot fully understand even one attribute of the divine nature. Neither do they know the times and seasons when God will work His great works upon the earth; even those He has partly revealed by His servants and prophets.

Second, they are not free from mistake, which is almost unavoidable, since those who "know but in part" are always liable to err concerning the things which they do not know. It is true that the children of God are not mistaken in things essential to salvation. But in unessential things they err frequently. The best and wisest of men are often mistaken even about facts. Even if they are not mistaken as to the fact itself, they may be about its circumstances. Therefore, they may believe some actions which were or are evil, to be good; and such as were or are good, to be evil. Also they may judge the characters of men inaccurately; not only by supposing good men to be better than they are, or wicked men to be worse than they are, but by believing certain wicked men to be good, or certain good men to be wicked.

Even regarding the Holy Scriptures themselves, the best of men are prone to be mistaken, especially in those parts that relate less directly to practice. Therefore, even the children of God are not agreed on the interpretation of many passages of Scripture. Their difference of opinion is not proof that they are not the children of God; but it is proof that we are no more infallible than we are omniscient.

Third, Christians are not free from infirmities. Let us understand this word properly. Let us not give that title to known sins, as some do. As one man tells us, "Every man has his infirmity, and mine is drunkenness." It is obvious that all you who speak in this way, if you do not repent, will, along with your infirmities, go suddenly into hell! But I refer not only to those which are properly termed bodily infirmities, but all those inward or outward imperfections that are not of a moral nature. These include weakness or slowness of understanding, incoherence of thought, fluctuating ability of imagination, or lack of a good memory. Of another kind are those which result from these; such as slowness of speech, poor vocabulary, and awkward pronunciation; along with a list of a thousand other defects, either in conversation or behavior. These infirmities are found in the best of men, to varying degrees. No one can hope to be perfectly free from these until his spirit returns to God that gave it. Nor can we expect, until then, to be completely free from temptation. Such perfection does not belong to this life.

By perfection I mean the humble, gentle, patient love for God and for our neighbor, ruling our tempers, words, and actions. I do not imply that it is impossible to fall from it, either partially or completely.

As to the means, I believe this perfection is always worked in the soul by a simple act of faith; therefore, in an instant. But I believe in a gradual work, both preceding and following that instant.

I do not consider the perfection spoken of here to be the perfection of angels. It is not possible for man always to think right, whose understanding is darkened; to whom error is as natural as ignorance; who cannot think at all except by using organs which are weakened and depraved like the other parts of his corruptible body. Therefore, his affections, depending on his understanding, are out of proportion. And his words and actions are influenced by the disorder both of his understanding and affections. Therefore, no man, while in the body, can possibly have angelic perfection.

Neither can any man, while he is in a corruptible body, achieve Adamic perfection. Adam's understanding was as clear as the angels', and his affections as consistent. Because of this, because he always perceived right, he was always able to speak and act right. Since man rebelled against God, however, this has not been the case. He is no longer able to avoid falling into countless mistakes; consequently, he cannot always avoid wrong affections; neither can he always think, speak, and act right. Therefore, man in his present state can no more attain Adamic perfection than angelic perfection.

Christian perfection, therefore, does not imply exemption from ignorance, mistakes, infirmities, or temptations. Actually, it is only another term for holiness. And so, everyone that is holy is, in the scriptural sense, perfect. Still, we may observe that there is no absolute perfection on earth; that is, a perfection that cannot be continually improved. To whatever degree any man is perfect, he still needs to "grow in grace," and to advance day by day in the knowledge and love of God.

The Perfection of Every Christian from Willful Sin

Then what is perfection? First, even babes in Christ are perfect in the sense that they do not commit sin. If anyone doubts this privilege of the sons of God, the question is not to be decided by abstract reasoning, nor by the experience of any particular person. Many may suppose they do not commit sin, even though they do; but this proves nothing either way. We appeal to the law and to the testimony. "Let God be true, and every man a liar." By His word we will stay.

Now the Word of God clearly declares, that those who are justified "do not continue in sin," that they cannot "live any longer therein" (Romans 6:1, 2). They are "planted together in the likeness of the death" of Christ; (v. 5) that their "old man is crucified with Him," the body of sin being destroyed, so that from that time forward they do not serve sin. Being dead with Christ, they are free from sin (vv. 6, 7); they are "dead unto sin, and alive unto God" (v. 11). "Sin has no more dominion over them," who are "not under the law, but under grace;" but they, "being free from sin, are become the servants of righteousness" (vv. 14, 18).

These words imply, at the very least, that all real Christians are free from outward sin. St. Peter expresses it this way: "He that hath suffered in the flesh, hath ceased from sin — that he no longer should live to the desires of men, but to the will of God" (1 Peter 4:1, 2). This ceasing from sin, even if it is interpreted even in the lowest sense, regarding outward behavior only, must mean the ceasing of any outward transgression of the law.

Clearest are the words of St. John, "He that committeth sin is of the devil; for the devil sinneth from the beginning. For this purpose the Son of God was manifested, that He might destroy the works of the devil. Whosoever is born of God doth not commit sin; for His seed remaineth in him: And he cannot sin because he is born of God" (1 John 3:8, 9). And "We know that whosoever is born of God sinneth not; but he that is begotten of God keepeth himself, and that wicked one toucheth him not" (5:18).

It is said by some that this means only that he does not sin willfully; or that he does not commit sin habitually; or, not as other men do; or, not as he did before. But by whom is this said? Not by St. John. There is no such word in the text; nor in the whole chapter; nor in his entire epistle; nor in any part of his writings.

If you want to prove that the Apostle's words, "He that is born of God sinneth not," are not to be understood according to their clear, natural, obvious meaning, you must find your proof in the New Testament, or you will fight as one beating the air. The first such "proof" is usually taken from the examples recorded in the New Testament. "The Apostles themselves," it is said, "committed sin; even the greatest of them, Peter and Paul: St. Paul, by his sharp contention with Barnabas; and St. Peter, by his division at Antioch." Well, suppose both Peter and Paul did commit sin at those times; what would you infer from that? That all the other Apostles committed sin sometimes? There is no shadow of proof in this. Or will you argue, "If two of the Apostles committed sin, then do not all other Christians, in all ages, commit sin as long as they live?" Alas, my brother! A child of common understanding would be ashamed of this reasoning. They had no compulsion to sin. The grace of God was sufficient for them, and it is sufficient for us today. Along with the temptation, there was a way to escape; as there is for every man in every temptation. Whoever is tempted to sin does not have to yield to it; for no man is tempted above what he is able to bear.

But here another difficulty may arise. How may we reconcile St. John with himself? In one place he declares, "Whosoever is born of God doth not commit sin;" and again, "We know that he which is born of God sinneth not:" Yet in another he says, "If we say that we have no sin, we deceive ourselves, and the truth is not in us;" and again, "If we say that we have not sinned, we make Him a liar, and His word is not in us."

This difficulty disappears if we observe that the tenth verse provides the meaning of the eighth. The phrase, "If we say we have no sin," in verse eight, is explained by the phrase, "If we say we have not sinned," in verse ten. The point we are discussing is not whether or not we have sinned before now, but whether or not a Christian still sins. These verses do not assert that we commit sin now. Third, the ninth verse explains both the eighth and tenth. "If we confess our sins, He is faithful and just to forgive us our sins, and to cleanse us from all unrighteousness:" It is as if he is saying, "I have already affirmed, 'The blood of Jesus Christ cleanseth us from all sin;' but let no man say, I do not need it; I have no sin to be cleansed from. If we say that we have no sin, that we have not sinned, we deceive ourselves: But 'if we confess our sins, He is faithful and just,' not only 'to forgive our sins,' but also 'to cleanse us from all unrighteousness:' that we may 'go and sin no more.'"

St. John is, therefore, consistent with himself, as well as with the other holy writers; as will be even more obvious if we look at all his assertions about this subject together. He declares, first, that the blood of Jesus Christ cleanses us from all sin. Second, that no man can say, "I have not sinned; I have no sin to be cleansed from." Third, God is ready both to forgive our past sins, and to save us from them in the future. Fourth, "These things write I unto you," says the Apostle, "that you may not sin. But if any man" should "sin," or has sinned, he does not need to continue in sin; seeing "we have an Advocate with the Father, Jesus Christ the righteous." So far all is clear. And should any doubt remain in a point of such great importance, the Apostle resumes this subject in the third chapter, and thoroughly explains his own meaning: "Little children," he says, "let no man deceive you" (To think that I had given any encouragement to those that continue in sin): "He that doeth righteousness is righteous, even as He is righteous. He that committeth sin is of the devil; for the devil sinneth from the beginning. For this purpose the Son of God was manifested, that He might destroy the works of the devil. Whosoever is born of God doth not commit sin: For His seed remaineth in him; and he cannot sin, because he is born of God. In this the children of God are manifest, and the children of the devil" (vv. 7-10). In conformity, then, both to the doctrine of St. John, and to the New Testament as a whole, we conclude that a Christian is at least as perfect so as not to commit sin.

The Further Perfection Possible

It is only those who are strong in the Lord, "and have overcome the wicked one," who can be said to be perfect in the sense that they are free from evil thoughts and evil tempers.

First, we will discuss the freedom from evil thoughts. Thoughts about evil are not always evil thoughts. A thought about sin and a sinful thought are very different. For example, a man may think of a murder which another has committed, but this is not an evil or sinful thought. Our blessed Lord certainly understood what was spoken by the devil, when he said, "All these things will I give thee, if thou wilt fall down and worship me." Yet he had no evil or sinful thought.

Where exactly should evil thoughts come from, in the servant who is like his Master? "Out of the heart of man" (if at all) "proceed evil thoughts" (Mark 7:21). If, therefore, his heart is no longer evil, then evil thoughts can no longer proceed out of it.

Just as Christians are free from evil thoughts, they are also free from evil tempers. This is clear from our Lord's declaration: "The disciple is not above his Master; but everyone that is perfect shall be as his Master" (Luke 6:40). He had been delivering, just before He said this, some of the greatest doctrines of Christianity, and some of the most difficult for flesh and blood. "I say unto you, love your enemies, do good to them which hate you; — and unto him that smiteth thee on the one cheek, offer also the other." In the next verse He removes the two great objections with which wise fools meet us at every turn: "These things are too difficult;" or, "They are too high to be attained." The Lord said, "'The disciple is not above his Master;' therefore, if I have suffered, be content to walk in My steps. And do not doubt, but I will fulfill My word. 'For everyone that is perfect shall be as his Master.'" But the Master was free from all sinful tempers. Therefore, so is His disciple.

He who lives in true believers has "purified their hearts by faith," to the extent that everyone that has Christ in him "purifieth himself, even as He is pure" (1 John 3:3). He is purified from pride; for Christ was lowly of heart. He is pure from self-will or desire; for Christ desired only to do the will of His Father, and to finish His work. And he is pure from anger, in the common sense of the word; for Christ was meek and gentle, patient and longsuffering. I say, "in the common sense of the word," because not all anger is evil. We read that our Lord once "looked round with anger" (Mark 3:5). But with what kind of anger? The next word explains, "being grieved for the hardness of their hearts." So then He was angry at the sin, and in the same moment grieving for the sinners; angry at the offense, but sorry for the offenders. With anger, even hatred, He looked on the thing; but with grief and love saw the persons. You that are perfect, go and do likewise. Be angry in this way, and you do not sin; disturbed by every offense against God, but feeling only love and tender compassion for the offender.

Jesus truly does "save His people from their sins:" And not only from outward sins, but also from the sins of their hearts; from evil thoughts, and from evil tempers. "True," some say, "we will be completely saved from our sins, but not until death; not in this world." But how are we to reconcile this with the clear word of St. John? "Herein is our love made perfect, that we may have boldness in the day of judgment. Because as He is, so are we in this world." The Apostle here, beyond all contradiction, speaks of himself and other living Christians, asserting that not only at death, but in this world, they are as their Master (1 John 4:17).

His words in the first chapter (v. 5, etc.) are in perfect agreement with this: "God is light, and in Him is no darkness at all. If we walk in the light, we have fellowship one with another, and the blood of Jesus Christ His Son cleanseth us from all sin." And again: "If we confess our sins, He is faithful and just to forgive us our sins, and to cleanse us from all unrighteousness." It is evident that the Apostle speaks of a deliverance that is accomplished in this world. For he does not say that the blood of Christ will cleanse at the hour of death, or in the day of judgment, but, it "cleanseth," at the present time, "us," living Christians, "from all sin." And it is equally evident, that if any sin remains, we are not cleansed from all sin. If any unrighteousness remains in the soul, it is not cleansed from all unrighteousness.

Neither let anyone say that this cleansing is the cleansing of justification only, or the cleansing from the guilt of sin. First, because this confuses what the Apostle clearly distinguishes, who first mentions forgiveness of sins and then cleansing from all unrighteousness. Second, because this would be asserting justification by works, making holiness necessary before justification. For if the cleansing here spoken of here is merely the cleansing from the guilt of sin, then we are cleansed from guilt, that is, are justified, not on the scriptural condition of faith, but by "walking in the light, as He is in the light."

We see, then, that the natural meaning of this verse is that Christians are saved in this world from all sin, from all unrighteousness; that they are now, in this sense, perfect, so as not to commit sins and to be free from evil thoughts and evil tempers.

(Editor's Note: The remainder of this essay is taken from the sermon entitled "On Perfection")

What then is the perfection of which man is capable while he lives in a corruptible body? It is complying with that kind command, "My son, give Me thy heart." It is "loving the Lord his God with all his heart, and with all his soul, and with all his mind." This is the sum of Christian perfection: it is love. The first part of it is the love of God. And just as he who loves God loves his brother also, it is inseparably connected with the second: "Thou shalt love thy neighbor as thyself." "On these two commandments hang all the Law and the Prophets." These express the whole of Christian perfection.

As St. Peter writes, "As He that hath called you is holy, so be ye holy in all manner of conversation" (1 Peter 1:15). According to this Apostle then, perfection is another name for holiness: inward and outward righteousness: holiness of life, arising from holiness of heart.

If any expressions can be stronger than these, they are those of St. Paul to the Thessalonians: "The God of peace himself sanctify you wholly; and may the whole of you, the spirit, the soul, and the body be preserved blameless unto the coming of our Lord Jesus Christ" (1 Thess. 5:23).

Response to Objections to Perfection

One common objection is that there is no promise of it in the Word of God. But there is a very clear promise that we will all love the Lord our God with all our hearts. We read, "Then will I circumcise thy heart, and the heart of thy seed, to love the Lord thy God with all thy heart, and with all thy soul" (Deut. 30:6). Equally clear is the word of our Lord, which is no less a promise, though in the form of a command: "Thou shalt love the Lord thy God with all thy heart, and with all thy soul, and with all thy mind" (Matthew 22:37). No words can be stronger than these; no promise can be more definite. Similarly, "Thou shalt love thy neighbor as thyself," is as definite a promise as it is a command.

And that unlimited promise which rules through the entire gospel age, "I will put My laws in their minds, and write them in their hearts," turns all the commands into promises; including this one, "Let this mind be in you which was also in Christ Jesus." This command is equivalent to a promise, and gives us reason to expect that He will work in us what He requires of us.

Regarding the fruit of the Spirit, the Apostle, in affirming that "the fruit of the Spirit is love, joy, peace, longsuffering, gentleness, goodness, faithfulness, meekness, self-control," affirms that the Holy Spirit actually works love and these other tempers in those that are led by Him. Here also we are walking on solid ground, for this scripture is also equivalent to a promise, and assures us that all these will be in us, if we are led by the Spirit.

The command of God given by St. Peter, "Be ye holy, as He that hath called you is holy, in all manner of conversation," implies a promise that we will be holy, if we are not unwilling. Nothing can be lacking on God's part. As He has called us to holiness, He is undoubtedly willing, as well as able, to work this holiness in us. For He cannot mock His helpless creatures, calling us to receive what He never intends to give. That He does call us to holiness is undeniable; therefore, He will give it if we are not disobedient to the heavenly calling.

The prayer of St. Paul for the Thessalonians, that God would "sanctify" them throughout, and "that the whole of them, the spirit, the soul, and the body, might be preserved blameless," is a prayer that will undoubtedly be heard on behalf of all the children of God. Therefore, all Christians are encouraged to expect the same blessing, that they also will be "sanctified throughout, in spirit, soul, and body;" and that "the whole of them shall be preserved blameless unto the coming of our Lord Jesus Christ."

But the great question is whether there is any promise in Scripture that we will be saved from sin. Undoubtedly there is. That promise, "He shall redeem Israel from all his sins" (Psalm 130:8); exactly corresponds to those words of the angel, "He shall save His people from their sins." And surely "He is able to save unto the uttermost them that come unto God through Him." This is the glorious promise given through the Prophet Ezekiel: "Then will I sprinkle clean water upon you, and ye shall be clean: From all your filthiness, and from all your idols, will I cleanse you. A new heart also will I give you, and a new spirit will I put within you: And I will take away the stony heart out of your flesh, and I will give you a heart of flesh. And I will put My Spirit within you, and cause you to walk in My statutes, and ye shall keep My judgments, and do them" (Ezekiel 36:25-27). This is what was pronounced by Zechariah, "The oath which He swore to our father Abraham, that He would grant unto us, being delivered out of the hand of our enemies" (such enemies as all our sins), "to serve Him without fear, in holiness and righteousness before Him, all the days of our life" (Luke 1:73-75). The last part of this promise is especially worthy of our observation. Should anyone say, "True, we shall be saved from our sins when we die," as if to destroy this argument, he says, "all the days of our life." With what humility then can anyone claim that no one will enjoy this liberty until death?

"But," some say, "this cannot be the meaning of the words, for the thing is impossible." It is impossible with men, but the things impossible with men are possible with God. "But this is impossible by nature, for a man cannot be saved from all sin while he is in a sinful body." There is a great deal of force in this objection. However, we have already allowed that while we are in the body we cannot be wholly free from error. In spite of all our carefulness, we will still be liable to discern wrongly in many instances. And a mistake in discernment will very frequently cause a mistake in practice. Further, a wrong judgment may cause something in the temper or passions that is not right. It may cause needless fear or ill-grounded hope, unreasonable love or unreasonable aversion. But this is in no way inconsistent with the perfection described above. It is quite consistent with salvation from sin, if sin is defined as a voluntary transgression of a known law.

"But does not St. Paul himself say, 'They that are in the flesh cannot please God?'" I am afraid that these words have deceived many who assume that the words, "they that are in the flesh," mean those that are in the body. No, the flesh, in this text, no more means the body than it does the soul. Abel, Enoch, Abraham, along with all those recited by St. Paul in Hebrews 11, did actually please God while they were in the body, as he himself testifies. Therefore, the expression used here means those that are unbelievers, in their natural state, and without God in the world.

But let us consider the reasoning of this issue. Why can the Almighty not sanctify the soul while it is in the body? Can He not sanctify you while you are in this house, as well as outside in the open air? Can the walls of brick or stone prevent Him? Neither can these walls of flesh and blood prevent Him for one moment from sanctifying you entirely. He can just as easily save you from all sin in the body as out of the body. "But has He promised to save us from sin while we are in the body?" Undoubtedly He has. For a promise is implied in every commandment of God, including, "Thou shalt love the Lord thy God with all thy heart, and with all thy soul, and with all thy mind." For this and every other commandment is given, not to the dead, but to the living. It is expressed in the words recited above, that we should walk "in holiness before Him all the days of our life."

But a more plausible objection remains, which is taken from

experience: that there are no living witnesses of this salvation from sin. In answer to this,

(1) I agree that there are not many. Such is our slowness to believe what both the prophets and apostles have spoken, that there are few true witnesses of this great salvation.
(2) I realize that there are false witnesses, who either deceive their own souls and speak of the things they do not know, or are hypocrites. Many do the same with regard to justification: they imagine they are justified, when they are not. But even though many imagine it falsely, still there are some that are truly justified. And though many imagine they are sanctified, and are not, still there are some that are really sanctified.
(3) I realize that some who once enjoyed full salvation have now lost it. They once walked in glorious freedom, giving God their whole heart, "rejoicing evermore, praying without ceasing, and in everything giving thanks." But all this is past. Perhaps they still have a sense of His pardoning love, but even this is often attacked by doubts and fears, so that they hold it with a trembling hand.

Some say that while it may please God to make some of His children unspeakably holy and happy, it is only for a time. They say that God never intended for it to continue to the end of their lives. But where is the proof? We know that in general, "the gifts and calling of God are without repentance." Why should we imagine that He will make an exception of the most precious gift on this side of heaven? Is He not as able to give it continually, as He is to give it once? As able to give it for fifty years, as for one day? How is this supposition that He is not willing consistent with the assertion of the Apostle, who says, "For this is the will of God concerning you in Christ Jesus." It is remarkable that after he had delivered that glorious promise (which it is) in the twenty-third verse, "The very God of peace shall sanctify you wholly: And the whole of you, the spirit, the soul, and the body, shall be preserved blameless unto the coming of the Lord Jesus Christ;" he adds again, "Faithful is He that hath called you, who also will do it." He will not only sanctify you completely, but will preserve you in that state until He comes to receive you to himself.

In fact, several persons have enjoyed this blessing, without any interruption, for many years. Several enjoy it now. And many enjoyed it until their death, as they declared with their last breath; calmly witnessing that God had saved them from all sin until their spirit returned to God.

As to any objections taken from experience, we observe that either the persons who claim perfection have attained Christian perfection or they have not. If they have not, the objections brought against them miss the mark, for they are not the persons we are referring to. Therefore, whatever they are or do is separate from the question. But if they have attained perfection, if they match the description given here, no reasonable objection can stand against them.

"But I never saw one," continues the objector, "that matched my idea of perfection." It may be so. And it is probable that you never will. For your idea includes too much; even freedom from those weaknesses which always accompany a spirit that is connected with flesh and blood. But if you keep to the account that is given above, and allow for the weakness of human understanding, you may see present, undeniable examples of scriptural perfection.

Questions for the Opponents of Perfection

Now permit me to ask, why are you so angry with those who

claim to have attained this? What rational objection can you have to loving the Lord your God with all your heart? Would it do you any harm? Would it lessen your happiness, either in this world or in the world to come? And why should you be unwilling that others should give Him their whole heart, or that they should love their neighbors as themselves, even "as Christ hath loved us?" Is it not rather highly desirable?

Why are you so averse to having in you the whole "mind which was in Christ Jesus," all the affections, all the tempers and dispositions, which were in Him while He dwelt among men? Would it be any worse for you if God were to form in you this very hour the mind that was in Him? If not, why should you keep others from seeking this blessing, or be displeased with those who think they have attained it? Is anything more lovely, or more to be desired by every child of man?

Why are you averse to having the whole "fruit of the Spirit:" "love, joy, peace, longsuffering, meekness, gentleness, faithfulness, goodness, self-control?" Because "against these there is no law," there cannot be any reasonable objection. Surely nothing is more desirable than for all these tempers to take root in your heart; and in the hearts of all that name the name of Christ; even all the inhabitants of the earth.

Is perfection being "sanctified throughout, in spirit, soul, and body?" What lover of God and man can be averse to this, or be afraid of it? Is it not, in your best moments, your desire to be consistent with yourself: all faith, all meekness, all love? And if you possessed this glorious liberty, would not you wish to continue in it, to be preserved "blameless unto the coming of our Lord Jesus Christ?"

Let me ask one more question. Why should any man of reason and religion be averse to salvation from all sin? Is sin not the greatest evil on this side of hell? If so, is not a complete deliverance from it one of the greatest blessings on this side of heaven? How earnestly then should all the children of God pray for it!

By sin I mean a voluntary transgression of a known law. Are you averse to being delivered from this? Are you afraid of such a deliverance? Do you love sin so much that you are unwilling to part with it? Surely not. You do not love either the devil or his works. Instead, you wish to be totally delivered from them; to have sin rooted out both of your life and your heart.

I have often observed with surprise that the opponents of perfection are more outspoken against it when it is stated in this way than in any other. They will allow everything you say of love for God and man; of the fruit of the Spirit; of complete holiness; of entire self-dedication; of sanctification in spirit, soul, and body; even the offering up of all our thoughts, words, and actions as a sacrifice to God. They will accept all of this if only we will allow sin, a little sin, to remain in us until death.

Contrast this with that remarkable passage in John Bunyan's "Holy War." "When Immanuel," he says, "had driven Diabolus and all his forces out of the city of Mansoul, Diabolus sent a petition to Immanuel, that he might have only a small part of the city. When this was rejected, he begged to have only a little room within the walls." But Immanuel answered that Diabolus would have no place in it at all; not even to rest the sole of his foot. Had not the good old man forgotten himself? Did not the force of truth prevail over him here so as to overturn his own system, and to declare perfection in the clearest way? For if this is not salvation from sin, I do not know what is.

Says one great man, "This is the error of errors: I hate it from my heart. I pursue it through all the world with fire and sword." Why are you so passionate? Do you seriously think there is no error equal to this? Here is something which I cannot understand. Why are those that oppose salvation from sin (with few exceptions) so eager, almost furious? Are you fighting "for God and your country?" For all that is near and dear to you? Why are you so fond of sin? What good has it ever done you? What good is it ever likely to do you, either in this world, or in the world to come? And why are you so violently opposed to those that hope for deliverance from it?

Have patience with us, if we are in an error. Allow us to enjoy our error. Even if we never attain it, the very expectation of this deliverance gives us comfort and gives us strength to resist those enemies which we expect to conquer. If you could persuade us to doubt that victory, we would surely give up the contest. Now "we are saved by hope." Do not be angry at those who are happy in their mistake. If you are, whether their opinion is right or wrong, your attitude is undeniably sinful. Be patient with us, just as we are with you; and see whether or not the Lord will deliver us; whether or not He is able and willing "to save them to the uttermost that come unto God through Him!"

6

A Plain Account of Christian Perfection

Editor's Note: This section is especially valuable for two reasons. First, it describes John Wesley's early progress in the development of the distinctive Wesleyan doctrines. Second, it provides an answer to opponents of these doctrines, primarily by clarification. Repetitious material has been deleted, including Wesley's summary of his sermon on perfection, since it is included in the preceding chapter of this volume.

My purpose in the following papers is to give a plain account of the steps by which I was led to embrace the doctrine of Christian perfection.

In 1725, at twenty-three years of age, I encountered Bishop Taylor's *Rule and Exercises of Holy Living and Dying*. I was very affected, especially by the part that relates to purity of intention.

Instantly I resolved to dedicate all of my life to God, all of my thoughts, words, and actions; being convinced that there is no middle ground; but that every part of my life must be either a sacrifice to God, or to myself, which is, in effect, to the devil. Can any serious person doubt this, or find a middle ground between serving God and serving the devil?

In 1726, I read Kempis's *Christian's Pattern*. The nature and extent of inward religion, the religion of the heart, now appeared to me in a stronger light than ever before. I saw that giving all of my life to God (assuming it was possible to do this), and going no farther would be of no benefit to me, unless I gave my whole heart to Him as well. I saw that "simplicity of intention, and purity of affection," one design in all we say or do, and one desire ruling all our tempers, are indeed "the wings of the soul," without which it can never ascend to the mountain of God.

A year or two later, William Law's *Christian Perfection* and *Serious Call* were put into my hands. These convinced me, more than ever, of the absolute impossibility of being half-Christian; and I determined, through His grace (the absolute necessity of which I was deeply conscious of), to be completely devoted to God, to give Him all my soul, my body, and my possessions. Will any thinking man say that this is carrying the matter too far, or that He who has given himself for us deserves anything less than ourselves, all we have, and all we are?

In 1729, I began to study the Bible as the only standard of truth and the only model of pure religion. There I saw the necessity of having "the mind which was in Christ," and of "walking as Christ also walked;" of having not only a part, but all of the mind which was in Him; and of walking as He walked, not only in many or in most aspects, but in all things. And this was the view that I had of religion, that it is a complete following of Christ, an entire inward and outward conformity to our Master. I was afraid of nothing more than adjusting this rule to fit my experience or the experiences of other men, to allow myself the least inconformity to our great Example.

Summary of Sermon on Circumcision of the Heart

On January 1, 1733, I preached before the University in St. Mary's church, on "the circumcision of the heart," which I described in these words: "It is that habitual attitude of the soul which, in the sacred writings, is called holiness; and which directly implies being cleansed from sin, 'from all filthiness both of flesh and spirit;' and, as a result, being given those virtues which were in Christ Jesus, being so 'renewed in the image of our mind,' as to be 'perfect as our Father in heaven is perfect.'" In this sermon I observed, "Love is the fulfilling of the law, the purpose of the commandment." It is not only "the first and great" command, but all the commandments in one. "Whatsoever things are just, whatsoever things are pure, if there be any virtue, if there be any praise," they are all contained in this one word, love. In this is perfection, and glory, and happiness. The royal law of heaven and earth is this, "Thou shall love the Lord thy God with all thy heart, and with all thy soul, and with all thy mind, and with all thy strength." The one perfect good will be your one ultimate goal.

"One thing you will desire for its own sake, — the fullness of Him who is all in all. One happiness you will propose to your souls, even a union with Him that made them, the 'fellowship with the Father and the Son,' being 'joined to the Lord in one spirit.' One plan you are to pursue: the enjoyment of God in time and in eternity. Desire other things only as far as they tend toward this; love the creature only as it leads to the Creator. Let every affection, and thought, and word, and action, be subject to this. Whatever you desire or fear, whatever you seek or avoid, whatever you think, speak, or do, let it be toward your happiness in God, the only end, as well as source, of your being."

I concluded with these words: "Here is the sum of the perfect law, the circumcision of the heart. Let the spirit return to God that gave it, with the whole spectrum of its affections. He does not desire other sacrifices from us, but He has chosen the living sacrifice of the heart. Let it be continually offered up to God through Christ, in flames of holy love. Let no creature be allowed to compete with Him; for He is a jealous God. He will not share His throne with another; He will reign without a rival. Let no intention or desire be accepted there, except that which has Him for its ultimate object."

And what is here that any man of understanding, who believes the Bible, can object to? What can he deny without flatly contradicting the Scripture?

Summary of Preface to a Volume of Hymns

In 1742, we published a volume of hymns. The preface included the following statements:

Perhaps the prejudice against Christian perfection arises mainly from a misunderstanding of it.

First, we insist there is no perfection in this life that implies any exemption from keeping all the ordinances of God, or from doing good to all men while we have time, though "especially unto the household of faith." We believe that not only the babes in Christ, but also those also who are "grown up into perfect men," must, as often as they have opportunity, eat bread and drink wine in remembrance of Him, and search the Scriptures. They must, by fasting and moderation, "keep their bodies under, and bring them into subjection;" and, above all, pour out their souls in prayer, both privately, and in the congregation.

Second, we believe that there is no perfection in this life that implies an entire deliverance from ignorance, or error in things not essential to salvation, or from various temptations, or from countless infirmities.

But whom then do you mean by "one that is perfect?" We

mean one who has "the mind which was in Christ," and who "walketh as Christ also walked;" a man "that hath clean hands and a pure heart," or that is "cleansed from all filthiness of flesh and spirit;" one who "does not commit sin." We mean one whom God has "sanctified throughout in body, soul, and spirit;" one who "walketh in the light as He is in the light, in whom is no darkness at all; the blood of Jesus Christ His Son having cleansed him from all sin."

This man can now testify to all mankind, "I am crucified with Christ: Nevertheless I live; yet not I, but Christ liveth in me." He is holy as God who called him is holy, both in heart and "in all manner of conversation." He "loveth the Lord his God with all his heart," and serves Him "with all his strength." He "loveth his neighbor as himself;" even those who "despitefully use him and persecute him." His soul is filled with love, and his life is consistent with love, full of "the work of faith, the patience of hope, the labor of love." "And whatever" he "doeth either in word or deed," he "doeth it all in the name," in the love and power, "of the Lord Jesus." In summary, he does "the will of God on earth, as it is done in heaven."

This is to be a perfect man, to be "sanctified throughout;" even "to have a heart so all-flaming with the love of God" (to use Archbishop Usher's words), "as to continually offer up every thought, word, and work, as a spiritual sacrifice, acceptable to God through Christ." In every thought of our hearts, in every word of our tongues, in every work of our hands, to "show forth His praise, who hath called us out of darkness into His marvelous light." O that we, together with all who sincerely seek the Lord Jesus, may "be made perfect in one!" It is to have "the mind which was in Christ," and to "walk as He walked;" to be inwardly and outwardly devoted to God; completely devoted in heart and life.

Doctrines Expressed at Preachers' Conferences 1744-47

We seriously considered the doctrine of sanctification, or perfection. The questions asked concerning it and the substance of the answers given were as follows:

QUESTION. What does it mean to be sanctified?

ANSWER. To be renewed in the image of God, "in righteousness and true holiness."

Q. What is implied in being a perfect Christian?

A. Loving God with all our heart, and mind, and soul (Deut. 6:5).

Q. Does this imply that all inward sin is taken away?

A. Undoubtedly; how else can we be said to be "saved" from all "our uncleannesses" (Ezek. 36:29)?

Q. When does inward sanctification begin?

A. The moment a man is justified. From that time a believer gradually dies to sin, and grows in grace. But sin still remains in him, even the seed of all sin, until he is thoroughly sanctified.

Q. How should we preach sanctification?

A. Hardly at all to those who are not pressing forward. To those who are, always by way of God's promises; always attracting, rather than driving.

Q. Which of our doctrines are accepted by our brothers who differ from us regarding entire sanctification?

A. They agree, (1) That everyone must be entirely sanctified at the time of death. (2) That until then a believer grows daily in grace, coming nearer and nearer to perfection. (3) That we ought to be continually pressing toward it, and urging all others to do so as well.

Q. Which of their doctrines do we accept?

A. We agree, (1) That many of those who have died in the faith were not perfected in love until shortly before their death. (2) That St. Paul continually applies the term *sanctified* to all that were justified. (3) That by this term alone, he rarely, if ever, means "saved from all sin." (4) That, consequently, it is not proper to use it in that sense, without adding the word *wholly*, *entirely*, or one similar. (5) That the inspired writers almost continually speak of or to those who were justified, but very rarely of or to those who were wholly sanctified [that is, to those alone, excluding all others; but they speak to them, along with others, almost continually]. (6) That, consequently, we should speak almost continually of justification; but more rarely [though in some places very frequently, strongly, and explicitly], of entire sanctification.

Q. What then is the point where our views diverge?

A. It is this: should we expect to be saved from all sin before the time of death?

Q. Is there any clear promise in Scripture that God will save us from all sin?

A. There is: "He shall redeem Israel from all his sins" (Psalm 130:8). This is expressed in greater detail in the prophecy of Ezekiel: "Then will I sprinkle clean water upon you, and you shall be clean; from all your filthiness and from all your idols will I cleanse you: I will also save you from all your uncleannesses" (Ezek. 36:25, 29). No promise can be more clear. And the Apostle plainly refers to this in that exhortation: "Having these promises, let us cleanse ourselves from all filthiness of flesh and spirit, perfecting holiness in the fear of God" (2 Cor. 7:1). Equally clear is that ancient promise: "The Lord thy God will circumcise thy heart, and the heart of thy seed, to love the Lord thy God with all thy heart and with all thy soul" (Deut. 30:6).

Q. But is there any statement like this in the New Testament?

A. There is. 1 John 3:8 reads: "For this purpose the Son of God was manifested, that he might destroy the works of the devil." This verse says the works of the devil, without any limitation or restriction; and all sin is the work of the devil. Parallel to it is the statement of St. Paul: "Christ loved the Church, and gave himself for it, that He might sanctify it, having cleansed it

. . . that He might present it to himself a glorious Church, not having spot or wrinkle, or any such thing, but that it might be holy and without blemish" (Eph. 5:25-27). To the same effect is his statement in Romans 8: 3, 4: "God sent His Son, that the righteousness of the law might be fulfilled in us, who walk not after the flesh, but after the Spirit."

Q. Does the New Testament give us any further reason to expect salvation from all sin?

A. Undoubtedly it does both in prayers and commands, which are the same as the strongest statements.

Q. What prayers do you mean?

A. Prayers for entire sanctification; which, if there were no such thing, would be a mockery of God. Specifically they are, (1) "Deliver us from evil." Now, when this is done, when we are delivered from all evil, there can be no sin remaining. (2) "Neither pray I for these alone, but for them also who shall believe on Me through their word; that they all may be one; as Thou, Father, art in Me and I in Thee, that they also may be one in us; I in them, and Thou in Me, that they may be made perfect in one" (John 17:20-23). (3) "I bow my knees unto the God and Father of our Lord Jesus Christ, that He would grant you...that you, being rooted and grounded in love, may be able to comprehend, with all saints, what is the breadth, and length, and depth, and height, and to know the love of Christ, which passeth knowledge; that you may be filled with all the fullness of God" (Eph. 3:14, etc.). (4) "The very God of peace sanctify you wholly. And I pray God, your whole spirit, soul, and body, may be preserved blameless unto the coming of our Lord Jesus Christ" (1 Thess. 5:23).

Q. What command is there to the same effect?

A. (1) "Be ye perfect, as your Father who is in heaven is perfect" (Matt. 5:48). (2) "Thou shalt love the Lord thy God with all thy heart, and with all thy soul, and with all thy mind" (Matt. 12:37). And if the love of God fills the heart, there can be no sin there.

Q. But how is this to be done before the time of death?

A. (1) From the very nature of a command, which is not given to the dead, but to the living. Therefore, "Thou shalt love God with all thy heart," cannot mean, "You will do this when you die; but not while you live."

(2) From clear texts of Scripture: "The grace of God, that bringeth salvation, hath appeared to all men; teaching us that, having renounced ungodliness and worldly lusts, we should live soberly, righteously, and godly in this present world; looking for the glorious appearing of our Lord Jesus Christ, who gave himself for us, that He might redeem us from all iniquity, and purify unto himself a peculiar people, zealous of good works" (Titus 2:11-14). "He hath raised up an horn of salvation for us, to perform the mercy promised to our fathers; the oath which He sware to our father Abraham, that He would grant unto us, that we, being delivered out of the hands of our enemies, should serve Him without fear, in holiness and righteousness before Him, all the days of our life" (Luke 1:69, etc.).

Q. Is there any example in Scripture of persons who attained this?

A. Yes; St. John, and all those of whom he says, "Herein is our love made perfect, that we may have boldness in the day of judgment; because, as He is, so are we in this world" (1 John 4:17).

Q. Are we able to continue in the joy of faith we receive at justification until we are perfected in love?

A. Why not? Holy grief at our need to be perfected does not quench this joy; since even while we deeply partake of the sufferings of Christ, we may rejoice with unspeakable joy.

Concluding Points

(1) Christian perfection is that love for God and for our neighbor which implies deliverance from all sin.

(2) This is received only by faith.

(3) It is given instantaneously, in one moment.
(4) We are to expect it, not at death, but at every moment; for now is the accepted time, now is the day of this salvation.

From the Bristol Conference in 1758

(1) Everyone is capable of making mistakes as long as he lives. (2) A mistake in opinion may cause a mistake in practice. (3) Every such mistake is a transgression of the perfect law. Therefore, (4) Every such mistake, if it were not for the blood of atonement, would cause eternal damnation. (5) Therefore, the most perfect Christians still have a continual need for the merits of Christ, even for their actual sins, and may say, "Forgive us our trespasses." This easily explains why some, who are not offended when we speak of the highest degree of love, still do not accept the possibility of living without sin. The reason is that they know all men are prone to errors in practice as well as in judgment. But they do not observe that this is not sin, even if love is the sole principle of action.

Q. But if they live without sin, does this not end their need for Christ, at least in His priestly office?

A. Far from it. None so entirely depend on Christ as these do. For Christ does not give life to the soul apart from himself. Therefore, His words are true of all men, whatever state of grace they are in: "As the branch cannot bear fruit of itself, except it abide in the vine; no more can you, except you abide in Me: Without Me you can do nothing." In every state we need Christ in the following ways: (1) Whatever grace we receive, it is a free gift from Him. (2) We receive it as a purchase, for which He paid the price. (3) We have this grace, not only from Christ, but in Him. For our perfection is not like that of a tree, which is nourished by the sap from its own root, but rather like that of a branch which, united to the vine, bears fruit; but, when severed from it, withers. (4) All our blessings, earthly, spiritual, and eternal, depend on His intercession for us, which is one part of His priestly office, which, therefore, we always need. (5) The best of men still need Christ in His priestly office, to atone for their omissions, their shortcomings, their mistakes in judgment and practice, and their defects of various kinds. For these are all deviations from the perfect law, and require an atonement. However, we infer from the words of St. Paul that they are not properly sins: "He that loveth, hath fulfilled the law; for love is the fulfilling of the law" (Rom. 13:10). Now mistakes, and whatever infirmities flow from our corruptible bodies, are not in any way contrary to love; nor are they therefore, in the scriptural sense, sin.

To explain this further, not only that which is properly called sin (that is, a voluntary transgression of a known law), but that which is improperly called such, (that is, an involuntary transgression of a divine law, known or unknown) needs the atoning blood. I believe there is no perfection in this life that excludes these involuntary transgressions which naturally result from the ignorance and mistakes inseparable from the human condition. A person filled with the love of God is still prone to these involuntary transgressions. You may call such transgressions sins, if you please. I do not, for the reasons I have given.

Q. What advice would you give to those that do, and those that do not, call mistakes sin?

A. Let those that do not call them sins never think that they are in such a state that they can stand before God's infinite justice without a Mediator. Let those who do call them so beware how they confuse these defects with sins, properly named. But how will they avoid it? How will these be distinguished from those, if they are all generally called sins? I am afraid that if we say that any so-called sins are consistent with perfection, few would limit the idea to those defects of which the statement could be true.

Q. How will we avoid setting the standard of perfection too

high or too low?

A. By keeping to the Bible, and setting it just as high as the Scripture does. It is nothing higher and nothing lower than this: our pure love for God and man; loving God with all our heart and soul, and our neighbor as ourselves. It is love governing the heart and life, penetrating all our tempers, words, and actions.

Q. How can we know for certain that a person is saved from all sin?

A. We cannot infallibly know that one is saved in this way (nor even that one is justified) unless it pleases God to give us discernment. But we consider these to be sufficient proofs for any reasonable man, which leave little room to doubt either the truth or depth of the work: (1) If we had clear evidence of his exemplary behavior for some time before this supposed change. This would give us reason to believe that he would not lie, but speak purely as he felt; (2) If he gave a detailed report of the time and manner in which the change was worked, with speech that could not be reproved; and, (3) If it appeared that all his words and actions which followed were holy and blameless. To state it briefly: (1) I have sufficient reason to believe that this person will not lie; (2) He testifies, "I feel no sin, but only love; I pray, rejoice, and give thanks without ceasing; and I have just as clear an inward witness that I am fully renewed, as that I am justified." If I have no reason to oppose this clear testimony, I ought to believe it.

It accomplishes nothing to object, "But I know several things in which he is mistaken." For it has been agreed that all who are in the body are prone to make mistakes; and that a mistake in judgment may cause a mistake in practice. For example, even one that is perfected in love may think that another person is more or less faulty than he really is. Therefore, he may speak to him with more or less severity than the truth would require. But this is no proof that the person speaking is not perfect.

Q. But can anyone who has a pure heart prefer pleasing food

to unpleasing food, or enjoy anything that is not strictly necessary? If so, how do they differ from others?

A. The difference between these and others in taking pleasant food is, (1) They need none of these things to make them happy, for they have a source of happiness within themselves. They see and love God. They rejoice forever in this, and in everything give thanks. (2) They may use these things, but they do not seek and value them. (3) They use them sparingly, and not for the sake of the thing itself. Having said this, we continue. Such a person may use pleasing food, without the danger which threatens those who are not saved from sin. He may prefer it to unpleasing, though equally wholesome, food, as a means of increasing his thankfulness, with a single eye toward God who gives us all things to enjoy. By the same principle, he may smell a flower, or eat a bunch of grapes, or take any other pleasure which does not lessen but increase his delight in God. Therefore, neither can we say that one perfected in love would be incapable of marriage or of worldly business. If he were called to it, he would be more capable than ever; being able to do everything without pressure or anxiety, without any spiritual distraction.

Q. When may a person consider himself to have attained this?

A. When, after having been fully convinced of his inherent sinfulness, by a deeper and clearer conviction than he experienced before justification, and after having experienced a gradual killing of it, he experiences a total death to sin, and an entire renewal in the love and image of God, rejoicing evermore, praying without ceasing, and in everything giving thanks. The mere feeling that one has only love and no sin is not a sufficient proof. Several have experienced this for a time before their souls were fully renewed. A person therefore ought not to believe that the work is done in his heart until there is added the testimony of the Spirit, witnessing his entire sanctification as clearly as his justification.

Q. But why do some imagine they are sanctified in this way, when in reality they are not?

A. It is because they do not judge by all the marks we have discussed, but either by part of them, or by others that are unclear. But I know of no instance of a person being deceived while he was attentive to them all. I believe there can be none in the world. If a man is deeply and fully convinced of his inherent sinfulness after justification; if he then experiences a gradual death of sin, and afterwards an entire renewal in the image of God; and if a clear, direct witness of this renewal is added to this change; I consider it impossible that this man should be deceived. And if one I know to be a man of truthfulness testifies of these things, I should not reject his testimony without sufficient reason.

Q. Is this death to sin and renewal in love gradual or instantaneous?

A. A man may be dying for some time; but he does not die until the instant his soul is separated from his body. In that instant, he lives the life of eternity. Likewise, he may be dying to sin for some time; but he is still not dead to sin until sin is separated from his soul; and in that instant he lives the full life of love. And, as could be said about physical death, the change accomplished when the soul dies to sin is of a different kind, infinitely greater than any before, and greater than anyone can imagine until he experiences it. And yet he still grows in grace, in the knowledge of Christ, and in the love and image of God; and will continue to do so, not only until death, but for all eternity.

Q. How are we to wait for this change?

A. Not in careless indifference, or lazy inactivity; but in vigorous, complete obedience, in zealously keeping of all the commandments, in watchfulness, in denying ourselves, and taking up our cross daily; as well as in earnest prayer and fasting and obedience to all the ordinances of God. If any man dreams of attaining it in any other way (or of keeping it once it is attained), he deceives himself. It is true that we receive it by simple faith. But God will not give that faith unless we look for it diligently, in the way that He has ordained. This consideration may satisfy those who ask why so few have received the blessing. Ask how many are looking for it in this way, and you have a sufficient answer. Prayer is especially lacking. Who continues in it? Who wrestles with God for this very thing? So, "you have not, because you ask not; or because you ask amiss," asking only that you may be renewed before you die. Will that make you content? Ask for it to be done today. Do not call this setting a time for God to act. Today is His time as well as tomorrow.

Q. But may we continue in peace and joy until we are perfected in love?

"A. Certainly, for the kingdom of God is not divided against itself; therefore, do not let believers become discouraged from "rejoicing in the Lord always." And yet we may suffer from the sinful nature that remains in us. It is good for us to have a piercing sense of this, and the strongest desire to be delivered from it. But this should only motivate us all the more zealously to run to our strong Helper, all the more earnestly to "press forward to the mark, the prize of our high calling in Christ Jesus." And when the sense of our sin abounds, the sense of His love should abound even more.

Q. How should we treat those who think they have attained perfection?

A. Examine them honestly, and urge them to pray that God would show them what is in their hearts. The most earnest exhortations to abound in grace and the strongest warnings to avoid all evil are given throughout the New Testament to those who are in the highest state of grace. But this should be done with the greatest tenderness; and without any harshness, sternness, or sourness. We should carefully avoid every appearance of anger, unkindness, or contempt. Leave it to Satan to tempt in this way, and to his children to cry out, "Let us test him with torture, so that we may know his meekness and prove his patience." If they are faithful to the grace given, they are in no danger of perishing by erring in this, even if they remain in that error until their spirit returns to God.

Q. But what harm can it do to deal harshly with them?

A. Either they are mistaken, or they are not. If they are, harshness may destroy their souls. This is not impossible, nor improbable. It may anger or discourage them to the point that they sink and rise no more. If they are not mistaken, it may grieve those whom God has not grieved, and do much harm to our own souls. For he that touches them, touches, as it were, the apple of God's eye. If they are full of His Spirit, to behave unkindly or contemptuously toward them is doing so also to the Spirit of grace. We also increase in ourselves evil thoughts and many wrong tempers. To specify one, what self-sufficiency this is, to set ourselves up as judges in these deep things of God! Are we qualified for this office? Can we determine, in all cases, how far infirmity reaches? Do we know what may or may not be consistent with perfect love in all circumstances? Can we precisely determine how it will influence the look, the gesture, or the tone of voice?

Q. But is it not a good thing to expose those who think they have attained perfection when they have not?

A. It is best to do it through mild, loving examination. But it is not good to triumph even over these. It is extremely wrong, if we find such a case, to rejoice as if we had gained something by conquest. Should we not rather grieve, be deeply concerned, and weep? Here is one who seemed to be a living proof of God's power to save completely; but, sadly, it is not as we hoped. Is this a matter of joy? Should we not rejoice a thousand times more, if we can find nothing but pure love? If he is deceived, it is a harmless mistake, while he feels nothing but love in his heart. It is a mistake which usually indicates great grace, a high degree both of holiness and happiness. This should be a matter of real joy; not the mistake itself, but the height of grace which causes it for a time. I rejoice that this soul is always happy in Christ, always full of prayer and thanksgiving. I rejoice that he feels no unholy temper, but the pure love of God continually. And I will rejoice if sin is suspended in him until it is totally destroyed.

Q. Is there no danger then when a man is deceived in this way?

A. Not at the time that he feels no sin. There was danger before, and there will be again when he comes into fresh trials. But so long as he feels nothing but love giving life to all his thoughts, words, and actions, he is in no danger; he is not only happy, but safe, and, for God's sake, let him continue in that love as long as he can. Meantime, you will do well to warn him of the danger that will be if his love grows cold and sin revives; that is, the danger of losing hope, and thinking that because he has not yet attained perfection, he never will.

Q. But what if no one has attained it yet? What if all who think so are deceived?

A. Convince me of this, and I will preach it no longer. But understand me correctly: I do not build any doctrine on this person or that person. Any particular man could be deceived, and I would not waver. But, if there are none made perfect yet, then God has not sent me to preach perfection. Put another way, for many years I have preached, "There is a peace of God which passes all understanding." If you can convince me that in all these years none have attained this peace; that there is no living witness of it today; I will no longer preach it. You may object, "But several persons have died in that peace." Perhaps so, but I need living witnesses. Of course I cannot be perfectly certain that this person or that person is a reliable witness; but if I knew there were no witnesses, I would have to give up this doctrine.

Q. But why does it matter whether any have attained it or not, since so many scriptures testify to it?

A. If I were convinced that none in England had attained

what has been so clearly and strongly preached by so many preachers, in so many places, and for so long a time, I would be clearly convinced that we had all mistaken the meaning of those scriptures; and that in the future, I too must teach that sin will remain until death.

Questions to Opponents of Perfection

Questions humbly proposed to those who deny perfection to be attainable in this life:

(1) Has God anywhere in Scripture commanded us more than He has promised to us?

(2) Are the promises of God concerning holiness to be fulfilled in this life, or only in the next?

(3) Is a Christian under any laws other than those which God promises to "write in our hearts?" (Jer. 31:31, etc.; Heb. 8:10).

(4) In what sense is "the righteousness of the law fulfilled in those who walk not after the flesh, but after the Spirit?" (Rom. 8:4).

(5) Is it impossible for anyone in this life to "love God with all his heart, and mind, and soul, and strength?" And is the Christian under any law which is not fulfilled in this love?

(6) Does the soul's going out of the body purify it from indwelling sin?

(7) If so, is it not something other than "the blood of Christ which cleanseth" it "from all sin?"

(8) If His blood cleanses us from all sin while the soul and body are united, is it not in this life?

(9) If it is not until death, is it not in the next life? And is this not too late?

(10) In the moment of death; what situation is the soul in, when it is neither in the body nor out of it?

(11) Has Christ ever taught us to pray for what He never

intends to give?

(12) Has He not taught us to pray, "Thy will be done on earth, as it is done in heaven?" Is it not done perfectly in heaven?

(13) If so, has He not taught us to pray for perfection on earth? Then does He not intend to give it?

(14) Did St. Paul pray according to the will of God when he prayed that the Thessalonians might be "sanct-fied wholly, and preserved" (in this world, not the next, unless he was praying for the dead) "blameless in body, soul, and spirit, unto the coming of Jesus Christ?"

(15) Do you sincerely desire to be free from indwelling sin in this life?

(16) If you do, did God not give you that desire?

(17) If so, did He give it to you in order to mock you, since it is impossible for it ever to be fulfilled?

(18) If you do not have enough sincerity to desire it, are you not concerned about matters too high for you?

(19) Do you ever ask God to cleanse the thoughts of your heart, that you may love Him perfectly?

(20) If you neither desire what you ask, nor believe it can be attained, do you not pray as a fool prays?

May God help you consider these questions calmly and impartially!

7

The Witness of the Spirit

Discourse I

"The Spirit itself beareth witness with our spirit, that we are the children of God."
Romans 8:16.

There are many who have mistaken the voice of their own imagination for the witness of the Spirit of God, and therefore assumed they were the children of God, even while they were doing the works of the devil! These are fanatics in the worst sense of the word. But it is difficult to convince them, for they consider all attempts to bring them to the knowledge of themselves to be fighting against God. Their passion and impulsiveness of spirit, which they call "defending the faith," makes them immune to all the usual methods of persuasion.

It is not surprising then that many reasonable men, seeing the awful effects of this delusion, and working to avoid it, sometimes tend toward the other extreme. They are reluctant to believe those who speak of having this witness. They are ready to consider fanatics those who use the expressions which have been so terribly abused. They may question whether the witness spoken of here is the privilege of *ordinary* Christians, or one of those *extraordinary* gifts which they suppose belonged only to the apostolic age.

But is it necessary to run toward either extreme? Surely we can find the middle by keeping a sufficient distance from that spirit of error and fanaticism, without denying the gift of God, and giving up the great privilege of His children. Let us then consider the following: first, what this witness of our spirit is; what the testimony of God's Spirit is; and how He does "bear witness with our spirit that we are the children of God;" and second, how this joint testimony of God's Spirit and our own differs from the presumption of a natural mind, and from the delusion of the devil.

Let us first consider what the witness of our spirit is. There are numerous texts of Scripture which describe the marks of the children of God. If anyone needs greater insight, he may receive it by giving attention to God's word, by meditating on it, and by conversing with those who know God's ways. And by the understanding that God has given him, every man can compare the scriptural marks to himself, to know if he is a child of God. If he knows that, "as many as are led by the Spirit of God," into all holy tempers and actions, "they are the sons of God;" and that, second, he is so "led by the Spirit of God;" he will easily conclude, "I am undoubtedly a son of God."

The clear declarations of St. John agree: "Hereby we know

that we do know Him, if we keep His commandments" (2:3). "Whoso keepeth His word, in him verily is the love of God perfected: Hereby know we that we are in Him;" that we are, in fact, the children of God (2:5). "If ye know that He is righteous, ye know that every one that doeth righteousness is born of Him" (2:29). "We know that we have passed from death unto life, because we love the brethren" (3:14). "Hereby we know that we are of the truth, and shall assure our hearts before Him" (3:19), because we "love one another, not in word, neither in tongue, but in deed and in truth." "Hereby know we that we dwell in Him, because He hath given us of His" loving "Spirit" (4:13). And, "hereby we know that He abideth in us by the" obedient "Spirit which He hath given us" (3:24).

It is evident that the apostles did not despise these marks of the children of God, for they applied them to their own souls for the confirmation of their faith. But this is nothing more than rational evidence, the witness of our spirit, our reason or understanding. It all comes to this: those who have these marks are children of God: we have these marks: therefore, we are children of God.

But how can we know that we have these marks? How can we know that we love God and our neighbor, and that we keep His commandments? Notice that the question is, "How do we know?" It is not, "How can we prove it to others?" I ask then, "How do you know that you are alive, and that you are now comfortable, and not in pain?" Are you not simply conscious of it? By the same kind of consciousness, you will know if your soul is alive to God; if you are saved from the pain of pride and anger, and have the comfort of a meek and quiet spirit. You know if you love, rejoice, and delight in God. You know if you love your neighbor as yourself; if you are full of gentleness and patience. And regarding the outward mark of the children of God, which is, according to St. John, the keeping of His commandments, you know in your own heart if you have it by God's grace. Your conscience informs you if you speak the name of God only with seriousness and devotion; if you keep the Sabbath day holy; if you honor your father and mother; if you do to all as you would have them do to you; if you keep your body in holiness and honor; and if, whether you eat or drink, you exercise moderation, and do all to the glory of God.

This is the testimony of our spirit; the testimony of our conscience, that God has given us holiness of heart and outward behavior. It is a consciousness of having received, by the Spirit of adoption, the tempers that, according to the Word of God, belong to His adopted children: a loving heart toward God and all mankind. It is a consciousness that we are inwardly conformed by the Spirit of God to the image of His Son, and that we walk before Him in justice, mercy, and truth, doing the things which are pleasing in His sight, and desiring nothing but Him.

But what is that testimony of God's Spirit which is added and connected to this? How does He "bear witness with our spirit that we are the children of God?" It is hard to find words in the language of men to explain "the deep things of God." There are none that will adequately express what the children of God experience. But perhaps one might say, "The testimony of the Spirit is an inward impression on the soul, by which the Spirit of God directly witnesses to my spirit that I am a child of God; that Jesus Christ has loved me, and has given himself for me; and that all my sins are blotted out, and that I am personally reconciled to God."

The fact that this testimony of the Spirit of God must precede the testimony of our own spirit arises from this one consideration: we must be holy in heart and life before we can be aware that we are so. But we must love God before we can be holy at all, this being the root of all holiness. And we cannot love God until we know He loves us. "We love Him, because He first loved us." And we cannot know His pardoning love for us, until His Spirit witnesses it to us. Since, therefore, this testimony of His pardoning love must precede our love for God and all holiness, it must also precede our consciousness that we have love and holiness. This inward consciousness is the testimony of our spirit.

It is not until the Spirit of God witnesses to our spirit that the Son "loved us, and hath washed us from our sins in His blood," that we "love God because He first loved us;" and, for His sake, love our brother also. Of this we must be conscious: we "know the things that are freely given to us of God." We know that we love God, and keep His commandments; and "hereby also we know that we are of God." This is the testimony of our spirit which, as long as we continue to love God and keep His commandments, is joined to the testimony of God's Spirit, "that we are the children of God."

It is not that the operation of the Spirit of God is separate from the testimony of our spirit. He not only works everything that is good, but also shows us what He has done. This is spoken of by St. Paul as one great purpose of receiving the Spirit, "that we may know the things which are freely given to us of God."

If one asks, "How does the Spirit of God 'bear witness with our spirit, that we are the children of God,' removing all doubt, and proving the reality of our sonship?" The answer is clear from what has been observed above. The soul knows just as intimately and clearly when it loves, delights, and rejoices in God, as when it loves and delights in anything on earth. Therefore, if this is good reasoning, he who loves God, who delights and rejoices in Him with a humble joy and an obedient love, is a child of God. A Christian, then, has a self-evident, inward proof that he loves God. So, the testimony of our own spirit is made known to our hearts by the Holy Spirit beyond all reasonable doubt, to prove the reality of our sonship.

I do not try to explain the way in which this divine testimony is revealed to the heart. This knowledge is too high for me: I cannot attain it. The wind blows, and I hear its sound; but I cannot tell how it comes or where it goes. But we do know that the

Spirit of God does give a believer a testimony of his adoption, such that, while it is present in his soul, he can no more doubt the reality of his sonship than he can doubt the shining of the sun while standing fully in its light.

How this joint testimony of God's Spirit and our spirit may be clearly distinguished from the presumption of a natural mind and from the delusion of the devil is the next thing to be considered. It is important for all who desire God's salvation to consider it most carefully, and not deceive their own souls. An error in this often has the most deadly consequences, because he that errs seldom discovers his mistake until it is too late.

First, how is this testimony distinguished from the presumption of a natural mind? It is certain that one who has never been convicted of sin is always ready to flatter himself, and to think of himself, especially in spiritual things, more highly than he should. It is not strange then that he, when he hears of this privilege of a true Christian, which he considers himself to be, would soon convince himself that he already possesses it. Such instances are commonplace and have been seen in every age. How then may the real testimony of the Spirit with our spirit be distinguished from this damning presumption?

I answer that the Holy Scriptures abound with marks which distinguish one from the other. They describe clearly the circumstances which go before, which accompany, and which follow, the true testimony of the Spirit of God with the spirit of a believer. Whoever carefully weighs these will not confuse darkness with light. He will perceive a vast difference between the real and the imagined witness of the Spirit. For him, there will be no possibility of confusing one with the other.

By these signs, one who mistakenly assumes that he has the gift of God could know, if he really wanted to, that he had been "given up to a strong delusion," and had believed a lie. For the Scriptures lay down those obvious marks that precede, accompany, and follow that gift, which were never in his soul. For instance, the Scripture describes repentance preceding this witness of pardon. So, "Repent ye, and believe the gospel" (Mark 1:15). "Repent, and be baptized every one of you for the remission of sins" (Acts 2:38). "Repent ye therefore, and be converted, that your sins may be blotted out" (Acts 3:19). But he is a stranger to this repentance. He has never known a broken and contrite heart. The reminder and burden of his sins have not caused him grief. In repeating words of repentance, he never meant what he said; he merely paid a compliment to God. The absence of this work of God should, by itself, be enough to convince him that he has grasped a mere shadow, and has never known the real privilege of the sons of God.

Again, the Scriptures describe the new birth, which must precede the witness that we are His children, as a vast and powerful change; a change "from darkness to light," as well as "from the power of Satan unto God;" as a "passing from death unto life," a resurrection from the dead. And so the Apostle writes to the Ephesians: "You hath he quickened who were dead in trespasses and sins" (2:1). And again, "When we were dead in sins, He hath quickened us together with Christ; and hath raised us up together, and made us sit together in heavenly places in Christ Jesus" (vv. 5,6). But what does the natural man know of such a change as this? He is unacquainted with this whole matter. This is a language which he does not understand. He knows of no time when he needed such a change. In this way also, if he allows himself to think, he could know that he is not born of the Spirit; that he has never known God; but has mistaken the voice of his own nature for the voice of God.

But even if we disregard the past, we can easily distinguish a child of God from a presumptuous self-deceiver by certain present marks. The Scriptures describe the joy in the Lord which accompanies the witness of His Spirit as a humble joy that makes a pardoned sinner cry out, "Now mine eye seeth You, I abhor myself in dust and ashes!" And wherever humility is, there is meekness, patience, gentleness, and longsuffering. There is a yielding spirit; a mildness and sweetness, a tenderness of soul which words cannot express. But do these fruits accompany the imagined testimony of the Spirit in a presumptuous man? Just the opposite. The more confident he is of the favor of God, the more he exalts himself; the more proud his behavior becomes. The stronger the witness he imagines himself to have, the more dominating he is to all around him; the more incapable of receiving correction; the more impatient toward contradiction. Instead of being more meek, and gentle, and teachable, more "swift to hear, and slow to speak," he is slower to hear, and swifter to speak; more unready to learn from anyone; and more fiery and forceful in his temper, and eager in his speaking. Perhaps there will even appear a kind of fierceness in his attitude, his manner of speaking, and his whole conduct, as if he were going to take the matter out of God's hands, and "devour the adversaries" himself.

Further, the Scriptures teach that the sure mark of our love for God is, "that we keep His commandments" (1 John 5:3). And our Lord said, "He that keepeth My commandments, he it is that loveth Me" (John 14:21). Love rejoices to obey; to do whatever is pleasing to the beloved. A true lover of God is quick to do His will on earth as it is done in heaven. But is this the character of the presumptuous pretender? No. Instead, his love gives him the liberty to disobey, to break, not keep, the commandments of God. Perhaps when he was in fear of God's anger, he labored to do His will. But now, seeing himself as not under the law, he thinks he is no longer required to observe it. Therefore, he is less eager to do good works; less careful to avoid evil; less watchful over his own heart and tongue. He is less willing to deny himself, and to take up his cross daily. The whole form of his life is changed, since he has imagined himself to be at liberty. He has found an easier way to heaven; a broad, smooth, flowery path; where he can say to his soul, "Soul, be at ease; eat, drink, and be merry." It follows, undeniably, that he does not have the true testimony of his spirit. He cannot be conscious of having those marks which he does not bear: that lowliness, meekness, and obedience. Nor can the Spirit of the God of truth bear witness to a lie; or testify that he is a child of God, when he is obviously a child of the devil.

Look at yourself, you poor self-deceiver! You who are confident of being a child of God; you who say, "I have the witness in myself," and therefore defy all your enemies. You are not humble in heart; therefore, you have not yet received the Spirit of Jesus. You are not gentle and meek; therefore, your joy is not joy in the Lord. You do not keep His commandments; therefore you do not love Him, nor are you a partaker of the Holy Spirit. It is as certain as the Scriptures can make it that His Spirit does not bear witness with your spirit that you are a child of God. Cry out to Him, so that the scales may fall from your eyes; that you may know yourself as you are; that you may hear Him say, "Be of good cheer: your sins are forgiven; your faith hath made you whole."

"But how can one who has the real witness in himself distinguish it from presumption?" How, I ask, do you distinguish day from night? How do you distinguish light from darkness; or the light of a candle from the light of the noonday sun? Is there not an inherent, obvious, essential difference between them? And do you not immediately see that difference if your senses are right? Likewise, there is an inherent, essential difference between the light of the Sun of righteousness, and that flickering light which arises only from the sparks we have kindled. And this difference is immediately seen if our spiritual senses are right.

To require more precise marks of the voice of God is to make an impossible demand, even for one who has the deepest knowledge of God. Suppose when Paul spoke before Agrippa, the Roman had said, "You speak of hearing the voice of the Son of God. How do you know it was His voice? Explain to me how you distinguish this voice from a human or angelic voice." Do you think that the Apostle would have attempted to answer this pointless demand? And yet, without a doubt, the moment he heard that voice, he knew it was the voice of God. But who is able to explain how he knew this?

When God tells any soul that his sins are forgiven, His voice must be known; otherwise He would speak in vain. And He is able to cause this, for He can do whatever He wills. That soul is absolutely sure, "This voice is the voice of God." Yet he who has that witness in himself cannot explain it to one who does not, nor should we expect him to. If there were a natural method to explain the things of God to those who have not experienced them, the natural man could understand the things of the Spirit of God. But this is contrary to the assertion of the Apostle, that "he cannot know them, because they are spiritually discerned." The natural man simply does not have these spiritual senses.

"But how can I know that my spiritual senses are right?" This is also a question of great importance, for if a man is mistaken in this, he may continue in his delusion. The confirmation is "the answer of a good conscience toward God." By the fruits He has worked in your spirit, you can recognize the testimony of the Spirit of God. By this you can know that you have not deceived your own soul. The fruits of the Spirit, ruling in the heart, are "love, joy, peace, a heart of mercy, humbleness of mind, meekness, gentleness, longsuffering." And the outward fruits are doing good to all men; doing evil to no one; and walking in the light, a passionate, complete obedience to all the commandments of God.

By the same fruits you can distinguish God's voice from any delusion of the devil. That proud spirit cannot humble you before God. He cannot soften your heart and melt it into a genuine longing for God, and then into love. It is not the enemy of God and man that enables you to love your neighbor; or to put on meekness, gentleness, patience, self-control, and the whole armor of God. He is not a destroyer of sin, which is his own work. Only the Son of God comes "to destroy the works of the devil." As surely as holiness is of God, and sin is the work of the devil, so surely the witness you have in yourself is not of Satan, but of God.

Knowing this you can say, "Thanks be unto God for His unspeakable gift!" Thanks be to God, who has "sent forth the Spirit of His Son into my heart, crying, Abba, Father," and even now, "bearing witness with my spirit that I am a child of God!" And make sure that not only your lips, but your life, declare His praise. He has marked you for His own; so glorify Him in both your body and spirit, which are His. Beloved, if you have this hope, purify yourself as He is pure. And as you see what manner of love the Father has given you, that you should be called a child of God; cleanse yourself "from all filthiness of flesh and spirit, perfecting holiness in the fear of God;" and let all your thoughts, words, and actions be a spiritual sacrifice, holy and acceptable to God through Christ Jesus!

8

The Witness of the Spirit

Discourse II

"The Spirit itself beareth witness with our spirit,
that we are the children of God."
Romans 8:16.

No one who believes the Scriptures to be the Word of God can doubt the importance of this truth, which is revealed there as a unique privilege of the children of God. It is necessary to explain and defend this truth, because there is a danger of going to extremes. On the one hand, if we deny this truth, there is a danger of our religion becoming mere formality. We could "have a form of godliness," but neglect, if not "deny, the power of it." On the other hand, if we accept it blindly and do not understand what we accept, we are liable to run into the wildness of fanaticism.

But what is the witness of the Spirit? It is the testimony "that God hath given unto us eternal life, and this life is in His Son." The testimony is given by the Spirit of God both to and with our spirit. What He testifies is "that we are the children of God." The immediate result of this testimony is "the fruit of the Spirit;" that is, "love, joy, peace, longsuffering, gentleness, goodness." Without these, the testimony cannot continue. It is inevitably destroyed, not only by the commission of outward sin or the omission of known duty, but by willingly yielding to any inward sin; to state it briefly, by whatever grieves the Holy Spirit of God.

I observed many years ago, "It is hard to find words in the language of men to explain the deep things of God. There are none that adequately express what the Spirit of God works in His children. But perhaps one might say, 'The testimony of the Spirit is an inward impression on the soul, by which the Spirit of God directly witnesses to my spirit that I am a child of God; that Jesus Christ has loved me, and given himself for me; that all my sins are blotted out, and that I am personally reconciled to God.'"

But recognize that I do not mean that the Spirit of God testifies by any outward voice; or always by an inward voice, though He may sometimes do this. Neither do I suppose that He always applies to the heart (though He often may) one or more texts of Scripture. But He works in the soul through His immediate influence and in a strong, though inexplicable manner, so that the stormy wind and troubled waves subside, and there is a sweet calm. The heart rests as in the arms of Jesus, and the sinner is clearly satisfied that he is reconciled to God, that all his "iniquities are forgiven, and his sins covered."

What then is the matter of dispute concerning this? It is not whether there is a witness of the Spirit. It is not whether the Spirit testifies with our spirit that we are the children of God. No one can deny this without flatly contradicting the Scriptures, and accusing God of lying. Therefore, the reality of the testimony of the Spirit is acknowledged by all.

It is equally certain that there is an *indirect* witness that we are the children of God. This is nearly, if not exactly, the same as the testimony of a good conscience towards God; and is the result of reflecting on what we feel in our own souls. Strictly speaking, it is a conclusion drawn both from the Word of God and from our own experience. The Word of God says that everyone who has the fruit of the Spirit is a child of God; experience, or inward consciousness, tells me that I have the fruit of the Spirit; and so I conclude, "I am a child of God." This is also agreed upon by all, and so is no matter of controversy.

We do not claim that there can be any real testimony of the Spirit without the fruit of the Spirit. We assert, on the contrary, that the fruit of the Spirit springs from this testimony; though not always in the same degree. Neither joy nor peace is always at the same level; nor love; neither is the testimony itself always equally strong and clear.

But the point in question here is whether there is any *direct* testimony of the Spirit other than that which comes from a consciousness of the fruit.

I believe there is, because that is the clear, natural meaning of the text, "The Spirit itself beareth witness with our spirit, that we are the children of God." It is evident that two witnesses are mentioned here, who together testify the same thing; the Spirit of God and our own spirit. What then is the other witness? This may be learned, as if the text itself were not already clear, from the preceding verse: "Ye have received, not the spirit of bondage, but the Spirit of adoption, whereby we cry, Abba, Father." It follows, "The Spirit itself beareth witness with our spirit, that we are the children of God."

This is further explained by a parallel text, "Because ye are sons, God hath sent forth the Spirit of His Son into your hearts, crying, Abba, Father" (Galatians 4:6). Is this not something *immediate* and *direct*, and not the result of reflection or argument? Does this Spirit not cry, "Abba, Father," in our hearts the moment it is given, before any consideration of our sincerity or any reasoning? Is this not the clear, natural sense of the words which strikes anyone as soon as he hears them? All these texts, therefore, obviously describe a direct testimony of the Spirit.

That the testimony of the Spirit of God must precede the testimony of our own spirit, may be seen from this consideration: we must be holy in heart and life before we can be conscious that we are so. But we must love God before we can be holy at all, this love being the root of all holiness. And we cannot love God until we know He loves us: "We love Him, because He first loved us." And we cannot know His love for us until His Spirit witnesses it to our spirit. Until then we cannot believe it; we cannot say, "The life which I now live, I live by faith in the Son of God, who loved me, and gave himself for me." Since, therefore, the testimony of His Spirit must precede love for God, and all holiness, it must precede our consciousness of it as well.

Let us now consider, in order to confirm this scriptural doctrine, the experience of the children of God; not the experience of two or three, but of a great multitude which no man can count. It has been confirmed, both in this and every age, by "a cloud" of living and dying "witnesses." It is confirmed by your experience and mine. The Spirit bore witness to my spirit that I was a child of God, gave me evidence of it, and I immediately cried, "Abba, Father!" And I did this (and so did you) before I was conscious of any fruit of the Spirit. It was from this testimony that love, joy, peace, and the whole fruit of the Spirit flowed.

But this is confirmed, not only by the experience of the children of God (thousands of whom can declare that they never knew they were in the favor of God until it was directly witnessed to them by his Spirit), but by all those who are convinced of their sinfulness, who feel God's anger remaining on them. These cannot be satisfied with anything less than a direct testimony from His Spirit, that He is "merciful to their unrighteousness, and remembers their sins and iniquities no more." Tell any one of these, "You may know whether you are a child by reflecting on what He has done in you, on your love, joy, and peace." Will he not immediately reply, "By all of this I know I am a child of the devil: I have no more love for God than the devil has; my carnal mind is opposed to God. I have no joy in the Holy Spirit; my soul is sorrowful. I have no peace; a storm rages in my heart." And how can these souls possibly be comforted, except by a divine testimony that God justifies the ungodly, the one who can do nothing that is truly good until he is aware that he is accepted by the free mercy of God, and not for any "works of righteousness which he hath done?" Can it be otherwise, if "a man is justified by faith, without the works of the law?" If so, what goodness can he be conscious of before his justification? Is not the consciousness of having nothing to pay, that "there dwelleth in us no good thing," necessary before we can be "justified freely, through the redemption that is in Jesus Christ?" Can any man be justified until he is brought to that point when he confesses, "My only plea is that I am damned except that You died?"

Anyone, therefore, who denies the existence of such a testimony, in effect denies justification by faith. It follows, either that he never experienced this, and never was justified, or that he has forgotten, as St. Peter writes, the purification from his former sins; the manner in which God worked in his soul when his sins were blotted out.

Even the experience of the children of the world confirms that of the children of God. Many of these have a desire to please God, and some of them try their hardest to please Him. But they consider it absurd for anyone to speak of knowing that his sins are forgiven. And yet many of them are conscious of their own sincerity. Many of them have, to some degree, a consciousness of their own uprightness. But this brings them no awareness that they are forgiven; no knowledge that they are the children of God. Usually, the more sincere they are, the more uneasy they are for the lack of this knowledge; showing that this cannot be adequately known merely by the testimony of our own spirit, without God directly testifying that we are His children.

Consideration of Objections to the Doctrine of a Direct Witness by the Spirit

It is objected that experience is not enough to prove a doctrine apart from Scripture. This is an important fact, but it does not affect this issue, for this doctrine is based on Scripture. Therefore, it is proper to use experience to confirm it.

Second, it is objected that madmen and fanatics of every kind have imagined they experienced this witness. That is true, and perhaps some of them did have the witness, even though they did not retain it for long. But this is no proof that others have not experienced it, just as a madman's imagining himself to be a king does not prove that there are no *real* kings. Many have fatally deceived themselves and are now incapable of being convinced, but a scriptural doctrine is still true, even if men abuse it to their own destruction.

A third objection is that if the fruit of the Spirit is a sufficient witness, then there is no need for any other. But it is not sufficient, first, in the total absence of the fruit of the Spirit, which is the case when the direct witness is first given; or, second, when one cannot perceive the fruit of the Spirit. For one may be unaware that he is in the favor of God apart from the testimony which is given for that purpose. We argue that the direct witness of the Spirit may shine clearly, even while the indirect one (the fruit of the Spirit) is under a cloud.

Fourth, it is objected that the purpose of this witness is to prove that the profession we make is genuine, which is something it cannot prove. But proving one's profession is not the purpose of it in the first place. It comes before we make any profession at all, except that of being lost, undone, guilty, helpless sinners. It is intended to assure those to whom it is given that they are the children of God; that they are "justified freely by His grace, through the redemption that is in Jesus Christ." And this does not suppose that their preceding thoughts, words, and actions conform to the rule of Scripture; it supposes just the opposite; that is, that they are sinners both in heart and life. Otherwise, God would justify the godly; and their own works would be counted to them for righteousness. It is evident that a belief that we are justified by works is at the root of all these objections, for whoever believes that God imputes righteousness without works to all that are justified, will easily accept that the witness of his Spirit precedes the fruit of it.

Fifth, it is objected that the direct witness of the Spirit does not ensure that we will be free from delusion; therefore, what good is it? I answer, to protect us from delusion, God gives us two witnesses that testify together that we are His children. And while they are joined, we cannot be deluded. They are able to be trusted completely, and need nothing else to prove what they assert.

Finally, it is objected that the greatest contenders for the direct witness of the Spirit are some of the proudest and most unkind among men. I respond that while some of the hottest contenders for it may be both proud and unkind, many of the firmest contenders for it are meek and lowly in heart; and, in all other respects also, true followers of their lamb-like Lord.

Conclusions

Two conclusions may now be drawn. First, let no one rest in any supposed testimony of the Spirit which is inconsistent with the fruit of it. If the Spirit of God truly testifies that we are the children of God, the immediate result will be the fruit of the

Spirit: "love, joy, peace, longsuffering, gentleness, goodness, faithfulness, meekness, self-control." Although this fruit may not be apparent to a tempted person for some time, the essential part of it still remains, even under the thickest cloud. It is true that joy in the Holy Spirit may be taken away during times of testing; and the goal may seem "exceeding sorrowful," yet this joy is usually restored in even greater abundance, until we rejoice "with joy unspeakable and full of glory."

The second conclusion is, let no one rest in any supposed fruit of the Spirit without the witness. There may be foretastes of joy, of peace, of love from God, long before the Spirit of God witnesses with our spirits that we have "redemption in the blood of Jesus, even the forgiveness of sins." Yes, there may be a degree of longsuffering, gentleness, faithfulness, meekness, and self-control, by the grace of God, before we "are accepted in the Beloved," and, consequently, before we have a testimony of our acceptance. But our souls are in danger if we rest here. If we are wise, we will continually cry out to God, until His Spirit cries in our heart, "Abba, Father!" This is the privilege of all the children of God, and without this we can never be sure that we are His children. Without this we cannot keep a steady peace, nor avoid perplexing doubts and fears. But when we have received this Spirit of adoption, this "peace which passeth all understanding will keep our hearts and minds in Christ Jesus." And when this has produced its genuine fruit, which is all inward and outward holiness, it is undoubtedly the will of Him that calls us to give us continually what He has given initially; so that we may keep the testimony of God's Spirit, and the testimony of our own spirit, the consciousness that we walk in all righteousness and true holiness.

9

The Witness of Our Own Spirit

"This is our rejoicing, the testimony of our conscience, that in simplicity and godly sincerity, not with fleshly wisdom, but by the grace of God, we have had our conversation in the world."
2 Corinthians 1:12.

The purpose of the following discourse is to show the nature and basis of a Christian's joy. We know it is that happiness and peace which arises from the testimony of his conscience, as described here by the Apostle. But in order to better understand this, it will be necessary to weigh all his words in order to know what the conscience is and what its testimony is; and also, how he that has this testimony always rejoices.

First, what are we to understand by *conscience?* God has made us thinking beings, capable of perceiving the present and looking back on the past. In particular, we are capable of perceiving whatever occurs in our own hearts or lives; of knowing what we feel or do both while it is occurring and when it is past. When we say that man is a *conscious* being, we mean this: he has a *consciousness*, or inward perception, of things present and past, relating to himself, and of his own tempers and outward behavior. But *conscience* implies more than this. It is not only the knowledge of our present life or the memory of our preceding life. To know either past or present things is the least concern of conscience. Its main business is to excuse or accuse, to approve or disapprove, to acquit or condemn. And according to the meaning of the term in Scripture, particularly in the Epistles of St. Paul, we understand that conscience is an ability, implanted by God in every soul, to perceive what is right or wrong in his own heart or life, in his tempers, thoughts, words, and actions.

But what is the rule by which men are to judge between right and wrong? By what is their conscience to be directed? The rule of heathens, as the Apostle teaches elsewhere, is "the law written in their hearts." "These," he says, "not having the" outward "law, are a law unto themselves: Who show the work of the law," that which the outward law requires, "written in their heart;" by the finger of God; "their conscience also bearing witness" whether or not they walk by this rule, "and their thoughts the meanwhile accusing, or even excusing them" (Romans 2:14, 15). But the Christian rule of right and wrong is the Word of God, all that the prophets and "holy men of God" wrote "as they were moved by the Holy Spirit;" all that Scripture which was given by inspiration of God, which is profitable for doctrine, or teaching the will of God; for reproving that which is contrary to it; for correcting error; and for instructing us in righteousness (2 Timothy 3:16). This is a lantern to a Christian's feet, and a light for all his paths. He calls nothing good except that which is commanded here, either directly or by clear implication; he considers nothing evil wxcept what is forbidden here, either directly or by clear implication. Whatever the Scripture neither forbids nor commands, he believes to be neutral; neither good nor evil in itself. Scripture is the only complete outward rule by which his conscience is to be directed in all things.

And if his conscience is actually directed by Scripture, then he has "the answer of a good conscience toward God." "A good conscience" is what is referred to elsewhere by the Apostle, "a conscience void of offense." So, what he at one time expresses in this way, "I have lived in all good conscience before God until this day" (Acts 23:1); he denotes at another, "Herein do I exercise myself, to have always a conscience void of offense toward God, and toward men" (24:16). Now in order for this to be true there is required, first, a right understanding of the Word of God, of His "holy, and acceptable and perfect will" for us as it is revealed there. For it is impossible to walk by a rule if we do not know what it means. Second, we need a true knowledge of ourselves; a knowledge both of our hearts and lives, of our inward tempers and outward behavior. If we do not know them, it is not possible for us to compare them with our rule. Third, there is required an agreement of our hearts and lives, of our tempers and conversation, of our thoughts, and words, and actions, with that rule, with the written word of God. Without this, our conscience can only be evil. Fourth, there is required an inward perception of this agreement. We must know that this habitual inward consciousness is a *good conscience*; or, in the other phrase of the Apostle, "a conscience void of offense toward God and toward men."

But whoever desires to have a good conscience must lay the right foundation. Let him remember, "Other foundation can no man lay, than that which is laid, even Jesus Christ." And let him also be mindful, that no man builds on Him except by a living faith, and no man partakes of Christ until he can clearly testify, "The life which I now live, I live by faith in the Son of God;" in Him who is now revealed in my heart; who "loved me, and gave himself for me." Faith alone is that evidence, that conviction, that demonstration of unseen things. It is by faith that we see all that is in ourselves, even the innermost stirrings of our souls. By this alone can the love of God be "shed abroad in our hearts," which enables us to love one another as Christ loved us. By this that gracious promise is fulfilled to all the Israel of God, "I will put My laws into their mind, and write them in their hearts" (Hebrews 8:10), bringing their souls into full agreement with His holy law, and "bringing into captivity every thought to the obedience of Christ." And, just as an evil tree bear good fruit, so a good tree cannot bear evil fruit. As the heart of a believer is thoroughly conformed to the rule of God's commandments, so also is his life, and being aware of this, he can give glory to God, saying with the Apostle, "This is our rejoicing, the testimony of our conscience, that in simplicity and godly sincerity, not with fleshly wisdom, but by the grace of God, we have had our conversation in the world."

"We have had our conversation." The Apostle, in the original language, expresses this with one word, but the meaning of it is very broad, taking in our whole conduct, yes, every inward as well as outward circumstance, whether relating to our soul or body. It includes every motion of our heart, of our tongue, of our hands; every part of our body. It extends to all our actions and words; to the use of all our abilities; to the use of every talent we have, with respect either to God or man.

"We have had our conversation in the world;" even in the world of the ungodly. Not only among the children of God but among the children of the devil, among those that live in wickedness. What a world this is! How thoroughly penetrated with the spirit it continually breathes. Just as our God is good, and does good, so the god of this world, and all his children, are evil, and do evil (as far as they are allowed) to all the children of God. Like their father, they are always lying in wait, or "walking about, seeking whom they may devour;" using fraud or force to destroy those who are not of the world; continually warring against our souls with weapons and devices of every kind, working to bring us back into the trap of the devil, and onto the broad road that leads to destruction.

"We have had our conversation," in such a world, "in simplicity and godly sincerity." First, in simplicity. This is what our Lord recommends under the name of a "single eye." "The light of the body," He said, "is the eye. If therefore thine eye be single, thy whole body shall be full of light." In other words, what the eye is to the body, the will is to all our words and actions. If then this eye of your soul has a single focus, all of your actions and conversation will be "full of light," of the light of heaven, of love, and peace, and joy in the Holy Spirit. We become simple of heart when the eye of our mind is fixed on God; when we aim toward God in all things, as our God, our portion, our strength, our happiness, our great reward, in time and eternity. This is simplicity; when a steady view, a single intention of promoting His glory, of doing and allowing His will, floods our soul, fills our heart, and is the constant spring of all our thoughts, desires, and purposes.

Second, "We have had our conversation in the world in godly sincerity." The difference between simplicity and sincerity seems to be this: simplicity regards the will itself, while sincerity pertains to its action. And this sincerity relates not only to our words, but to all our behavior, as described above. It implies that we speak and do everything to the glory of God; that all of our actions flow in an even stream, always serving this great purpose; and that we are continually moving straight toward God, walking steadily in the paths of justice, mercy, and truth.

This sincerity the Apostle calls, "godly sincerity;" to prevent us from confusing it with the sincerity of the heathens, for they also had a kind of sincerity among them, which they claimed to honor. By calling it the sincerity of God, he also points to the Author of it, the "Father of lights from whom every good and perfect gift descends."

"Not with fleshly wisdom." It is as if he said, "We cannot live this way in the world by any natural understanding, or by any naturally acquired knowledge or wisdom. We cannot gain this simplicity or practice this sincerity by good sense or good breeding. It surpasses all our inherent courage and resolve, as well as all our principles of philosophy. The power of custom is not able to train us in this, nor the most developed rules of human education. Neither could I, Paul, ever attain this as long as I was in the flesh, in my natural state, and pursued it only by fleshly, natural wisdom." Surely, if any man could, Paul might have attained this by natural wisdom, for few, if any, were more highly favored with gifts both of nature and education. Besides his natural abilities, which were not in the least inferior to those of any person then alive, he had all the benefits of learning, studying at the University of Tarsus, and afterwards trained by Gamaliel, one respected both for his knowledge and integrity by the whole Jewish nation. And he had all the possible advantages of religious education, being a Pharisee, and the son of a Pharisee, trained up in the very strictest sect. He had surpassed many by his zeal, and was, "as touching the righteousness of the law, blameless." But he would never attain this simplicity and godly sincerity in this way. All of it was wasted effort toward that goal. In a deep, piercing sense of this, he cried out, "The things which were gain to me, those I counted loss for Christ: Yea, doubtless, and I count all things but loss, for the excellency of the knowledge of Christ Jesus my Lord" (Philippians 3:7, 8).

It was impossible for him attain this except by the "excellent knowledge of Jesus Christ;" that is, "by the grace of God." "The grace of God" is sometimes to be understood as that free love, that unmerited mercy, by which I, a sinner, through the merits of Christ, am reconciled to God. But here it means the power of God the Holy Spirit, which "worketh in us both to will and to do of His good pleasure." As soon as the grace of God in His pardoning love is made known to our souls, the grace of God in the power of His Spirit works there also. Now we can do, through God, what was impossible for man. Now we can do all things in the light and power of that love, through Christ who strengthens us. We now have "the testimony of our conscience," which we could never have by fleshly wisdom, "that in simplicity and godly sincerity, we have our conversation in the world."

This is the basis of a Christian's joy. We can easily see how the one who has this testimony always rejoices. He is able to say, "I rejoice in Him, who, out of His own unmerited love, out of His own free and tender mercy, has called me into this state of salvation where, through His power, I now stand. I rejoice, because His Spirit bears witness to my spirit that I am bought with the blood of the Lamb; and that, believing in Him, I am a member of Christ, a child of God, and an heir of the kingdom of heaven. I rejoice, because the sense of God's love for me has, by the same Spirit, produced in me love toward Him, and, for His sake, love for every man. I rejoice because He gives me 'the mind that was in Christ.' He gives me *simplicity*, a single motive to love Him with all of my heart; power to focus the loving eye of my soul on Him who 'loved me, and gave himself for me;' to aim toward Him alone, and at His glorious will in all I think, or speak, or do. He gives me *purity*, desiring nothing more than God; 'crucifying the flesh with its affections and lusts;' and 'setting my affections on things above, not on things of the earth.' He gives me *holiness*, a recovery of the image of God, a renewal of soul 'after His likeness.' And he gives me *godly sincerity*, directing all my words and actions to contribute to His glory. In this I also rejoice because my conscience bears witness in the Holy Spirit, by the light He continuously pours in on it, that I 'walk worthy of the vocation wherewith I am called;' that I 'abstain from all appearance of evil,' running from sin as from a snake; that, as I have opportunity, I do good, in every possible way, to all men; that I follow my Lord in all my steps, and do what is acceptable in His sight. I rejoice, because I both see and feel, through the inspiration of God's Holy Spirit, that all my works are worked in Him, and that it is He who works all my works in me. I rejoice in seeing, through the light of God which shines in my heart, that I have power to walk in His ways; and that by His grace, I do not turn to the right or to the left."

This is the basis and the nature of that joy by which a mature Christian continually rejoices. And from all of this we may easily reason, first, that this is not a *natural* joy. It does not arise from any natural cause. It is not from some cause that gives only temporary joy, for the Christian always rejoices. It cannot be due to bodily health and strength, for it is equally strong in sickness and pain, and perhaps even stronger than before. Many Christians never experience anything equal to the joy which filled their soul when their body was almost worn out with pain or consumed with sickness. Least of all can it be attributed to outward prosperity, to the favor of men, or an abundance of worldly goods; for it is especially when their faith has been tested by all kinds of outward afflictions, that the children of God have rejoiced in Him with unspeakable joy. And men have never rejoiced like those who were treated as "the filth and offscouring of the world;" who wandered, being desperately needy; in hunger, in cold, in nakedness; who had trials, not only of "cruel mockings," but, "moreover of bonds and imprisonments;" who, at last, "counted not their lives dear unto themselves, so they might finish their course with joy."

Second, from the preceding considerations we may conclude that a Christian's joy does not arise from any blindness of conscience, from not being able to discern good from evil. Quite the opposite is true, for he was a complete stranger to this joy until the eyes of his understanding were opened; he did not know it until he had spiritual senses, capable of discerning spiritual good and evil. And the eye of his soul was never so keen before. His ability to perceive even the smallest things is quite amazing to the natural man. As a speck of dust is visible in the sunbeam, every speck of sin is visible to him who is walking in the light, in the beams of the uncreated Sun,. Nor does he close the eyes of his conscience any more. His soul is always awake. He is always standing on the tower, listening for what his Lord will say concerning him.

To conclude, Christian joy is joy in obedience; joy in loving God and keeping His commandments. And yet it is not in keeping them as if we were fulfilling the terms of the covenant of works in this way; as if we were to gain pardon and acceptance with God by any works or righteousness of our own. We are already pardoned and accepted through the mercy of God in Christ Jesus. It is not as if we were, by our own obedience, to gain life, freed from the death of sin. We already have this through the grace of God. Us "hath He quickened, who were dead in sins," and now we are "alive to God, through Jesus Christ our Lord." But we rejoice in walking according to the covenant of grace, in holy love and happy obedience. We rejoice in knowing that we are "justified through His grace," that God has freely reconciled us to himself through the blood of the Lamb,. We run, in the strength which He gives us, in the way of His commandments. We gladly "fight the good fight of faith." We rejoice to "lay hold of eternal life" through Him who lives in our hearts by faith. This is our joy, that as our "Father worketh hitherto," so (not by our own might or wisdom, but through the power of His Spirit, freely given in Christ Jesus) we also work the works of God. And may He work in us whatever is pleasing in His sight! To whom be the praise for ever and ever!

10

The Means of Grace

"Ye are gone away from Mine ordinances, and have not kept them."
Malachi 3:7.

Are there any means ordained of God to be the usual channels of His grace? This question could never have been asked in the apostolic church, except by a heathen; for all Christians agreed that Christ had ordained certain outward means for conveying His grace into men's souls. They confirmed this by their actions, for "they continued steadfastly in the teaching of the Apostles, and in breaking of bread, and in prayers" (Acts 2:42).

But, in time, when the love of many grew cold, some began to mistake the means for the end, and found their religion in doing those outward works, rather than in a heart renewed after the image of God. They forgot that "the end of" every "commandment is love, out of a pure heart," loving the Lord their

God with all their heart, and their neighbor as themselves; and being purified from pride, anger, and evil desire. Others imagined that although religion did not principally consist of these outward means, somehow these means would make them acceptable in God's sight, even while they neglected the weightier matters of the law, such as justice, mercy, and love for God.

It is evident that, for those who abused them, these means did not lead to the end for which they were ordained. Rather, they only brought a curse on their head. Instead of growing more heavenly in heart and life, they became more the children of hell than before. Others, seeing that these means did not convey the grace of God to those children of the devil, began to assume that they were not means of conveying His grace at all.

Still, there were many more who abused the ordinances of God than those who rejected them altogether until certain men arose, men not only of great understanding, but who also appeared to be men of love, who were personally acquainted with true, inward religion. Some of these were shining lights, famous in their generations for standing against ungodliness. At first, they probably only intended to show that outward religion is worth nothing without the religion of the heart; that "God is a Spirit, and they who worship Him must worship Him in spirit and in truth;" that, consequently, external worship is a wasted effort without a heart devoted to God; that the outward ordinances of God are of great benefit when they advance inward holiness, but are useless when they do not advance it; and when they are used in place of holiness, they are an abomination to the Lord.

It is not strange, then, that some of these men, seeing the horrible profaning of the ordinances of God which had spread throughout the whole church and almost driven true religion out of the world, out of their fervent zeal for the glory of God and the recovery of souls from that fatal delusion, spoke as if outward religion were absolutely nothing, as if it had no place in the religion of Christ. It is not surprising at all that they did not always express themselves with sufficient caution; causing unwary hearers to believe that they condemned all outward means as unprofitable and not designed by God to be the ordinary channels of conveying His grace into men's souls. It is likely that some came to this opinion who, not by choice, but by the providence of God, were cut off from these ordinances; perhaps wandering without a home, or hiding in dens and caves. These men, who experienced the grace of God in themselves though deprived of all outward means, might have concluded that the same grace would be given to those who purposely abstained from these means.

Experience shows how easily this idea spreads, especially among those who are thoroughly awakened from the sleep of death, and begin to feel that the weight of their sins is a burden too heavy to carry. These persons are usually impatient; and, trying to escape from that burden, they are always ready for any new method of relief or happiness. They have probably tried most of the outward means, and found no relief in them; though perhaps more remorse, and fear, and sorrow, and condemnation. It is easy, therefore, to persuade these that it is better for them to abstain from those means. They are already weary of their seemingly useless effort, and are glad for any excuse to cast aside that which their soul finds no pleasure in, to give up the painful struggle, and sink down into laziness.

Limitations of the Means of Grace

In the following discourse, I propose to examine thoroughly whether there are any *means of grace*. By this I mean those outward signs, words, or actions which are ordained by God, and appointed to be the ordinary channels by which He conveys to men His preceding, justifying, or sanctifying grace. I use this expression, *means of grace*, because I know of none better; and because it has been used in the Christian church for many ages, and in particular by our own church [the Church of England], which directs us to thank God, both for the means of grace, and the hope of glory; and teaches us that a sacrament is "an outward sign of inward grace, and a means whereby we receive the same."

The principal means are prayer, whether in private or in the congregation; searching the Scriptures (which implies reading, hearing, and meditating on them); and receiving the Lord's supper, eating bread and drinking wine in remembrance of Him. We believe these are ordained of God as the ordinary channels of conveying His grace into men's souls.

The value of the means depends on their actual use for the purpose of religion; consequently, all these means, when separated from their purpose, are meaningless and useless. If they do not actually lead us to know and love God, they are not acceptable in His sight; instead, they are an abomination to Him, a stench in His nostrils. Above all, if they are used to replace the religion they were designed to serve, it is not easy to find words for this foolish and wicked turning of God's weapons against himself; of keeping Christianity out of the heart by those very means which were ordained to bring it in.

Likewise, all outward means, if separated from the Spirit of God, are unable to assist us either in knowing or loving God. Unquestionably, whatever help that is given on earth, He alone gives. It is He alone who, by His own power, works in us what is pleasing in His sight; and all outward things, unless He works through them, are only weak, impoverished elements. Therefore, whoever imagines that there is intrinsic power in any of these means errs greatly, not knowing the Scriptures or the power of God. We know that there is no inherent power in the words that are spoken in prayer, in the letter of Scripture read, or the sound of it, or in the bread and wine received in the Lord's Supper; it is God alone who is the Giver of every good gift, the Author of all grace. We know also that He would be able to give the same grace even if there were no such means on earth. In this sense, we can affirm that with God there is no such thing as means; since He is able to do whatever pleases him, either by any means or by none at all.

We also agree that the use of these or any other means will never atone for one sin; for it is the blood of Christ alone that reconciles a sinner to God; there being no other propitiation for our sins, no other fountain where we can be cleansed from sin and uncleanness. Every believer in Christ is deeply convinced that there is no merit except in Him; that there is no merit in any of his own works; not in uttering the prayer, or searching the Scripture, or hearing the Word of God, or eating of that bread and drinking of that cup. So that if no more is intended by the expression some have used, "Christ is the only means of grace," than that He is the only cause of it, it cannot be disputed by any who know the grace of God.

Further, we agree, though it is a sad truth, that many of those who are called Christians still abuse the means of grace to the destruction of their souls. This is certainly the case with all who are content with a form of godliness, but without its power. Either they assume they are Christians already because they do this or that (although Christ has not yet been revealed in their hearts, nor the love of God poured out in them), or else they suppose they will become so simply because they use these means. They imagine (even though they may be hardly aware of it) either that there is some kind of power in them by which, sooner or later, they will be made holy; or that there is a kind of merit in using them, which will move God to give them holiness or accept them without it.

They understand so little of that great foundation of the entire Christian building, "By grace are ye saved." You are saved from your sins, from their guilt and power, and you are restored to the favor and image of God, not because of any works or merits of your own, but by the free gift of God's mercy through the merits of His beloved Son. You are saved, then, not by any power, wisdom, or strength which is in you; but only through the grace or power of the Holy Spirit.

The Biblical Emphasis of the Means of Grace

But the central question remains: "We know this salvation is the gift and the work of God; but how can I gain it?" If you say, "Believe, and you will be saved!" he answers, "True. But how must I believe?" You reply, "Wait on God." "But how am I to wait? Am I to wait for the grace of God by using these means, or by laying them aside?"

It is not possible for the Word of God to provide no direction regarding so important a point; or for the Son of God, who came down from heaven for our salvation, to have left unanswered a question that is so important to our salvation. We must only consult the oracles of God to see what is written there. If we abide by their decision, no doubt can remain.

According to Scripture, all who desire the grace of God are to wait for it by the means that He has ordained. First, all who desire the grace of God are to wait for it in prayer. This is the direction of our Lord himself. In His Sermon on the Mount, after explaining what religion consists of, and describing the main parts of it, He adds, "Ask, and it shall be given you; seek, and ye shall find; knock, and it shall be opened unto you: For every one that asketh receiveth; and he that seeketh findeth; and to him that knocketh it shall be opened" (Matthew 7:7, 8). Here we are clearly directed to ask, as a means of receiving; to seek, in order to find the grace of God, the pearl of great price; and to knock, to continue asking and seeking, if we desire to enter into His kingdom.

So that no doubt might remain, our Lord emphasizes this point in a more peculiar manner. He appeals to every man's heart: "What man is there of you, who, if his son ask bread, will he give him a stone? Or, if he ask a fish, will he give him a serpent? If ye then, being evil, know how to give good gifts unto your children, how much more shall your Father which is in heaven give good things to them that ask Him?" (7:9-11). Or, as He expresses himself on another occasion, "How much more shall your heavenly Father give the Holy Spirit to them that ask Him?" (Luke 11:13). Our Lord directs them to use this means, and promises that it would happen as He said; that by asking they should receive the Holy Spirit.

The absolute necessity of using this means, if we want to receive any gift from God, also appears from that passage which immediately precedes these words: "And He said unto them," whom He had just been teaching how to pray, "Which of you shall have a friend, and shall go unto him at midnight, and shall say unto him, Friend, lend me three loaves: And he from within shall answer, Trouble me not; I cannot rise and give thee. I say unto you, though he will not rise and give him, because he is his friend, yet because of his importunity, he will rise, and give him as many as he needeth. And I say unto you, Ask, and it shall be given you" (Luke 11:5, 7-9). How could our blessed Lord be more clear that, by persistently asking, we may receive from God that which we otherwise would not receive at all?

"He spake also another parable, to this end, that men ought always to pray, and not to faint," until by this means they should receive from God whatever they asked of Him: "There was in a city a judge which feared not God, neither regarded man. And there was a widow in that city, and she came unto him, saying, Avenge me of my adversary. And he would not for a while; but afterwards he said within himself, Though I fear not God, nor regard man, yet because this widow troubleth me, I will avenge her, lest, by her continual coming, she weary me" (Luke 18:1–5). Our Lord explained this himself: "Hear what the unjust judge saith!" Because she continues to ask, because she will not be denied, therefore I will avenge her. "And shall not God avenge His own elect, which cry day and night unto Him? I tell you He will avenge them speedily," if they pray and do not give up.

He has also given us a direction to wait for the blessings of God in private prayer, together with a promise, saying, "Enter into thy closet, and, when thou hast shut thy door, pray to thy Father which is in secret; and thy Father, which seeth in secret, shall reward thee openly" (Matthew 6:6).

Second, all who desire the grace of God are to wait for it by searching the Scriptures. Our Lord's direction, with regard to using this means, is plain and clear. "Search the Scriptures," He said to the unbelieving Jews, "for they testify of Me" (John 5:39). For this very purpose He directed them to search the Scriptures, that they might believe in Him. That God's blessing accompanies the use of this means appears from what is recorded concerning the Bereans; who, after hearing St. Paul, "searched the Scriptures daily, whether those things were so. Therefore many of them believed," or, put another way, found the grace of God in the way which He had ordained (Acts 27:11, 12). It is likely that for some of them faith came by hearing, and was only confirmed by reading the Scriptures. As we observed earlier, under the general heading of searching the Scriptures, both hearing, reading, and meditating are included.

This is a means by which God not only gives, but also confirms and increases true wisdom, as we learn from the words of St. Paul to Timothy: "From a child thou hast known the Holy Scriptures, which are able to make thee wise unto salvation through faith which is in Christ Jesus" (2 Timothy 3:15). The same truth (that is, that this is the great means God has ordained for conveying His grace to man) is found in the words which immediately follow: "All Scripture is given by inspiration of God;" consequently, all Scripture is infallibly true; "and is profitable for doctrine, for reproof, for correction, for instruction in righteousness" so "that the man of God may be perfect, thoroughly furnished unto all good works" (vv. 16, 17).

It should be observed that this is spoken directly of the Scriptures which Timothy had known as a child; which must have been those of the Old Testament, for the New was not yet written. St. Paul then was far from making light of the Old Testament! See here, you who put such a small value on one half of the Word of God! The Holy Spirit clearly declares that half "profitable," as a means ordained of God.

Nor is this profitable only for the men of God, those who already walk in the light; but also for those who are still in darkness, seeking the One they do not know. And so St. Peter says, "We have also a more sure word of prophecy." Literally, "And we have the prophetic word more sure;" confirmed by our being "eye-witnesses of His Majesty," and "hearing the voice which came from the excellent glory." And to that prophetic word, which he calls the Holy Scriptures, "ye do well that ye take heed, as unto a light that shineth in a dark place, until the day dawn, and the Day-star arise in your hearts" (2 Peter 1:19). Let all who desire that day to dawn in their hearts wait for it by searching the Scriptures.

Third, all who desire an increase of the grace of God are to wait for it by partaking of the Lord's supper, for this also is a direction the Lord has given. "The same night He was betrayed, He took bread, and brake it, and said, Take, eat; this is My body;" that is, "the sacred sign of My body:" "This do in remembrance of Me." Likewise, "He took the cup, saying, This cup is the new testament," or covenant, "in My blood;" the sacred sign of that covenant; "this do ye in remembrance of Me." "For as often as ye eat this bread, and drink this cup, ye do show forth the Lord's death until He come" (1 Corinthians 11:23, etc.). By these visible signs, you show your solemn remembrance of His death until He comes in the clouds of heaven. Only "let a man examine himself," whether he understands the nature and design of this holy institution, and whether he really desires to conform to the death of Christ; and then, without doubting, "let him eat of that bread, and drink of that cup" (v. 28). Here the direction given by our Lord is repeated by the Apostle: "Let him eat; let him drink" (both imperative in the Greek); words not implying a permission only, but a clear command to all those who either already are filled with peace and joy in believing, or those who can truly say, "The remembrance of our sins grieves us, the burden of them is intolerable."

That this is also an ordinary means of receiving the grace of God is evident from those words of the Apostle which occur in the preceding chapter: "The cup of blessing which we bless, is it not the communion," or *communication*, "of the blood of Christ? The bread which we break, is it not the communion of the body of Christ?" (1 Corinthians 10:16). Is the eating of that bread and the drinking of that cup then not the outward, visible means by which God conveys into our souls all that spiritual grace, that righteousness, and peace, and joy in the Holy Spirit, which were purchased by the body and blood of Christ for us? Therefore, let all who truly desire the grace of God eat of that bread and drink of that cup.

Objections to the Use of the Means of Grace

As clearly as God has pointed the way in which He will be sought after, countless objections have been raised against it. It is necessary to consider a few of these; not because they have weight in and of themselves, but because they have often been used to mislead those who were running well until Satan appeared as an angel of light.

The first and foremost of these objections is, "You cannot use these means without trusting in them." But where is this written? I expect you to show me a basis in Scripture for your assertion. Otherwise, I will not receive it, because I am not convinced that you are wiser than God. If what you say is true, then Christ must have known it. And if He had known it, He surely would have warned us. Therefore, because there is not the slightest evidence of this in the whole revelation of Jesus Christ, I am as fully assured that your assertion is false, as I am that this revelation is of God. They suggest, "Abandon these means for a short time, to see whether or not you trusted in them." So I am to disobey God, in order to know whether I trust in obeying Him? But they claim, "If you are troubled when you stop using them, it is evident that you trusted in them." By no means. If I am troubled when I willfully disobey God, it is clear that His Spirit remains in me; but if I am not troubled by willful sin, it is just as clear that I have been given up to a reprobate mind. But what do you mean by "trusting in them?" Is it looking for the blessing of God in them, believing that, if I wait in this way, I will attain what I otherwise would not? This is what I do! By the grace of God I will so trust in them until the day of my death. And since God has promised to bless me in this way, I trust it will be according to His word.

Second, it has been objected, "This is seeking salvation by works." But what is seeking salvation by works? In the writings of St. Paul, it means either seeking to be saved by observing the ritual works of the Mosaic law; or expecting salvation for the sake of our own works, by the merit of our own righteousness. But how is either of these implied when I wait in the way God has ordained, expecting that He will meet me there, because He has promised to do so? I expect that He will fulfill His word, that He will meet and bless me in this way. Yet not for the sake of anything I have done, nor because of my own righteousness; but only through the merits, sufferings, and love of His Son.

Third, it has been argued that "Christ is the only means of grace." I answer that this is simply playing with words. Explain your terms, and the objection vanishes. When we say, "Prayer is a means of grace," we mean a channel through which the grace of God is conveyed. When you say, "Christ is the means of grace," you mean the only price and purchaser of it; or, that "no man cometh unto the Father, but through Him." And who denies that? This objection is separate from the question.

Fourth, "But does the Scripture not direct us to wait for salvation? Does David not say, 'My soul waiteth upon God, for of Him cometh my salvation?' And does Isaiah not teach us the same thing, saying, 'O Lord, we have waited for Thee?'" This cannot be denied. Since it is the gift of God, we are to wait on Him for salvation. But how are we to wait? If God himself has appointed a way, can you find a better way of waiting for Him? The Prophet's own words put this beyond question. For the whole sentence reads: "In the way of Thy judgments," or ordinances, "O Lord, have we waited for Thee" (Isaiah 26:8). And David waited in the very same way, as his own words testify: "I have waited for Thy saving health, O Lord, and have kept Thy law. Teach me, O Lord, the way of Thy statutes, and I shall keep it unto the end."

I will mention one more objection, because it has been so frequently raised. "Does St. Paul not say, 'If ye be dead with Christ, why are ye subject to ordinances?' (Colossians 2:20). Therefore, a Christian, one that is dead with Christ, does not need to use the ordinances any more." So you say, "If I am a Christian, I am not subject to the ordinances of Christ!" Surely you must see that the ordinances mentioned here cannot be the ordinances of Christ. They are the Jewish ordinances, which a Christian is certainly no longer subject to. The same appears from the words immediately following, "Touch not, taste not, handle not;" all evidently referring to the ancient ordinances of the Jewish law. This objection is the weakest of all. And, in spite of all this, that great truth stands unshaken, that all who desire the grace of God are to wait for it by the means which He has ordained.

The Order of Using the Means

We recognize that there is an order that God usually uses in bringing a sinner to salvation. One who is spiritually unconscious is going along in his own way, not having God in his thoughts, when God comes on him unexpectedly, perhaps by an awakening sermon or conversation, perhaps by some act of providence, or even by a sudden stroke of His convicting Spirit, without any outward means at all. Now having a desire to escape from the judgment to come, he purposely goes to *hear* how it may be done. If he finds a preacher who speaks to the heart, he is amazed, and begins searching the Scriptures to see whether these things are so. The more he *hears* and *reads*, the more convinced he is; and the more he meditates on this day and night. Perhaps he finds some other book which explains and enforces what he has heard and read in Scripture. By all these means, the arrows of conviction sink deeper into his soul. He also begins to *talk* about of the things of God, which are always in his thoughts; and even to talk to God; to *pray* to him; although, out of fear and shame, he hardly knows what to say. Doubting whether God will listen to a sinner like him, he wants to pray with those who know God in the congregation. Here he observes others going up to *the table of the Lord*. He considers, "Christ has said, 'Do this!' But I am too sinful. I am not worthy." After struggling with these thoughts awhile, he breaks through. And so he continues in God's way, in hearing, reading, meditating, praying, and partaking of the Lord's supper, until God, in the way that pleases Him, speaks to his heart, "Thy faith hath saved thee. Go in peace."

By observing this order of God's working, we learn what means of grace is appropriate for any particular soul. If any means will reach a careless sinner, it is probably hearing, or conversation. To the careless, therefore, we might recommend these, if he ever has any thoughts about salvation at all. To one who begins to feel the weight of his sins, not only hearing the word of God, but reading it too, perhaps along with other serious books, may be a means of deeper conviction. You could also advise him to meditate on what he reads, so that it may have its full effect on his heart, and to discuss it with others who walk in the same way. When trouble and heaviness take hold of him, you should urge him to pour out his soul to God; and when he feels the worthlessness of his own prayers, remind him to go into the house of the Lord, and to pray with those that fear God. If he does this, he will learn the Lord's last command, and this is the time when we should reinforce the leadings of the Holy Spirit. This way we can lead him, step by step, through all the means which God has ordained; not according to our own will, but as the providence and the Spirit of God prepare the way.

Yet, since we find no command in Scripture for any particular order to be observed, so neither do the providence and the Spirit of God follow a certain order. Rather, the means by which different men are led and find the blessing of God are varied and combined together in different ways. Still, our wisdom is to follow the leadings of His providence and His Spirit; to be guided in this (especially as to the means by which we ourselves seek the grace of God), partly by His outward providence, which gives us the opportunity of using a variety of means, and partly by our experience, to know by which means His Spirit is most pleased to work in our hearts. In the meantime, the certain and general rule for all who long for the salvation of God is this: whenever opportunity allows, use all the means which God has ordained; for who knows exactly how God will meet you with the grace that brings salvation?

The Manner of Using the Means

As to the manner of using them, which determines whether they convey any grace at all to the user; we would be wise, first, to remember that God is above all of these means. Be careful not to limit the Almighty. He does whatever He pleases, and at the time of His choosing. He can convey His grace, either with or without any of the means He has appointed. Expect His appearing at every moment! Whether it is at the time when you are using His means; or before, or after that time. Even when you are prevented from using them, He is not. He is always ready, always able, always willing to save.

Second, before you use any means, let it be deeply impressed on your soul that there is no *power* in this. Separate from God, it is only a dry leaf, a shadow. Neither is there any *merit* in using this; nothing inherently pleasing to God; nothing by which I deserve any favor from Him. But because God commands it, I do it; because He directs me to wait in this way, I wait for His free mercy, from which comes my salvation. Settle this in your heart, that the work itself is of no benefit; there is no *power* to save but in the Spirit of God, no *merit*, but in the blood of Christ; therefore, even what God ordains conveys no grace to your soul if you do not trust in Him alone. On the other hand, he that does trust in Him cannot fail to receive the grace of God, even if he were cut off from every outward means, or imprisoned in the center of the earth.

Third, in using these means, desire God alone. In every outward thing, look only to the power of His Spirit and the merits of His Son. Take care that you do not focus on the work itself; if you do, it is all wasted effort. Nothing less than God can satisfy your soul. Remember to use all means only *as means*; as ordained not for their own sake but in order to renew your soul in righteousness and true holiness. If they actually lead toward this, all is well. If not, they are only dung and dross.

Finally, after you have used any of these, take care not to congratulate yourself as though you have done some great thing. This is turning it all into poison and increasing your sins. Remember, if God is not there, what does this accomplish? If God is there, if His love flows into your heart, you will, in a sense, forget the outward work. You see, you know, you feel that God is all in all. Be humbled. Bow low before Him. Give Him all the praise. "Let God in all things be glorified through Christ Jesus."

11

A Caution Against Bigotry

"And John answered Him, saying, Master, we saw one casting out devils in Thy name, and he follows not us: And we forbad him, because hefollows not us. But Jesus said, Forbid him not."
Mark 9:38-39.

Some may not consider this event to be relevant to us, assuming that the task of casting out devils no longer exists. That we may take full advantage from this occasion in Scripture, I intend to, first, show in what sense men still cast out devils; second, identify who he is that "follows not us;" third, explain our Lord's direction, "Forbid him not;" and draw a conclusion from it.

What it Means to Cast Out Devils

First, I will show in what sense men still cast out devils. We should remember that as God dwells and works in the children of light, so the devil dwells and works in the children of darkness. As the Holy Spirit possesses the souls of good men, so the evil spirit possesses the souls of the wicked. Therefore, the Apostle calls him "the God of this world;" from the uncontrolled power he has over worldly men. For this reason, our blessed Lord calls him "the prince of this world," because his dominion over it is so complete.

For the devil is not to be considered only "a roaring lion, going about seeking whom he may devour;" nor only a subtle enemy, who comes secretly upon poor souls and leads them captive, but also he who rules worldly men and all their dark schemes and actions by possessing their hearts, and setting up his throne there. And he is not idle in his dwelling place. He is continually "working in" these "children of disobedience." He works in them with power, with mighty energy, transforming them into his own likeness, disfiguring what remains of the image of God and preparing them for every evil word and work.

It is, therefore, an unquestionable truth, that the god and prince of this world still possesses all who do not know God. It is only the manner of this possession which now differs from that of long ago. At that time he openly tormented their bodies as well as their souls; now he torments their souls only (except in some rare cases), acting as covertly as possible. The reason for this difference is clear. His purpose used to be to drive mankind into superstition; therefore, he worked as openly as he could. But now his purpose is to drive us into unbelief; therefore, he works as privately as he can, for the more secret he is, the more he succeeds.

Yet, if we can believe historians, there are countries, even now, where he works just as openly as before. But why in savage, uncivilized countries only? Why not in Italy, France, or England?

The reason is clear: he knows his men; and he knows what he must do with each. To the heathen he appears unmasked, in order to hold them in superstition and idolatry. But with you he is pursuing a different strategy. He wants to make you idolize yourselves; to make you wiser in your own eyes than God himself. In order to do this, he must not appear in his own shape. That would frustrate his plan. Instead, he uses all his skill to make you deny his existence until he has you securely in hell.

He reigns in different ways, but just as completely in one land as in another. He has the unbelievers in his teeth, as surely as the heathens. But the unbelievers are asleep in the mouth of the lion, who is too wise to wake them. So he merely plays with them for the time being; and, when he pleases, swallows them up! It is not to his benefit to frighten them, for then they might run to the God of heaven. The prince of darkness, therefore, does not show himself while he rules over his willing subjects. The conqueror holds his captives more securely because they think they are free. Neither the Deist nor the nominal Christian suspects he exists; so they and the devil are perfectly at peace with each other.

During this time he works actively in them. He blinds the eyes of their understanding, so that the light of the glorious gospel of Christ cannot shine on them. He chains their souls with their own evil desires. He binds them to the earth with the love of the world, of money, of pleasure, and of praise. And by pride, envy, anger, hate, and vengefulness, he brings their souls closer to hell; encountering no resistance, because they do not know that he is working in them.

If you consider this, you will see in what sense men still cast out devils. Every minister of Christ casts them out, as the Lord works through him. By the power of God accompanying his message, he brings sinners to repentance: an entire inward as well as outward change, from all evil to all good. This is casting devils out of the souls where they have lived. This is how the Son of God "destroys the works of the devil." The understanding of the sinner is now enlightened, and his heart is drawn toward God. His desires are refined, and his affections purified. Being filled with the Holy Spirit, he grows in grace until he is not only holy in heart, but in behavior as well.

The Identity of the Person Who "Follows Not Us"

But should we forbid one who "casts out devils," if "he follows not us?" This was the opinion and practice of the Apostle until he asked his Master. "We forbad him," he said, "because he follows not us," which he considered a sufficient reason. What we may understand by this expression, "He follows not us," is the next point to be considered. One circumstance in which this might occur arises simply because we do not labor in the same organization. When our Lord is pleased to send many laborers into His harvest, they cannot all act in connection with each other. Furthermore, they cannot all be personally acquainted, or even know of one another. There will be many in different regions of the harvest that will be absolute strangers to each other, as if they had lived in different ages. So then, we could easily say, "He follows not us," regarding any of these whom we do not know.

A second use of this expression may be to mean that a person is not of our party. It has long been a cause of concern to all who pray for the peace of Jerusalem, that so many parties still exist among those who are called Christians. This has been especially obvious among our own countrymen, who have been continually dividing from each other over points of no importance, and often over things unrelated to religion. The pettiest of circumstances have given rise to different parties, which have continued for many generations; and each of these would be ready to say of one who was on the other side, "He follows not us."

A third way the expression may be used is to mean a person who differs from us in our religious opinions. How quickly differences of opinion arose in the church of Christ; and not in false but in real Christians: even in the Apostles themselves! It is not surprising, then, that infinite varieties of opinion are now found in the Christian Church. A likely result of this is that whenever we see someone "casting out devils," he will be one that does not share our opinion. It is hard to imagine that he will be like-minded in all things, even religion. He may think differently even on several subjects of importance; such as the nature and use of the moral law, the eternal decrees of God, the sufficiency and efficacy of His grace, and the perseverance of His children.

Fourth, he may differ from us, not only in opinion, but also in some specific practice. He may not approve of the manner in which our congregation of worships God; and may consider a manner originating with Calvin or Luther to be more beneficial. He may have many objections to the liturgy which we approve; and many doubts concerning the form of church government we consider to be both apostolic and scriptural. Perhaps he may depart even farther from us than this. He may, from a principle of conscience, refrain from the bread-breaking which we believe to be ordained by Christ. Or, though he may agree that it is ordained by God, there may remain a difference between us as to how or to whom it should be served. The unavoidable result of any of these differences will be that he who differs from us must separate himself from us, at least in the observation of these points. In this sense, then, "he follows not us."

But, in a far stronger sense, the person who "follows not us," is not only of a different church, but of a church that we consider to be in many respects anti-scriptural and anti-Christian; a church that we believe to be completely false and erroneous in her doctrines, as well as dangerously wrong in her practice; guilty of superstition as well as idolatry; a church that has added to the holy faith which was delivered to the saints long ago; that has abandoned one whole commandment of God, and voided several others by her traditions; and, while pretending to have the highest respect for the ancient church and the strictest conformity to it, has brought in countless innovations, without basis either in history or Scripture. Now, most certainly, "he follows not us," who stands at so far away from us.

Still, there may be an even wider difference than this. He who differs from us in judgment or practice may also stand apart from us in affection. Differences which begin in points of opinion seldom end there. They usually spread into the affections and separate close friends. No animosities are as deep and irreconcilable as those that spring from disagreement in religion. For this reason a man's bitterest enemies are the members of his own household. And so a father rises against his own children, and the children against their father; perhaps persecuting each other even to the death, thinking all the while they are serving God. Therefore, we may expect those who differ from us, either in religious opinions or practice, to develop a sharpness, or even a bitterness toward us as their prejudice grows, until they have as bad an opinion of our persons as they do of our principles. An almost inevitable result of this will be that they will speak of us as they think of us. They will undermine our work, since it does not appear to them to be the work of God. He that thinks, speaks, and acts in this manner, in the highest sense, "follows not us."

I do not imagine that the person of whom the Apostle speaks in the text went so far as this. We have no reason to suppose that there was any substantial difference between him and the apostles; much less that he had any prejudice either against them or their Master. We may conclude this from our Lord's words, which follow the verses quoted: "There is no man which shall do a miracle in My name, that can lightly speak evil of Me." My purpose, however, was to state the case as extremely as possible, in order that we may be warned of the temptation at its worst, and not yield to it, nor fight against God.

What It Means to "Forbid Him Not"

Suppose, then, that a man has no interaction with us, suppose he is not of our party, suppose he separates from our Church, and widely differs from us in opinion, practice, and affection. And yet, if we see even this man "casting out devils," Jesus says, "Forbid him not." I must explain this important direction of our Lord.

If we see this man casting out devils, it would be best for us to believe what we see with our eyes, and not deny the testimony of our own senses. We are extremely reluctant to believe that any man casts out devils who "follows not us" in all or most of the senses described above. We may easily learn, even from what happens in our own hearts, how unwilling men are to recognize anything good in others who do not agree with them in all things.

But what is a sufficient, reasonable proof that a man does (in the above sense) cast out devils? The answer is easy. Is there a shameless sinner who has left his sins and lives a Christian life because of hearing this man preach? If this is undeniable, then you have proof (proof that you cannot resist without committing willful sin) that this man casts out devils.

Then "forbid him not." Beware of your attempts to hinder him, either by your authority, or arguments, or persuasions. Do not in any way fight to prevent him from using all the power God has given him. If you have authority over him, do not use that authority to stop the work of God. Do not furnish him with reasons why he should no longer speak in the name of Jesus. Satan will supply him with these without your help. If he should yield to the devil and to you, many souls might die in their sins, but God would require their blood at your hands.

But if you claim not to know if he is sent by God, those whom he has brought from Satan to God might understandably be amazed. "If this man were not of God, he could do nothing." If you doubt the fact, question the parents of the changed man:

ask his brothers, friends, and acquaintances. But if you cannot doubt that a miracle has been worked, then how in good conscience can you command him whom God has sent, "not to speak any more in His name?"

It is helpful if whoever preaches has permission from the church authority as well as an inward call from God, but I deny that it is absolutely necessary. In the eighth chapter of Acts we read, "There was a great persecution against the Church which was at Jerusalem; and they were all scattered abroad throughout the regions of Judea and Samaria, except the Apostles" (Acts 8:1). "Therefore they that were scattered abroad, went everywhere preaching the word" (8:4). Now, were all these ordained by the church to preach? No sensible man can think so. This proves that which was the practice of the apostolic age. Here you see a multitude of preachers that were sent only by God.

Do you fear God? Then "forbid not His servants," either directly or indirectly. There are many ways of doing this. You indirectly forbid him when you either deny or despise the work which God has done through him. You indirectly forbid him when you discourage him in his work by drawing him into disputes concerning it, by raising objections against it, or by frightening him with results that may never happen. You forbid him when you show any unkindness toward him, either in speech or behavior; and when you speak of him to others either with unkindness or contempt. You are forbidding him all the while you are speaking evil of him, or putting no value on his work. "Forbid him not" in any of these ways; nor by forbidding others to hear him, by discouraging sinners from hearing that word that is able to save their souls!

If you want to observe the full meaning of our Lord's direction, then remember His words: "He that is not for us is against us; and he that gathereth not with Me, scattereth." He that does not gather men into the kingdom of God certainly scatters them from it. There can be no neutral side in this war. Everyone is either on God's side or on Satan's. Are you on God's side? Then you will not only not forbid any man that casts out devils, but you will labor, to the full extent of your power, to move him forward in this work. You will acknowledge the work of God and confess the greatness of it. You will remove all difficulties and objections, as far it is possible, out of his way. You will strengthen his hands by speaking honorably of him before all men and affirming the things which you have seen and heard. You will encourage others to hear him whom God has sent. And you will not withhold any love which God gives you an opportunity to show him.

The Danger of Bigotry

If we willingly fail in this, if we either directly or indirectly forbid him, "because he follows not us," then we are bigots. This is the inference I draw from what has been said. Bigotry is too strong an attachment to, or fondness for, our own party, opinion, church, and religion. Therefore, he is a bigot who is so fond of these, so strongly attached to them, that he forbids anyone who casts out devils simply because that one differs from himself in any or all of these particulars.

Beware of this, and examine yourself! Do I directly forbid him because he is not of my party? Because he does not share my opinions? Because he does not worship God according to that style of religion which I have received from my fathers?

Examine yourself again! Am I sorry that God should recognize and bless the ministry of a man that holds such erroneous opinions? Do I discourage him because he is not of my church, by arguing with him about it, by raising objections, and by troubling his mind with distant and uncertain consequences? Do I show anger, contempt, or unkindness of any sort, either in my words or actions? Do I mention his faults behind his back? His defects or infirmities? Do I keep sinners from hearing him speak? If you do any of these things, you are most certainly a bigot.

In order to examine ourselves thoroughly, let the case be stated in the strongest manner. What if I were to see a Papist, an Arian, or a Socinian, casting out devils? If I did, I could not forbid even him, without convicting myself of bigotry.

Stand clear of this! But go beyond simply not forbidding those who cast out devils. In every instance, whatever the instrument may be, acknowledge the finger of God. Rejoice in God's work, and praise His name with thanksgiving. Speak well of whomever God is pleased to use; wherever you are, defend his character and his mission. Enlarge his sphere of action to the extent that you are able; show him all kindness in word and deed; and do not stop crying out to God on his behalf, so that he may save both himself and them that hear him.

I need to add one caution. Do not think that the bigotry of another is any excuse for your own. It is possible that one who casts out devils himself may forbid you so to do. In fact, this is the very case mentioned in the text. The apostles did not permit another to do what they did themselves. But it is not for you to return evil for evil. Another's neglect of our Lord's direction is no reason why you should neglect it too. If he forbids you, do not forbid him. Instead, labor, watch, and pray all the more, in order to confirm your love toward him. If he speaks evil of you, speak good (that is true) of him. Imitate that glorious saying of a great man [Zwingli] (O that he had always breathed the same spirit!), "Let Luther call me a hundred devils; I will still reverence him as a messenger of God."

Editor's note: We can see from Wesley's own practice that he did not intend to imply that erroneous doctrine should not be refuted, or that we should be silent when we see that a doctrine will inevitably be harmful. For examples of balancing statements, see Wesley's comment about the followers of Zinzendorf in the third paragraph of the chapter entitled "On Sin in Believers," and the closing comment of the chapter entitled "A Dialogue with a Predestinarian and His Friend."

12

The Spirit of Unity

Editor's Note: This sermon was originally entitled "Catholic Spirit." This expression has been changed in the title and throughout the sermon, since the term catholic *today is not usually understood in its original meaning.*

"And when he was departed thence, he lighted on Jehonadab the son of Rechab coming to meet him: And he saluted him, and said to him, Is thine heart right as my heart is with thy heart? And Jehonadab said, It is. If it be, give me thine hand." 2 Kings 10:15.

It is agreed even by those who do not pay this great debt, that love is owed to all mankind; for the law, "Thou shalt love your neighbor as yourself," is proof in itself. And it does not come with the limitation some place on it, "Thou shalt love your relation, acquaintance, and friend, but hate your enemy." Not so, "I say unto you," says our Lord, "Love your enemies, bless them that curse you, do good to them that hate you, and pray for them that despitefully use you, and persecute you; that ye may be the children of your Father which is in heaven; who maketh His sun to rise on the evil and on the good, and sendeth rain on the just and on the unjust."

But it is certain that there is a special love that we owe to those that love God. Therefore David said, "All my delight is upon the saints that are in the earth, and upon such as excel in virtue." And, likewise, One greater than he said, "A new commandment I give unto you, that ye love one another; As I have loved you, that ye also love one another. By this shall all men know that ye are My disciples, if ye have love one to another" (John 13:34, 35). This is that love on which the Apostle John so strongly insists: "This is the message that ye heard from the beginning, that we should love one another" (1 John 3:11). "Hereby perceive we the love of God, because He laid down His life for us: And we ought," if love should call us to, "to lay down our lives for the brethren" (3:16). And again: "Beloved, let us love one another: For love is of God. He that loveth not, knoweth not God; for God is love" (4:7, 8). "Not that we loved God, but that He loved us, and sent His Son to be the propitiation for our sins. Beloved, if God so loved us, we ought also to love one another" (4:10, 11).

All men approve of this, but do all men practice it? Daily experience shows the opposite. Where are even the Christians who "love one another as He has given us commandment?" The greatest hindrance is that they cannot all think alike; and, as a result, do not all walk alike. Invariably, their practices will differ according to the difference of their opinions.

But even if a difference in opinions or forms of worship may prevent organizational unity; must it prevent our unity of affection? Though we cannot think alike, can we not love alike? May we not be of one heart, though we are not of one opinion? Certainly, all the children of God may unite in this, even though they have these smaller differences.

It is certain that as long as our knowledge is imperfect, all men will not see all things alike. It is an unavoidable result of the weakness of human understanding that men will have various opinions about religion as well as common life. It has been this way from the beginning of the world, and so it will be until the restoration of all things.

Furthermore, although every man believes that every particular opinion he holds is true (for to believe an opinion not to be true is the same as not to hold it); no man can be sure that all his opinions, collectively, are true. In fact, every thinking man is sure they are not; since to be ignorant of many things, and to be mistaken in some, is the inevitable condition of humanity. Therefore, he recognizes this in himself as well. He knows, in general, that he is mistaken; although in what, specifically, he does not know.

And perhaps he cannot know, for who can tell how far ignorance or prejudice extends? Prejudice is often so established in tender minds that it is impossible to pull up what is rooted so deeply. And who could say, unless he knew every circumstance involved, to what degree any mistake is blameworthy? All guilt requires some consent of the will, which only He who sees the heart can judge.

Every wise man, therefore, will allow others the same liberty of thinking which he desires for himself; and will no more insist that they embrace his opinions than he would want them to insist that he embrace theirs. He has patience with those who differ from him, and asks him with whom he desires to unite in love just one question: "Is your heart right, as my heart is toward yours?"

But even among the upright, men who desire to have a clear conscience, as long as there are various opinions, there will be various ways of worshipping God; since variety in opinion causes variety in practice. And as men have always widely differed in their opinions concerning the Supreme Being, so widely do they differ in their manner of worshipping Him. Had this been the case only in the heathen world, it would not have been surprising at all. But is it not strange that, even in the Christian world, although all agree that, "God is a Spirit; and they that worship Him must worship Him in spirit and in truth;" still the particular modes of worshipping God vary almost as much as among the heathens?

How then will we choose among so much variety? No man can choose for another. Everyone must follow his own conscience in godly sincerity. He must be fully persuaded in his own mind, and then act according to the best light he has. No creature has the power to force another to walk by his own rule. God has given no right to any of the children of men to be lord over the consciences of his brothers, but every man must judge for himself, for every man must give an account of himself to God.

Therefore, although every follower of Christ is obligated, by the nature of the Christian institution, to be a member of some particular congregation (which implies a particular manner of worshipping God, for they could not worship together unless they agreed on the manner), no one can be required by any power on earth but his own conscience to prefer one congregation over another, or to choose a particular manner of worship. It is commonly supposed that the place of our birth determines the church to which we ought to belong; for example, that one who is born in England ought to be a member of the Church of England, and to worship God in the manner which is prescribed by that Church. I was once a zealous proponent of this idea, but no longer, for it seems to have difficulties that no reasonable man can get over. One problem with the view is that it would allow no reformation from popery; since it destroys the right of private judgment on which the whole Reformation stands.

I do not dare, therefore, impose my mode of worship on any other person. While I believe it is true to the apostles' teaching, my belief is no rule for another. Therefore, I do not ask him with whom I would unite in love, "Do you belong to my church?" "Do you have the same form of church government, and allow the same church officers?" "Do you join in the same form of prayer by which I worship God?" I do not ask whether you receive the Lord's Supper in the same manner that I do, nor whether you agree with me in the manner of baptism, or the age of those to whom it should be administered. I do not ask (although it is clear in my own mind) even whether you allow baptism and the Lord's Supper at all. Let these things wait; we will speak of them, if necessary, at a more convenient time; my only question now is this, "Is your heart right, as my heart is toward yours?"

What Is Necessary for Hearts to Unite

But what is properly implied in this question? What should a follower of Christ mean by it when he offers it to any of his brothers? The first thing it implies is this: is your heart right with God? Do you believe His being, and His perfections; His eternity, immensity, wisdom, power; His justice, mercy, and truth? Do you believe that He "upholds all things by the word of His power;" and that He governs even the smallest, even the most unpleasant, for His own glory, and the good of those who love Him? Do you have divine evidence, a supernatural conviction, of the things of God? Do you "walk by faith, not by sight," not looking at earthly things, but at those things which are eternal?

Do you believe in the Lord Jesus Christ, "God over all, blessed forever?" Is He revealed in your soul? Do you know Jesus Christ and Him crucified? Does He live in you, and you in him? Is He formed in your heart by faith? Having discarded any claim to your own righteousness, have you "submitted yourself unto the righteousness of God," which is by faith in Christ Jesus? And are you, through Him, "fighting the good fight of faith, and taking hold of eternal life?"

Is your faith filled with the energy of love? Do you love God "with all your heart, and with all your mind, and with all your soul, and with all your strength?" Do you look for all your happiness in Him alone? And do you find what you are looking for? Does your soul continually "magnify the Lord, and your spirit rejoice in God your Savior?" Having learned "in everything to give thanks," do you find it is a joyful and pleasant thing to be thankful? Is God the center of your soul? Is He the sum of all your desires? Are you then laying up your treasure in heaven, and considering everything else dung and dross? Has the love of God thrown the love of the world out of your soul? Then you are "crucified to the world;" you are dead to all that is below; and your "life is hid with Christ in God."

Are you busy doing, "not your own will, but the will of Him that sent you?" Are you fulfilling the plan of Him that sent you down to spend a few days in a strange land, until, having finished the work He has given you to do, you return to your Father's house? Is it your meat and drink "to do the will of your Father which is in heaven?" Is your single motive to honor Christ in all things? Are you always looking to Jesus in whatever you do: all your labor, your business, your conversation? Is your only goal the glory of God in whatever you do, either in word or deed, doing it all in the name of the Lord Jesus; giving thanks to the Father, through Him?"

Does the love of God cause you to serve Him with fear? Are you more afraid of displeasing God, than of death or hell? Is nothing so terrible to you as the thought of offending the eyes of His glory? On this basis, do you "hate all evil ways," every violation of His holy and perfect law; and, in this, "exercise yourself to have a conscience void of offense toward God and toward man?"

Is your heart right toward your neighbor? Do you love, as yourself, all mankind without exception? Do you "love your enemies?" Is your soul full of goodwill, of tender affection, toward them? Do you love even the enemies of God, the unthankful and unholy? Could you "wish yourself" now "accursed" for their sake? And do you show this by "blessing them that curse you, and praying for those that despitefully use you and persecute you?"

Do you show your love by your actions? While you have time, and as you have opportunity, do you "do good to all men," neighbors or strangers, friends or enemies, good or bad? Do you do for them all the good you can, trying to supply all their needs; assisting them both in body and soul, to the best of your ability? If this is your attitude, then every Christian may say, "Your heart is right, as my heart is with yours."

What It Means to Take Another's Hand

I do not mean, "Be of my opinion." I do not expect or desire it. Neither do I mean, "I will be of your opinion." I cannot; it does not depend on my choice. I can no more choose what to think, than I can choose what to see or hear. Keep your opinion, and I will keep mine. You do not need to try to come to my opinion, or bring me to yours. I do not want you to argue those points, or to hear or speak one word concerning them. Leave all these opinions alone on both sides. Only, "give me your hand."

I do not mean, "Embrace my mode of worship;" or, "I will embrace yours." This also is a thing which does not depend either on your choice or mine. We must both act as each of us is fully persuaded in his own mind. Hold to that which you believe is most acceptable to God, and I will do the same. I believe the Episcopal form of church government is scriptural and apostolic. If you think the Presbyterian or Independent form is better, then think so, and act accordingly. I believe infants ought to be baptized, and that this may be done either by dipping or sprinkling. If you believe otherwise, continue to do so, and follow your own belief. It appears to me that written prayers are useful, particularly in the congregation. If you consider extemporaneous prayer to be more useful, act according to your own judgment. My belief is that I ought to teach baptism; and that I ought to eat bread and drink wine as a memorial of my dying Master. However, if you are not convinced of this, live by the light that you have. I have no desire to argue with you for one moment on any of the preceding topics. Let these smaller points stand aside. "If your heart is as my heart," if you love God and all of mankind, I ask no more than for you to "give me your hand."

I mean, first, love me. Not only as you love all of mankind; not only as you love your enemies, or the enemies of God, those that hate you, that "despitefully use you and persecute you;" not only as a stranger, as one of whom you know nothing, either good or evil. I am not satisfied with this. If your heart is right, as mine is with your heart, then love me with a very tender affection, as a friend that is closer than a brother; as a brother in Christ, a fellow citizen of the New Jerusalem, a fellow soldier engaged in the same battle, under the same Captain of our salvation. Love me as a companion in the kingdom and patient endurance of Jesus, and a joint heir of His glory.

Love me (but in a higher degree than you do the rest of mankind) with a love that is longsuffering and kind; with a love that is patient if I am ignorant or misguided, that lifts and does not increase my burden. Remain tender, soft, and compassionate. Love me with a love that does not envy if at any time God prospers me in His work more than you. Love me with the love that is not provoked, either at my foolishness or my infirmities; or even when I do not act (if it sometimes appears that way to you) according to the will of God. Love me so as not to think evil of me; to put away all jealousy and presumptions of evil. Love me with the love that covers all things; that never reveals my faults or infirmities. Love me with a love that is always willing to believe the best about all my words and actions. And hope to the end that whatever is wrong, will, by the grace of God, be corrected; and whatever is lacking, supplied through the riches of

His mercy in Christ Jesus.

Second, I mean lift me to God in all your prayers; wrestle with Him on my behalf, that He would quickly correct what He sees is wrong with me, and supply what is lacking in me. Beg of Him that my heart may be more as your heart, more right toward both God and man; that I may have a fuller conviction of things not seen, and a stronger view of the love of God in Christ Jesus; that I may walk more steadily by faith, not by sight; and more earnestly grasp eternal life. Pray that love for God and for all mankind may increase in my heart; that I may be more passionate in doing the will of my Father; more zealous to do good works, and more careful to avoid every appearance of evil.

Third, I mean urge me on to love and to do good works. Reinforce your prayer, as you have the opportunity, by speaking to me in love whatever you believe to be for the good of my soul. Motivate me in the work which God has given me to do, and instruct me how to do it better. Correct me whenever I appear to you to be doing my own will, rather than the will of Him that sent me. Speak and do not withhold whatever you believe may help; for correcting my faults, strengthening my weaknesses, building me up in love, or making me more fit for the Master's use!

Finally, I mean love me not only in word, but also in deed. As far as you can with a clear conscience (retaining your own opinions, and your own manner of worshipping God), join with me in the work of God, and let us go on hand in hand. This far, it is certain, you may go. Wherever you are, speak honorably of the work of God, and kindly of His messengers. And, if you are able, not only sympathize with them when they are in any difficulty or distress, but give them cheerful and effective assistance, that they may glorify God because of you.

Two things should be noted with regard to what has been spoken under this last topic. First, whatever duties of love, whatever spiritual or earthly assistance I ask of him whose heart is right, I am ready, according to my ability, to give him the same. Second, I have not claimed this for myself only, but for all whose hearts are right toward God and man, that we may all love one another as Christ has loved us.

Observations Regarding a True Spirit of Unity

From what has been said, we may learn what a spirit of unity is. There is hardly any expression which has been more misunderstood, and more dangerously misapplied than this. But we may learn, first, that a spirit of unity is not an indifference to all opinions. This unsettledness of thought, this being "driven to and fro, and tossed about with every wind of doctrine," is a great curse, not a blessing; an irreconcilable enemy, not a friend, to true unity. A man with a true spirit of unity is not still trying to find his religion. He is as established as the sun in his judgment concerning the main parts of Christian doctrine. It is true that he is always ready to hear and evaluate evidence against his principles; but this does not show any doubt in his own mind, and neither does it cause any. He does not hesitate between two opinions, nor try uselessly to blend them into one. Pay attention, you who do not know to whom you belong; who call yourselves men with a spirit of unity, only because you have no clear understanding; because your mind is all in a fog; because you have no settled, consistent principles, but want to jumble all opinions together. Be convinced that you have completely lost your way; you do not know where you are. Go and learn the basic truths of the gospel of Christ, and then you will learn to have a true spirit of unity.

Second, we may learn from what has been said that a spirit of unity is not an indifference to rules of practice. It is not indifference to public worship, or to the outward manner of performing it. This, likewise, would not be a blessing, but a curse. Far from being a help, it would be a great hindrance to worshipping God in spirit and in truth. But the man with a spirit of unity, having considered carefully the things pertaining to the sanctuary, has no doubt concerning the particular mode of worship in which he participates. He is clearly convinced that this manner of worshipping God is both scriptural and rational. He knows of none in the world which is more scriptural, and none which is more rational. Therefore, without rambling here and there, he holds close to it, and praises God for the opportunity to do so.

Third, we may learn from this that a spirit of unity is not indifference to all congregations. This is far removed from a man of a true spirit of unity. He is firmly set in his congregation as well as in his principles. He is united to this church, not only in spirit, but by all the outward ties of Christian fellowship. This is where he receives the Lord's Supper. This is where he pours out his soul in public prayer, and joins in public praise and thanksgiving. This is where he rejoices to hear the word of reconciliation, the gospel of the grace of God. Here he joins with his most-beloved brethren, on solemn occasions, to seek God by fasting. He watches over these in love, as they do over his soul; exhorting, comforting, reproving, and in every way building each other up in the faith. He regards these as members of his own household; and therefore, according to the ability God has given him, naturally cares for them, and provides all that they need for life and godliness.

But while he is established in his religious principles, in what he believes to be the truth; while he firmly adheres to that worship of God which he considers most acceptable in His sight; and while he is united by the tenderest and closest ties to one particular congregation, his heart is enlarged toward all mankind. He embraces both those he knows and those he does not with strong affection. He that has this love has a spirit of unity. For love alone is a spirit of unity.

If, then, we take this word in the strictest sense, a man of a spirit of unity is one who, in the way we have just described, gives his hand to all whose hearts are right. He values and praises God for all the advantages he enjoys: the knowledge of the things of God, the true scriptural manner of worshipping Him, and his union with a congregation which fears God and works righteousness. He keeps these blessings with great care, while at the same time loving all those, of whatever opinion, or worship, or congregation, who believe in the Lord Jesus Christ; who love God and man; who, rejoicing to please and fearing to offend God, are careful to avoid evil, and zealous for doing good. He is the man of a true spirit of unity, who carries all these continually in his heart; who, having an unspeakable tenderness for them, and longing for their welfare, never ceases commending them to God in prayer, as well as pleading their cause before men. He speaks encouragingly to them and works by all his words to strengthen their hands in God. He assists them to the full extent of his ability in all things, spiritual and earthly. He is ready to spend and be spent for them; even to lay down his life for them.

Man of God, think about these things! If you already follow in this way, continue. If you have missed the path, praise God who has now brought you back! Run the race which is set before you, in the royal way of universal love. Be careful, or you will either become wavering in your judgment, or narrow in your bones. So keep an even pace, rooted in the holy faith which was given to the saints long ago, and grounded in true unifying love, until you are swallowed up in love for ever and ever!

13

A Letter to a Roman Catholic

I am sure you have heard ten thousand stories about us who are Protestants, and if you believe even one in a thousand, you must think very badly of us. But this is contrary to our Lord's rule, "Judge not, that ye be not judged;" and has many harmful results; especially that it leads us to think just as badly of you. We are then both less willing to help one another and more ready to hurt each other. As a result, brotherly love is completely destroyed; and each side, seeing the other as monsters, surrenders to anger, hatred, malice, and every unkind action; which have frequently resulted in practices so inhuman, they are rarely found even among the heathens.

Can anything be done, while allowing each of us to retain our own opinions, for the softening of our hearts toward one another, stopping this flood of unkindness and restoring at least some degree of love among our neighbors and countrymen? Do you not also want this? Are you not fully convinced that malice, hatred, revenge, and bitterness, whether in our hearts or yours, are an abomination to the Lord? Whether our opinions are right or wrong, these tempers are undeniably wrong. They are the broad road that leads to destruction, to the deepest hell.

I do not pretend that all the bitterness is on your side. I know there is too much on our side also. I fear that many Protestants (so-called) will be angry at me as well for writing to you in this manner; and will say, "It is showing them too much favor; they deserve no such treatment from us."

But I think you do. I think you deserve the most tender regard I can show, even if it were only because the same God has formed you and me from the dust of the earth, and has made us both capable of loving and enjoying Him eternally; even if it were only because the Son of God has bought you and me with His own blood. And how much more, if you are a person who fears God (as many of you are), and tries to have a conscience free of offense towards both God and man?

I will try then, as inoffensively as I can, to remove some of the reasons for your unkindness, by clearly stating what our belief and practice is; so that you can see that we are not all the monsters you have imagined us to be. A true Protestant will express his belief in words similar to these:

Just as I am assured that there is an infinite and independent Being, and that it is impossible for there to be more than one; so I believe that this One God is the Father of all things, especially of angels and men; that He is, in a special sense, the Father of those whom He regenerates by His Spirit, whom He adopts in his Son, as co-heirs with Him, and crowns with an eternal inheritance; but He is also, in an even higher sense, the Father of His only Son, whom He has begotten from eternity. I believe this Father of all is not only able to do as He pleases, but also has an eternal right to make whatever, whenever and however He pleases, freely possessing or disposing of all that He has made;

and that He, out of his own goodness, created heaven and earth and all that is in them.

I believe that Jesus of Nazareth was the Savior of the world, the long-awaited Messiah; that, being anointed with the Holy Spirit, He was a Prophet, revealing to us the complete will of God; that He was a Priest who gave himself as a sacrifice for sin and still intercedes for sinners; that He is a King who has all power in heaven and on earth and will reign until He has brought all things under himself. I believe He is the proper, natural Son of God, God of God, very God of very God; and that He is the Lord of all, having absolute, supreme, universal dominion over all things; but He is more specially our Lord, the Lord of all who believe in Him, whether by conquest, purchase, and voluntary obligation. I believe that He was made man, joining the human nature with the divine in one person; being conceived by the unique operation of the Holy Spirit, and born of the blessed Virgin Mary, who both after as well as before she gave birth to Him continued as a pure and unspotted virgin. I believe He was afflicted with inexpressible pain in both body and soul and, at last, suffered the death of the cross, at the time Pontius Pilate governed Judea, under the Roman Emperor; that His body was then laid in the grave, and His soul went to the place of separate spirits; that on the third day He rose again from the dead; that He ascended into heaven; where He remains at the throne of God, in the highest power and glory, as Mediator until the end of the world, as God to all eternity; and that, in the end, He will come down from heaven to judge every man according to his works; both those who will be alive then, and all who died before that day.

I believe the infinite and eternal Spirit of God, equal with the Father and the Son, to be not only perfectly holy in himself, but the direct cause of all holiness in us; enlightening our understandings, correcting our wills and affections, renewing our natures, uniting our persons to Christ, assuring us of our adoption as sons, leading us in our actions; purifying and sanctifying our souls and bodies, to a full and eternal enjoyment of God.

I believe that Christ, by His apostles, gathered to himself a Church, to which He has continually added those who will be saved; that this catholic, or universal Church, extending to all nations and all ages, is holy in all its members who have fellowship with God the Father, Son, and Holy Spirit; that these have fellowship with the holy angels, who constantly minister to these heirs of salvation; and with all the living members of Christ on earth, as well as all who have passed away in His faith and fear.

I believe God forgives all the sins of those who truly repent and genuinely believe His holy gospel; and that, at the last day, all men will rise again, each one with his own body. I believe that even as the unjust will, after their resurrection, be tormented in hell forever, so the just will enjoy inconceivable happiness in the presence of God for all eternity.

Now, is there anything wrong in this? Is there any one point in which you do not believe as strongly as we do? But you think we ought to believe more. We will not enter into that dispute now. Only let me ask, if a man sincerely believes this much, and practices accordingly, can anyone possibly persuade you to think that such a man will perish eternally?

Perhaps you ask, "But does he practice accordingly?" If he does not, we acknowledge that all his faith will not save him. And this leads me to show you, in a few clear words, what the practice of a true Protestant is. I say a true Protestant; for I disown all common swearers, Sabbath-breakers, drunkards; all whoremongers, liars, cheats, and extortioners; in short, all that live in open sin. These are not Protestants; they are not Christians at all. Give them their own name: they are heathens. They are the curse of the nation, the poison of society, the shame of mankind, the scum of the earth.

A true Protestant believes in God, has full confidence in His mercy, fears Him with a son's reverence, and loves Him with all his soul. He worships God in spirit and in truth, gives thanks to Him in everything; calls on Him with his heart as well as his lips, at all times and in all places; honors His holy name and His word, and serves Him all the days of his life. Now, do you not approve of this yourself? Is there any one point you can condemn? And do you not practice as well as approve of it? Can you ever be happy if you do not? Can you ever expect true peace in this world, or glory in the world to come, if you do not believe in God through Christ, and if you do not fear and love God in this way? My dear friend, please understand that I am not trying to persuade you to leave or change your religion, but to follow after that fear of and love for God without which all religion is vain. I will not say a word to you about your opinions or outward manner of worship. But I will say that all worship is an offense to the Lord unless you worship Him in spirit and in truth; with your heart, as well as your lips; with your spirit, and also with your understanding. Let your form of worship be what it will, but give Him thanks in everything; or else it is all a wasted effort. Use whatever outward observances you please, but put all of your trust in him. Honor His holy name and His word, and serve Him all the days of your life.

Further, a true Protestant loves his neighbor as himself; that is, he loves every man, whether friend or enemy, good or bad, just as he loves his own soul, even as Christ loved us. And as Christ laid down His life for us, so he is ready to lay down his life for his brothers. He shows this love by doing to all men as he wants them to do to him. He loves, honors, and obeys his father and mother, and helps them to the best of his ability. He honors and obeys the king, and all that are in authority under him. He gladly submits to all his governors, teachers, spiritual pastors, and masters. He behaves humbly and respectfully toward those of a higher class than himself. He hurts no one either in word or deed. He is true and just in all his dealings. He holds no malice or hatred in his heart. He keeps himself from all evil speaking, lying, and slandering; neither is he deceitful. Knowing his body to be the temple of the Holy Spirit, he keeps it in soberness, self-control, and purity. He does not desire other men's possessions; but is content with what he has. He works for his own living, and to do the complete will of God in that state of life to which God has called him.

Do you see anything here that needs correction? Are you not the same as he is in these things? If not (tell the truth), are you not condemned both by God and your own conscience? Can you fall short in any of these points without falling short of being a Christian? Come, my brother, and let us reason together. Are you right if you only love your friend and hate your enemy? Do not even the heathens and publicans do as much? You are called to love your enemies; to bless those who curse you, and to pray for those who despitefully use you and persecute you. But are you obedient to the heavenly calling? Does your tender love to all men, not only the good, but also the evil, confirm that you are child of your Father which is in heaven? Otherwise, no matter what you may believe or practice, you are of your father the devil. Are you ready to lay down your life for your brothers? And do you do to all as you want them to do to you? If not, do not deceive yourself: you are still only a heathen. Do you love, honor, and obey your father and mother, and help them to the best of your ability? Do you honor and obey all in authority, all your governors, spiritual pastors, and masters? Do you behave humbly and respectfully toward those of a higher class than yourself? Do you hurt no one either in word or deed? Are you true and just in all your dealings? Do you pay whatever you owe? Do you feel any malice, or envy, or revenge, any hatred or bitterness toward any man? If you do, it is clear that you are not of God, for all these are tempers of the devil. Do you speak the truth from your heart to all men, in tenderness and love? Do you keep your body in soberness, self-control, and purity, knowing it is the temple of the Holy Spirit, and that, if any man defiles the temple of God, God will destroy him? Have you learned to be content in every circumstance? Do you work for your own living, abhorring laziness as you do the fires of hell? The devil tempts men; but a lazy man tempts the devil. A lazy man's brain is the devil's shop, where he is continually working mischief. Are you diligent in business? Whatever your hand finds to do, do you do it with all your strength? And do you do it all as for the Lord, as a sacrifice to God, acceptable in Christ Jesus? This alone is the old religion. This is true, original Christianity. When will it spread over all the earth? When will it be found both in us and you? Without waiting for others, let each of us, by the grace of God, correct ourselves.

Do we not agree on this much? Let us thank God for this, and receive it as a fresh example of His love. And if God loves us, we ought to love one another. We should, without this endless noise about opinions, motivate one another to love and to do good works. Let the points in which we differ stand aside; here are enough in which we agree, enough to be the basis of every Christian attitude and action. Brothers, let us not still argue along the way! I hope to see you in heaven. If I practice the religion described above, you do not dare say I will go to hell. You cannot think so. Your own conscience tells you the opposite. If we cannot think alike in all things, at least we may love alike. We cannot possibly do wrong in this. For one point no one can doubt: "God is love; and he that dwelleth in love, dwelleth in God, and God in him."

In the name and in the strength of God, let us resolve, first, not to hurt one another; to do nothing unkind or unfriendly to each other, nothing which we would not want done to ourselves. Instead, let us try to demonstrate kind, friendly, and Christian behavior towards each other. Second, let us resolve not to speak harshly or unkindly of each other. The sure way to avoid this is to say all the good we can, both of and to one another. In all our conversation, let us use only the language of love; speaking with the most affectionate expressions that are consistent with truth and sincerity. Third, let us resolve to keep no unkind thought, no unfriendly attitude, towards each other. Let us examine all that arises in our hearts, and allow no attitude to remain that is contrary to tender affection. Then we will easily keep from unkind actions and words, once the very source of bitterness is removed. Fourth, let us try to help each other forward in whatever we agree leads to the kingdom. To the extent that we are able, let us always find joy in strengthening each other's hands in God. Above all, let us each one watch himself (since each must give an account of himself to God), so that he does not fall short of the religion of love. Let you and I (no matter what others may do) press on toward the prize of our high calling! So that, being justified by faith, we may have peace with God through our Lord Jesus Christ; that we may rejoice in God through Jesus Christ, by whom we have received the atonement; and so that the love of God may be poured out in our hearts by the Holy Spirit which is given unto us. Let us count all things as loss for the excellency of the knowledge of Jesus Christ our Lord; being ready to lose all things for His sake, considering them only dung, that we may win Christ.

14

The Nature of Fanaticism

Editor's Note: This sermon was originally entitled "The Nature of Enthusiasm." Because our understanding of the term enthusiasm *has changed, the term* fanaticism *better expresses Wesley's meaning.*

"And Festus said with a loud voice, Paul, thou
art beside thyself."
Acts 26:24.

Fanaticism Falsely Charged

So say all the men who do not know God, regarding those who follow Paul's example as he followed Christ. There is a kind of religion which may be practiced without any such accusation, which is usually considered to be consistent with common sense. It is a religion of form, a set of outward duties performed in a conventional manner. You may add orthodoxy to it, a system of right opinions, and some amount of heathen morality; and still few will say, "Much religion has made you mad." But if you speak of the religion of the heart, if you talk of "righteousness, and peace, and joy in the Holy Spirit;" then it will not be long before your sentence is passed, "Thou art beside thyself [out of your mind]."

The men of the world pay you no compliment with this statement. For once, they mean what they say. They actually believe that every man is beside himself, who says "the love of God is shed abroad in" his "heart by the Holy Spirit given unto him;" and that God has enabled him to rejoice in Christ "with joy unspeakable and full of glory." If a man is alive to God and dead to all things below; if he continually sees Him that is invisible, walking by faith and not by sight; then they consider it a clear case: "much religion has made him mad."

It is easy to observe the things by which the world recognizes madness: that utter contempt for all earthly things, and the steady pursuit of eternal things; that divine evidence of the unseen; that joy of being in God's favor; that happy, holy love for God; and that testimony of His Spirit with our spirit that we are the children of God; that is, the whole spirit, and life, and power of the religion of Jesus Christ.

They will agree that in other things this man acts and talks like he is a reasonable man. It is only in these instances that his head is touched. It is acknowledged then that the madness he has is of a particular kind; so they distinguish it by a particular name: fanaticism.

Description of Fanaticism

This is a term which is frequently used, yet seldom understood even by those who use it most. It may be helpful, therefore, if I explain the meaning of this term and show what fanaticism is. It may serve as an encouragement to those who are wrongly accused of it; and may help some who are rightly accused of it; and still others who might become guilty, if they are not warned of it.

As to the nature of fanaticism, it is a disorder of the mind which greatly hinders the exercise of reason. Sometimes it sets reason aside completely. It not only dims but shuts the eyes of the understanding. It may, therefore, be considered a kind of madness rather than foolishness. A fool is one who draws wrong conclusions from true premises; whereas a madman draws right conclusions, but from false premises. So does a fanatic. If his premises were true, his conclusions would be. But here is his mistake: his premises are false. He imagines himself to be what he is not. Therefore, by starting out wrong, the farther he goes, the more he loses his way.

Every fanatic, then, is truly a madman. But in this case his madness has religion for its object. The fanatic usually speaks of religion, of God, or of the things of God; but in such a way that every reasonable Christian can discern his disorder. Fanaticism, generally speaking, may be defined in this way: a religious madness arising from some falsely imagined influence or inspiration of God; or, at the very least, from expecting something from God which should not be expected from Him.

Types of Fanaticism

There are countless types of fanaticism. Those which are most common, and therefore most dangerous, I will try to summarize under a few general categories. The first type of fanaticism I will mention is that of those who imagine they have the grace which they do not have. And so, some imagine, even though it is not true, that they have redemption through Christ, "even the forgiveness of sins." These are usually ones who have no deep repentance or thorough conviction. "They receive the word with joy," but "because they have no deepness of earth," no deep work in their heart, the seed "immediately springs up."

There is a sudden superficial change, which, together with that joy, joins with the pride of their unbroken heart and their self-love, easily persuading them they have already "tasted the good word of God, and the powers of the world to come."

This is an example of the first type of fanaticism. It is a kind of madness arising from the imagination that they have that grace which they do not have, so that they deceive their own souls. And it may be rightly termed madness, for the conclusions of these men would be right, if their premises were; but since their premises are created by their own imaginations, all that is built on them falls. The foundation of their thinking is this: they imagine themselves to have faith in Christ. If they had this, they would be "kings and priests to God!" possessing "a kingdom which cannot be moved." But they do not have it; consequently, their behavior is as far from truth and soberness as that of the ordinary madman, who, believing himself to be an earthly king, speaks and acts accordingly.

There are many other fanatics of this type, such as the fiery zealot for religion; or, more appropriately, for the opinions and modes of worship which he calls religion. This man also imagines himself to be a believer in Jesus, a champion of the holy faith that was given to the saints long ago. Accordingly, his conduct is based on that vain imagination. If his supposition were true, he might have an excuse for his behavior; but now it is too evidently the effect of a fevered brain, as well as a fevered heart.

These fanatics who imagine themselves to be Christians abound, not only in all parts of our land but in most parts of the earth. It is undeniable that they are not Christians, if we are to believe the oracles of God. Christians are holy; these are unholy: Christians love God; these love the world: Christians are humble; these are proud: Christians are gentle, these are angry: Christians have the mind which was in Christ; these are far from it. Consequently, they are no more Christians than they are archangels. And yet they imagine themselves to be; and they can give several reasons for it: they have been called Christians ever since they can remember; they were christened many years ago; they embrace the Christian opinions that are popularly called the Christian faith; they use the Christian forms of worship as their fathers did before them; they live what is called a good Christian life, as the rest of their neighbors do. And who will dare to say that these men are not Christians? But what is a Christian without one grain of true faith in Christ, or of real, inward holiness; without ever having tasted the love of God or having been "made partakers of the Holy Spirit?"

Poor self-deceivers! You are not Christians. You are fanatics in a high degree. Your whole life is fanaticism; based on the imagination that you have received that grace of God which you do not have. You blunder on day after day, playing a role that does not belong to you. From this arises that clear inconsistency that fills your entire behavior; which is an awkward mixture of real heathenism and imaginary Christianity. Yet, because you have such an overwhelming majority on your side, you will always shape popular opinion by mere force of numbers, leading the masses to believe that you are the only men in your right minds, and that everyone is a lunatic who is not as you are. But this does not change the nature of things. In the sight of God and His holy angels, and in the eyes of all the children of God here on earth, you are only madmen, merely fanatics! Are you not? Are you not walking in a shadow, a shadow of religion, a shadow of happiness? How long? Perhaps until death brings you back to your senses, to mourn your foolishness forever!

A second type of fanaticism is that of those who imagine they have gifts from God that they do not have. Some have imagined themselves to have the power to work miracles, to heal the sick by a word or a touch, to restore sight to the blind, or even to raise the dead. Others have begun to prophesy, to foretell things with the greatest accuracy. But time usually convinces these fanatics. When facts run contrary to their predictions, experience shows them what reason could not, and brings them to their senses.

To the same group belong those who, in preaching or prayer, imagine themselves to be influenced by the Spirit of God in a way that they are not. I realize that without Him we can do nothing, especially in our public ministry. I know that all our preaching is completely useless unless it is accompanied by His power; and our prayer is also, unless His Spirit strengthens our weaknesses. I know that if we do not both preach and pray by the Spirit, it is all wasted effort. But while there is a real influence of the Spirit of God, there is also an imaginary one, and many mistake one for the other. Many suppose themselves to be under that influence when it is far from them. And many others suppose they are more under that influence than they really are. This includes all those who imagine that God dictates the very words they speak; and that, consequently, it is impossible for them to speak anything wrong, either in content or manner. How many fanatics of this type have appeared during this century; some of whom speak in a more authoritative manner than St. Paul or any of the Apostles!

The same kind of fanaticism is also found in men who are not preachers. They may likewise imagine themselves to be directed by the Spirit when they are not. It is true, "If any man have not the Spirit of Christ, he is none of His;" and that if ever we either think, speak, or act rightly, it is through the assistance of that blessed Spirit. But how many expect things from Him without any rational or scriptural basis! These imagine that they receive specific directions from God, and not only in important things, but even in the most trivial circumstances of life. In these instances God has given us our own reason for a guide, though never excluding the unseen assistance of His Spirit.

People usually tend toward this kind of fanaticism if they expect to be directed by God in an extraordinary manner, either in spiritual things or in common life. By this I mean through visions or dreams, or by strong impressions or sudden impulses on the mind. I do not deny that God has, in the past, revealed His will in this manner, or that He can do so now. I believe he does in some very rare instances. But how frequently are men mistaken in this! How they are misled by pride and an active imagination to ascribe impulses or impressions, dreams or visions, to God, which are completely unworthy of Him! This is all pure fanaticism; as far from religion as it is from truth and soberness.

Perhaps some may ask, "Should we not ask what the will of God is in all things? And should His will not be the rule which guides our practice?" Certainly it should. But how is a reasonable Christian to know the will of God? By waiting for supernatural dreams? By expecting God to reveal it in visions? By looking for any particular impressions or sudden impulses on his mind? No! It is only by consulting the oracles of God. This is the usual method of knowing what is "the holy and acceptable will of God."

"But how can I know the will of God in a particular case, when it is not specified in Scripture." I answer, the Scripture gives you a general rule, which can then be applied to all particular cases: "The will of God is our sanctification." It is His will that we should be inwardly and outwardly holy; that we should be good, and do good, in every way and to the highest degree that we are able. Here we walk on firm ground. This is as clear as the shining of the sun. In order, therefore, to know the will of God in a particular case, we only need to apply this general rule.

Suppose, for example, it were proposed to a reasonable man to marry or to enter into a new business. In order to know whether this is the will of God, and being assured, "It is the will of God for me to be as holy and to do as much good as I can," he needs only to ask, "In which of these states can I be most holy and do the most good?" This is to be determined partly by reason and partly by experience. Experience tells him what advantages he has in his present state, either for being or doing good; and reason will show which ones he will most likely enjoy in the proposed state. By comparing these, he may judge which of the two will most assist his being and doing good; and to the extent that he knows this, he can be certain of the will of God.

In the meantime, the assistance of God's Spirit is assumed during this whole process. It is not easy to say just in how many ways that assistance is given. He may remind us of many circumstances; may place some in a clearer light; may open our mind to receive conviction, and establish that conviction in our hearts. And along with the agreement of these circumstances, which confirms what is acceptable to Him, He may add such a peace of mind, and such a measure of His love, that we can have no doubt of His will.

This is the clear, scriptural, rational way to know the will of God in a particular case. But considering how seldom this way is taken, and what a flood of fanaticism must rush over those who try to know the will of God by unscriptural, irrational means; the expression, "the will of God," should be used more sparingly. Using it as some do, on the most trivial occasions, is a way of taking the name of God in vain, and shows great irreverence toward Him. Would it not be far better to use expressions that are not liable to such objections? For example, instead of saying, "I want to know what the will of God is;" would it not be better to say, "I want to know what will work for my improvement; and what will make me most useful?" This way of speaking is clear and unobjectionable. It places the matter on a clear, scriptural issue, without any danger of fanaticism.

A third common type of fanaticism (perhaps like the former) is that of those who expect to attain a goal by the immediate power of God, without using the natural means of attaining it. If those means were unavailable, they would not fall under this accusation. God can, and sometimes does, exert His own immediate power in situations like this. But those who expect this when they have means and will not use them are fanatics. These expect to understand the Holy Scriptures without reading them and meditating on them and without using all available helps. These purposely speak in the public assembly without any forethought. I say purposely, because there may be circumstances that make this unavoidable. But whoever rejects preparation as a means of helping them speak beneficially is, to that extent, a fanatic.

It may be expected that I should mention what some have considered to be a fourth type of fanaticism; that is, wrongly attributing things to the providence of God. But I do not know what things do not belong to the providence of God. I exclude nothing but sin; and even in the sins of others, I see the providence of God to me. I do not say, "His general providence;" for I consider this an expression that means nothing. And if there is a particular providence, it must extend to all persons and all things. Our Lord understood this, or He never would have said, "Even the hairs of your head are all numbered;" and, "Not a sparrow falls to the ground, without" the will of "your Father" which is in heaven. But if God rules over the whole universe as over every single person and over every single person as over the whole universe; what is it (except our own sins) which we are not to attribute to His providence? I cannot see any room here for the charge of fanaticism.

If it is objected, "When you attribute this to providence, you imagine you are the favorite of heaven:" I answer, you have forgotten some of the words I have just spoken: "His providence is over all men in the universe, as much as over any single person." Do you not see that he who believes this, and attributes anything which happens to him to providence, does not make himself any more the favorite of heaven than he supposes every man to be? Therefore you have no basis here to charge him with fanaticism.

We must guard ourselves diligently against every sort of fanaticism, considering its dreadful effects. Its immediate offspring is pride; which continually increases the source out of which it flows; and so it alienates us more and more from the favor and life of God. It dries up the springs of faith and love, of righteousness and true holiness; seeing that all of these flow from grace: for "God resisteth the proud, and giveth grace to the humble."

Along with pride there will naturally arise an unteachable spirit. So that into whatever error the fanatic falls, there is little hope for his recovery. Reason will have little weight with him who imagines he is led by a higher guide, the immediate wisdom of God. And as he grows in pride, so he must grow in unteachableness and in stubbornness also. He must be less and less capable of being convinced, less open to persuasion; more attached to his own judgment and his own will, until he is completely immovable.

Being fortified both against the grace of God, and against all advice from men, he is left to the guidance of his own heart, and of the king of the children of pride. It is no wonder, then, that every day he becomes more deeply rooted in his contempt for all mankind, in furious anger, in every unkind disposition, in every earthly and devilish temper. Neither can we wonder at the terrible outward effects which have flowed from such attitudes in every age: all kinds of wickedness, and all the works of darkness, committed by those who call themselves Christians. Such is the nature and the dreadful effects of that many-headed monster, fanaticism!

Guidelines for Our Own Behavior

First, if fanaticism is a term so seldom understood, take care not to use the word until you understand it. As in all other things, learn to think before you speak. First know the meaning of this word; and then use it, if you must. But if so few understand this dark, ambiguous word, beware of calling any man a fanatic on account of a rumor. This is not a sufficient basis on which to accuse any man. To bring such a serious charge without proof is inconsistent with both justice and mercy.

But if fanaticism is so great an evil, watch and pray that you do not fall into the temptation. Take care that you do not think of yourself more highly than you should. Do not imagine you have attained that grace of God which you have not attained. Cry out to God that He would not allow you, blind as you are, to lose your way; that you may never think you are a believer in Christ until Christ is revealed in you, and until His Spirit witnesses with your spirit that you are a child of God.

Take care that you do not run with the common herd of fanatics, thinking you are a Christian when you are not. Do not dare to assume that name unless you have a clear, scriptural title to it; unless you have the mind which was in Christ and walk as He walked.

Take care that you are not a fiery, persecuting fanatic. Do not imagine that God has called you (contrary to the Spirit of Him you call your Master) to destroy men's lives rather than to save them. Never dream of forcing men into the ways of God. Think for yourself, and let others think as well. Use no coercion in matters of religion. Do not force even those who are farthest out of the way to come in by any means other than reason, truth, and love.

Take care that you do not fall into the second sort of fanaticism, imagining you have those gifts from God which you do not have. Do not trust in visions or dreams; in sudden impressions, or strong impulses of any kind. Remember, it is not by these that you are to know the will of God on any particular occasion. Instead, apply the clear rule of Scripture, with the help of experience and reason, and the ordinary assistance of the Spirit of God. Do not use the name of God carelessly; do not speak of the will of God on any and every occasion; but let your words, as well as your actions, be tempered with reverence and godly fear.

Finally, take care that you do not try to obtain the end without using the natural means to it. If He so pleases, God can give the end without any means at all; but you have no reason to think He will. Therefore constantly and carefully use all those means which He has appointed to be the ordinary channels of His grace. Use every means which either reason or Scripture recommends as beneficial (through the free love of God in Christ) either for obtaining or increasing any of the gifts of God. If you do, you can expect a daily growth in that pure and holy religion which the world has always called fanaticism; but which, to all who are saved from real fanaticism, from merely nominal Christianity, is "the wisdom of God, and the power of God;" the glorious image of the Most High; "righteousness and peace;" a "fountain of living water, springing up into everlasting life!"

15

The Use of Money

"I say unto you, Make to yourselves friends of the mammon of unrighteousness; that, when ye fail, they may receive you unto everlasting habitations."
Luke 16:9.

The right use of money is a part of Christian wisdom. Money is a subject discussed often by men of the world, but not sufficiently considered by Christians. These do not sufficiently consider the value of this excellent talent. Neither do they understand how to take full advantage of it.

It has been the way of poets, orators, and philosophers, in almost every age and nation, to decry money as the corrupter of the world, the enemy of virtue, the pest of human society. One writer urges his countrymen, in order to banish all evil at once, to throw all their money into the sea. But is there any wisdom in this? Not at all. Though the world is corrupt, is gold or silver to blame? "The love of money is the root of all evil," but not the thing itself. The fault does not lie in the money, but in those who use it. It may be used wrongly, but it may likewise be used well.

If we use money according to Christian wisdom, it is a means of doing all kinds of good. In the hands of God's children, it is food for the hungry, drink for the thirsty, clothes for the naked. It gives to the traveler and stranger a place to lay his head. It enables us to provide a defense for the oppressed, a means of health for the sick, a relief to them that are in pain. It may be as eyes to the blind, as feet to the lame, even a rescue from the gates of death!

It is important then that all who fear God know how to use this valuable talent in order that it may fulfill these glorious purposes to the highest degree. Perhaps all the instructions which are necessary may be summarized in three clear rules, which show us how to be faithful stewards.

I. Gain All You Can

Here we may speak like the children of the world. It is our duty to gain all we can. But it is certain that we should not gain money at the expense of our lives, nor at the expense of our health. Therefore, no gain should influence us to work at any employment requiring labor which will impair our physical nature. Neither should we begin or continue in any business which continually deprives us of proper times for food and sleep. Some employments are entirely unhealthy; such as those which require working with arsenic, or other harmful minerals, or breathing air tainted with the steam of melting lead, which will eventually destroy even the firmest physical nature. Others may not be absolutely unhealthy except for persons whose bodies are already weakened. We may not submit to anything that is destructive to health or strength; since "the life is more" valuable "than meat, and the body than raiment." If we are already engaged in such employment, we should, as soon as possible, find another which, even if it lowers our income, will not lessen our health.

Second, we are to gain all we can without harming our mind. Therefore, we may not engage in any sinful trade; any that is contrary to the law of God or our country. These necessarily imply robbing the king of his lawful customs. For it is at least as sinful to defraud the king of his right, as it is to rob our fellow subjects. There are other businesses which, however innocent in and of themselves, cannot be followed innocently at the present, such as those which require cheating or lying, or conformity to some custom which is not consistent with a good conscience. These are to be avoided, for in gaining money we must not lose our souls. There are still others which many are able to pursue innocently, without hurting either their body or mind; while you, however, cannot. Either they may entangle you in those evil influences which would destroy your soul, as you have found by repeated experiments, or there may be something in the make-up of your soul which makes that employment deadly to you, but which another may safely pursue. Therefore, no one can decide for anyone else; but every man must judge for himself, and keep away from whatever he finds to be harmful to his soul.

Third, we are to gain all we can without harming our neighbor. We cannot, if we love everyone as ourselves, defraud anyone of his possessions. We cannot devour his possessions by gambling, by overcharging him, or by taking excessive or illegal interest. This prohibits all pawnbroking, since whatever good we might do by it is exceeded by the evil. And even if it were otherwise, we are still not allowed to "do evil that good may come." We cannot, to be consistent with brotherly love, work to ruin our neighbor's business in order to advance our own; nor can we lure away any of the workmen he relies on. No one can profit by swallowing up his neighbor's possessions without gaining the damnation of hell!

Neither can we gain by harming our neighbor's body.

Therefore we may not sell anything which will impair health. Such is that liquid fire, alcoholic liquor. It is true that it may have a place in medicine. Therefore, those who prepare and sell it only for this purpose may keep their consciences clear. But who prepares it only for this purpose? Do you know ten such distillers in England? Then excuse these few. But all who sell it to any that will buy are poisoners. They murder His Majesty's subjects. They drive them to hell like sheep. And what is their gain? Is it not the blood of these men? Who would envy their large estates and luxurious palaces then? A curse is in them: the curse of God clings to their stones, timbers, and furniture! The curse of God is in their gardens, walks, and groves; a fire that burns to the deepest hell! Blood is there: the foundation, the floor, the walls, the roof, are all stained with blood!

Partakers of the same guilt, though to a lesser degree, are those surgeons, pharmacists, or physicians, who purposely lengthen the pain or disease which they are able to relieve quickly, in order to rob the patient of his money. Can any man be innocent before God who does not shorten every illness as much as he can, and relieve all sickness and pain as soon as he can? He cannot, for it could not be more obvious that he does not "love his neighbor as himself;" and that he does not "do unto others, as he would they should do unto him."

This unjust gain is too costly. And so is whatever is gained by harming our neighbor's soul; by appealing to his impurity or lack of self-control. All should consider this who have anything to do with taverns, opera houses, playhouses, or any other places of public, popularly-accepted entertainment. If these are beneficial to the souls of men, your work is good, and your gain is innocent; but if they are either sinful in and of themselves, or are natural inlets for sin of various kinds, then you will have a sad report to make. Beware, or God will say in that day, "These have perished in their sins, but I require their blood at your hands!"

Observing these cautions, it is the duty of all who are

engaged in business to follow that first rule of Christian wisdom with respect to money, "Gain all you can." Gain all you can by honest effort. Be diligent in your calling. Waste no time. If you understand yourself and your relation to God and man, you know that you have none to spare. The business in which you are placed, if you pursue it earnestly, will make no allowance for silly, unprofitable distractions. You will always have something better to do that will profit you. And "whatsoever thy hand findeth to do, do it with thy might." Do it as soon as possible. Never leave anything until tomorrow which you can do today. And do it as well as possible. Do not grow weary or lazy in doing it. Put your whole strength to the work. Let nothing be half-done or done carelessly. Let nothing in your business be left undone if it can be done by labor or patience.

Gain all you can by common sense, by using in your business all the understanding which God has given you. It is amazing how few do this; how men continue on in the same dull rut as their forefathers. But regardless of what those godless men do, this is to be no rule for you. You should be continually learning, from the experience of others, or from your own experienced reading and reflection, to do everything you have to do better today than you did yesterday. And see that you put into practice whatever you learn, so that you can make the best of all that is in your hands.

II. Economize All You Can

Having gained all you can by honest wisdom and hard work, the second rule of Christian stewardship is, "Economize all you can." Do not throw the precious talent into the sea. Do not throw it away in unnecessary expenses, which is just the same as throwing it into the sea. Spend no part of it simply to satisfy the *desire of the flesh*, the *desire of the eye*, or the *pride of life*.

Do not waste any part of such a precious talent by gratifying the *desires of the flesh*; by indulging the pleasures of sense, of whatever kind; but especially the pleasure of tasting. I do not mean only that you should avoid gluttony and drunkenness. An honest heathen would condemn these. There is, however, a popularly accepted sensuality which does not immediately sicken the stomach, nor impair the understanding; and yet it cannot be maintained without great expense. Cut off this needless expense! Reject delicacy and variety and be content with what the simplicity of nature requires.

Do not waste any part of this precious talent by gratifying the *desire of the eye*, by unnecessary or expensive clothing, or by needless ornaments. Waste no part of it adorning your houses in unnecessary or expensive furniture; or in costly painting, gilding, pictures or books; or in elegant gardens rather than useful ones. Let your neighbors who do not know any better do this.

Spend nothing to gratify the *pride of life*, to gain the admiration or praise of men. Men are expensive in diet, clothing, and furniture, not only to please their appetite, or to gratify their eye, or their imagination, but their vanity too. As long as you are "clothed in purple and fine linen, and farest sumptuously every day," many will applaud your elegance of taste, your generosity and hospitality. But do not spend your money on their applause. Instead, be content with the honor that comes from God.

Who would spend any amount to gratify these desires if he realized that gratifying them only increases them? Experience teaches that the more they are indulged the more they increase. Did you not have enough vanity, sensuality, and curiosity already? Was there need of any more? And would you pay for it too? What manner of wisdom is this? Would literally throwing your money into the sea not be less foolish?

And why should you throw away money for your children's sake any more than for your own, in delicate food, in colorful or expensive clothing, in luxuries of any kind? Why should you purchase for them more pride or lust, more vanity, or foolish and harmful desires? Why should you pay to increase their temptations, and to pierce them with more sorrows?

Do not leave it to them to throw away. If you have reason to believe that they would waste what is now in your possession, for the sake of your soul and theirs, do not set these traps in their way. Have pity on them, and remove whatever you see would increase their sins, and consequently plunge them deeper into everlasting ruin! And to think there are parents who believe they can never leave their children enough! What! Can you not leave them enough foolish and harmful desires? Not enough of pride, lust, ambition, and vanity?

If I had a considerable fortune to leave and had one child, older or younger, who knew the value of money, one who I believed would put it to good use, I would consider it my absolute duty to leave that child the bulk of my fortune; and to the others just enough to allow them to live in the manner they had been accustomed to. But if all my children were equally ignorant of the true use of money, I would give each one that which would keep him from poverty; and give the remaining sum in a manner I would judge to be most for the glory of God.

III. Give All You Can

But do not let any man think that he has done anything by going this far, by gaining and economizing all he can. All this is nothing, if a man does not go forward, if he does not aim all this at a farther purpose. A man cannot properly be said to save anything if he simply stores it away. You may as well throw your money into the sea or bury it in the earth. And you would do just as well to bury it in the earth as to put it in your chest or in the bank. Not to use it is essentially to throw it away.

In order to see the reason for this, consider that when the Possessor of heaven and earth brought you into being, and placed you in this world, he placed you here, not as an owner, but as a steward. And He has told you clearly how you are to use your possessions for Him, that it may be all a holy sacrifice, acceptable through Christ Jesus. And He has promised to reward this easy task with an eternal glory.

The directions which God has given us concerning the use of our possessions as faithful stewards are as follows: first, provide things needed for yourself; food to eat, clothing to wear, whatever nature requires for preserving your body in health and strength; second, provide the same for your wife, your children, your servants, and any others you consider part of your household; third, if there is a surplus left when this is done, then "do good to them that are of the household of faith;" and last, if there is still some remaining, "as you have opportunity, do good unto all men." In doing this, you give all you can; even everything you have. For all that is spent this way is really given to God. You give to God the things that are God's, not only by what you give to the poor, but also by that which you spend in providing things needed for yourself and your household.

If a doubt should arise in your mind at any time concerning what you are going to spend, either on yourself or any part of your family, you have an easy way to remove it. Calmly and seriously consider,

(1) In spending this money, am I acting according to my proper responsibility, not as an owner, but as a steward of my Lord's possessions?
(2) Am I doing this in obedience to His word? Where in Scripture does He require me to do this?
(3) Can I consider this expense a sacrifice to God through Jesus Christ?
(4) Do I have reason to believe that I will have a reward for this work at the resurrection of the just?

If any doubt still remains, you may further examine yourself by prayer. See whether you can say to the Searcher of hearts, with a clear conscience, "Lord, you see I am going to spend this amount on that food, clothing, or furniture. And you know I act in this as a steward of Your possessions. You know I do this in obedience to Your word, as You command it. Let this, I pray, be a holy sacrifice, acceptable through Jesus Christ! And give me a witness in myself, that for this labor of love I will have a crown when you reward every man according to his works." Now, if your conscience bears witness in the Holy Spirit that this prayer is pleasing to God, then you have no reason to doubt that the expense is right.

This is the nature of Christian stewardship as it relates to the use of money. Gain all you can, without harming either yourself or your neighbor in soul or body, by working diligently, and with all the understanding which God has given you. Save all you can, by eliminating every expense which serves only to indulge foolish desire; to gratify either the desire of the flesh, the desire of the eye, or the pride of life; waste nothing, during your life or at your death, on sin or foolishness, whether for yourself or your children. Then, give all you can; that is, give all you have to God. Do not limit yourself to some percentage. Give to God, not a tenth, not a third, not half; but all that is God's, by using all on yourself, your household, the household of faith, and all of mankind, in such a way that you may give a good account of your stewardship.

Brothers, can we be faithful stewards, unless we manage our Lord's possessions in this way? We cannot, as not only the Word of God, but our own conscience, tells us. Then why should we delay? Why should we confer any longer with men of the world? Our kingdom, our wisdom, is not of this world. Heathen customs mean nothing to us. We follow no man any farther than he is a follower of Christ. From this moment forward, do His will. I urge you, in the name of the Lord Jesus, to live up to the dignity of your calling! No more laziness! No more waste! Use whatever God has entrusted you with to do all the good that is possible, both to the household of faith, and to all men! Give all you have, as well as all you are, as a spiritual sacrifice to Him who did not withhold from you His only Son.

16

Advice to the Methodists Regarding Dress

Many years ago I observed several aspects of Christian practice among the people called Quakers. I particularly noticed their plainness of speech and plainness of dress. I willingly adopted a form of both, but especially plainness of dress. I recommended the same to you when God first called you out of the world; and now, after more than twenty years of experience, I recommend it to you still.

But I ask you, in the name of God, to remain open to conviction. Whatever prejudices you have acquired from education, custom, or example, lay them aside as far as possible. Be willing to receive light either from God or man. Be glad to see more than you did before; to "have the eyes of your understanding opened." Receive the truth, out of love for the truth, and you will have a reason to thank God forever.

It is not that I would advise you to imitate the Quakers in those peculiarities of dress which serve no purpose other than to distinguish them from all other people. To be different only for difference's sake is not the responsibility of a Christian. I do not, therefore, advise you to wear a hat of certain dimensions, or a coat of a particular form. Rather, in things that are of no consequence at all, humility and courtesy require you to conform to the customs of your country.

But I advise you to imitate them, first, in the neatness of their clothing. This is most appropriate to your Christian calling. Let all your clothing be as clean as your situation in life will allow. Certainly the poor cannot be as clean as they would like, wearing the same clothes day after day. But let even these be as clean as proper care and diligence can keep them. In fact, they have a particular need for this; because cleanliness is a part of good stewardship. It is also better for one's health than is generally realized. Let the poor, then, try especially to be clean.

Second, I advise you to imitate them in the plainness of their clothing. Two things are implied in this:

(1) That your clothing be inexpensive, far more inexpensive than others in your circumstances wear, or than you would wear if you did not know God;
(2) That it be serious, not colorful, airy, or showy; not conforming to the latest fashions. These simple rules may be applied both to the materials of which it is made, and the manner in which it is worn.

Would you like a further rule to govern these two? Then, "do everything with a single motive;" and this will guide you in every circumstance. Let a single intention to please God determine both what clothing you buy, and how you wear it. In other words, let all you do be done so that you may offer it to God as a sacrifice acceptable through Christ Jesus; so that it may increase your reward and brighten your crown in heaven. And it will do so, if it is consistent with Christian humility, seriousness, and love.

Should I be even more specific? Then I urge all those who want me to watch over their souls to wear no gold, no pearls, or precious stones; avoid curled hair, or expensive clothing. I advise those who are able to accept this to buy no velvet, no silk, no fine linen, no mere ornaments, even though they are in fashion. Wear nothing of a glaring color, or in any way bright, glittering, or showy; nothing made in the very height of fashion, nothing intended to attract the eyes of bystanders. I do not advise women to wear rings, earrings, necklaces, lace, or ruffles. Neither do I advise men to wear colored waistcoats, shining stockings, glittering or expensive buckles or buttons, either on their coats or on their sleeves. It is true that these are very little things, none of which are worth defending; therefore, give them up, for fear that a little needle may cause much pain in your flesh, and a little self-indulgence may do much harm to your soul.

For this I have the authority of God, in the clearest terms: "I will that women" (and logically, men too) "adorn themselves in modest apparel, with shamefacedness and sobriety; not with broidered [curled] hair, or gold, or pearls, [one kind of precious stones representing all] or costly apparel; but (which becometh women professing godliness) with good works" (1 Timothy 2:9, 10). Again, "Whose adorning let it not be that outward adorning of plaiting [curling] the hair, and of wearing of gold, or of putting on of apparel. But let it be the ornament of a meet and quiet spirit, which is in the sight of God of great price" (1 Peter 3:3, 4). Nothing can be more obvious; the wearing of gold, of precious stones, and of expensive clothing, together with the curling of hair, is forbidden here by name. Nor is there any exception allowed, either here, or in any other verse of Scripture. Therefore, whoever says, "There is no harm in these things," may as well say, "There is no harm in stealing or adultery."

Let "them adorn themselves," says St. Paul, "not with curling of hair, or with gold, pearls, or costly apparel; but (which becometh women professing godliness) with good works." The last clause is added for clear and significant reasons. For:

(1) The forbidden adornment cannot spring from godliness; from either love for or fear of God; from a desire to conform to His will, or from the mind which was in Christ Jesus;
(2) It does not tend to increase godliness; it does not lead toward any holy passion; Instead,
(3) It tends to destroy the attitudes which are most essential to godliness. It has no positive influence on humility; whether we aim at pleasing others or ourselves by it. Either way, it will increase pride rather than lowliness of heart.

Furthermore, because they are unnecessary expenses, they take the place of spending for good works. Consequently, they destroy the love which is fed by good works, hardening our hearts to the cries of the poor and needy.

Unnecessary expenses of this kind, whether large or small, are senseless and foolish. We challenge every living man to overcome this, if he agrees that there is a world beyond this one. For there is no reward in heaven for spending your money for ornaments or expensive clothing; but you may have an eternal reward for whatever you give on earth.

Consider this more closely. Here are two possible ways of spending a certain amount of money. I may spend it on expensive clothing for myself, or on necessary clothing for my neighbor. The former will please my own eye, or that of others; the latter will please God. Now even if there were no more harm in one than in the other; is there as much good in it? If they were equally innocent, are they also equally wise? By the one, I gratify the desire of the eye, and gain a pleasure that fades; by the other I gain a larger share of those pleasures that are at God's right hand for eternity. By the former, I obtain the applause of men; by the latter, the praise of God. In one way, I am admired by fools; in the other, I hear from the Judge of all, "Well done, good and faithful servant; enter thou into the joy of thy Lord."

But we may be sure that the wisdom of the world will offer many objections to this. It is argued, first, "If God has given us great fortunes, if we are placed in a higher class of life, we ought to dress according to our rank; that is, in gold and expensive clothing." But where is this written? Bring me clear, scriptural proof for your assertion, or I cannot allow it.

"But did God not give a direct command by Moses, that some among His chosen people should be adorned with gold and precious stones, and the finest garments?" Yes, He did; He specifically commanded this for Aaron and his successors in the High Priesthood. But this direction which God gave for the Jewish high priest has no effect on anyone in England. Second, the Jews were under a different dispensation. The glory of that Mosaic dispensation was chiefly visible and external; but the glory of the present Christian dispensation is of an invisible and spiritual nature.

"But what then are gold and precious stones for? Why were they created?" What if I say I do not know? There are many things in creation which have no obvious, necessary purpose. What are crocodiles, lions, tigers, and scorpions for? Why are there so many poisons in creation? Whatever they are for, they are certainly not to be used in a way that God has forbidden.

"But we cannot carry on our business without dressing like other people." If you only mean conforming to those styles of your countrymen that are neither showy nor expensive, why should you not dress like other people? I really think you should.

Let an Englishman dress like other Englishmen, not like a Turk or a Tartar. Let an English woman dress like other English women, not like a French woman or a German. But if you mean conforming to them in a way that God has forbidden, the answer is obvious. If you cannot carry on your business without breaking God's command, you must not continue in it. But I know of no business which cannot be carried on by one who dresses plainly and modestly. I fear that you love these things so much that you have come to think they are necessary. Your heart confuses your judgment; if you were not fond of them, you would never dream of needing them.

In one particular case these things may be unavoidable: the case of women who are under the rule of self-willed, unreasonable husbands or parents. These may be forced into doing what they otherwise would not. And they are blameless in this if they use every possible argument, asking to be excused from it; and, when they see they cannot win, submit to it only as far as they are forced.

And now, brothers, what remains for me is to ask you who are not under anyone's rule, who are, under God, the directors of your actions, to set prejudice, stubbornness, and fashion aside, and yield to Scripture, to reason, and to truth.

And why should my advice, based on Scripture and reason, not carry enough weight with you? I will tell you why:

(1) You are surrounded with saints of the world, those who are religious in a fashionable way. These constantly oppose all who would go farther in religion than themselves. These are continually warning you against going to extremes, and trying to mask the simplicity of the Gospel.

(2) You have closeby even more dangerous enemies than these: the antinomians, who, when any specific Christian practice is taught, come in like the cuckoo,

"The law, the law!" and while they glory in their shame, they make you ashamed of what should be your glory.

(3) You have suffered by false teachers in our own ranks, who undermined the doctrine you had received, by not publicly insisting on it, by not urging you to dress as persons professing godliness (because not to speak for a Christian duty is, in effect, to speak against it). They have joked privately about your preciseness in observing the rule of Scripture, or made personal remarks which, even though you did not mind them then, afterward weakened your soul.

(4) You have been in danger among false brothers. And I do not mean only those of other congregations, who consider strictness the same as bondage, but even many of our own who were once clearly convinced of the truth; but have since fallen away from it, and now try to harden others against it (at least by example) by returning again to the foolishness from which they had once escaped. But of what value is anyone's example when it contradicts Scripture and reason? I have warned you a thousand times to disregard any example which contradicts reason or Scripture. If it should ever be that I or my brother, my wife or his, or all of us together, set an example which is contrary to Scripture and reason, I beg of you to disregard it completely; let Scripture and reason prevail.

You who have passed the morning, or even the noon of life, and who find the shadows of the evening approaching, should set a better example for the generation that is now dawning. For you the day of life is nearly spent; the night of death is almost here. You have no time to lose; see that you use every moment that remains. Remove everything out of the way, even if it is small (though showy or expensive clothing is not small), that might in any way obstruct your holiness and meekness, your seriousness of spirit, your single intention to glorify God in all your thoughts and words and actions. Let no unnecessary expense keep you from being, to the highest degree possible, "rich in good works, ready to distribute, willing to communicate," until you are clothed with glory and immortality. Our bodies will soon fall into the dust; then let the survivors adorn them with flowers. In the meantime, let us value only those ornaments that will accompany us into eternity.

You that are in the morning of your days, do not make your appearance noticeable; rather let it lie hidden in plain clothing. If you want to speak highly of yourself by your dress, is anything better than plain neatness? What kind of people will you please with showy or expensive clothing? Probably none that will make you happy; this kind of dress pleases only the silliest and worst of men. At best, it pleases only the silliest and worst motives in those who are of a better character.

Let us walk more generously and more wisely in the future! Let us now throw aside whatever is not appropriate for men and women professing godliness; whatever does not spring from and serve our love for and fear of God. Let all who see us know that we are not of this world. Let our adorning be that which does not fade away; which is righteousness and true holiness. Do not grieve the Holy Spirit of God. Do you ask, "But what should I do with the showy or expensive clothing and the ornaments that I already have? Should they be wasted? Should I not wear them, now that I have them?" Wearing them is the greatest loss of all. But what then should you do with them? Burn them, rather than wear them; throw them into the sea. Or, if you can with a clear conscience, sell them and give the money to those who are in need; but buy no more at the risk of your soul. Be a faithful steward. After providing those in your own household with the things they need for life and godliness, feed the hungry, clothe

the naked, comfort the sick, the prisoner, and the stranger with all that you have. Then will God clothe you with glory and honor in the presence of men and angels, and you will shine "as the stars for ever and ever."

17

On Dress

"Whose adorning let it not be that outward adorning of wearing of gold, or of putting on of apparel; "But let it be the hidden man of the heart, in that which in not corruptible, even the ornament of a meek and quiet spirit, which is in the sight of God of great price."
1 Peter 3:3, 4.

St. Paul urges all those who desire to be "transformed by the renewal of their minds," and to approve "that good and acceptable and perfect will of God," not to be "conformed to this world," This message applies especially to the *wisdom* of the world, which is opposed to God's "good and acceptable and perfect will." But it also refers to the *customs* of the world, which naturally flow from its wisdom and spirit, and are consistent with them.

Some of these directions apply even to the way Christians *dress*. Both this text and the parallel one of St. Paul are as clear as possible. St. Paul's words are, "I will that women adorn themselves in modest apparel; not with gold, or pearls, or costly array; but (which becometh women professing godliness) with good works" (1 Timothy. 2:9, 10).

"But is it not strange," some say, "that God should bother to notice such trivial things? For what does it matter, if we care for our souls, what the body is covered with, whether with silk or sackcloth? What harm can there be in wearing gold, or silver, or precious stones, or any of the other beautiful things God has provided? May we not apply to this what St. Paul has said on another occasion, that 'every creature of God is good, and nothing to be rejected?'"

It is certain that many who sincerely fear God have embraced this opinion. And their practice is consistent with it. They place no restrictions on conformity to the world. They put on, as often as they have occasion, either gold, or pearls, or expensive clothing. And they are not pleased with those that reject these things; since they consider using them to be part of Christian liberty. Some have gone so far as to influence those who had stopped using them to use them again, assuring them that it was only superstition to think there was any harm in them. It is therefore worthwhile to ask whether there is any harm in putting on gold, or jewels, or expensive clothing.

But before we begin the subject, let us observe that sloppiness has no part in religion; and no text of Scripture condemns neatness. Certainly neatness is a duty, not a sin. Everyone should give attention to this, so that the good in him is not spoken of as evil.

The question is, "What harm does it do to adorn ourselves with gold, or pearls, or expensive garments, assuming that you can afford it; that is, it does not hurt or impoverish your family?" The first harm it does is to cause and increase pride. Whoever closely observes what happens in his own heart will clearly see this. Nothing is more natural than to think of ourselves as better because we are dressed in better clothes; and it is nearly impossible for a man to wear expensive clothing without, to some degree, valuing himself because of it. One of the old heathens realized this, so that, when he wanted to harm to a poor man, he first distorted the man's thinking by giving him a suit of fine clothes. The man would then imagine himself to be better than his neighbor because he was so fashionable. How many thousands, and not only men of nobility and wealth, but also honest merchants, reason the same way, assuming the superior value of a person from the value of his clothes!

"Cannot a person dressed in sackcloth," you ask, "be as proud as one who is dressed in gold?" He certainly may. I suppose no one doubts it. But what conclusion can you draw from this? Think of it this way. One man that drinks a cup of wholesome wine may become as sick as another that drinks poison. But does this prove that the poison has no greater tendency to harm a man than the wine? Or does it excuse any man for drinking that which has a natural tendency to make him sick? Now, experience shows that fine clothes have a natural tendency to make a man sick with pride; plain clothes do not. Although it is true that you may be sick with pride in these also, it remains that they have no natural tendency either to cause or increase this sickness. Therefore, all who desire to be clothed with humility, stay away from that poison.

Second, wearing colorful or expensive clothing naturally tends to cause and increase vanity. By vanity I mean the desire to be admired and praised. Every one of you that is fond of dress has a sense of this in your heart. Whether you confess it or not, you know in your heart that you adorn yourself in order to be admired; and that you would not if no one could see you but God and His holy angels. Make it your goal to please God alone, and all these ornaments will fall away.

Third, wearing colorful and expensive clothing naturally tends toward anger, and every violent passion. This is why the Apostle shows this "outward adorning" to be the direct opposite of the "ornament of a meek and quiet spirit." No one can easily imagine, except by experience, the difference between the "outward adorning," and this "quietness of spirit." You can never truly enjoy this sense of inward peace, while you are still fond of external appearances. It is only when you place little value on that "outward adorning," that you can in "patience possess your soul." Only when you have abandoned your fondness for dress will the peace of God reign in your hearts.

Fourth, colorful and expensive clothing tends to create and inflame lust. The fact is obvious; it has this effect both on the wearer and the beholder. To the wearer, our poet, Cowley, addresses these lines:

The' adorning yourself with so much art
Is only a barbarous skill;
It's like the poisoning of a dart,
Already too able to kill.

That is, you poison the beholder with far more of this fleshly desire than he would otherwise feel. Did you not know that this would be the natural result of your elegant adorning? Did you not intend for this to happen? Meanwhile, you cannot escape the trap which you have set for others. The dart flies back, and you are infected with the same poison. You kindle a flame which consumes both you and your admirers. And we can only hope that it will not plunge both you and them into the flames of hell!

Fifth, wearing expensive garments is directly opposed to being adorned with good works. The more you spend on your own clothing, the less you have left to clothe the naked, to feed the hungry, to shelter the strangers, to comfort those that are sick and in prison, and to lessen the countless afflictions which we suffer in this valley of tears. Every penny you save on your own clothing you can spend in meeting the needs of the poor. Therefore, every penny which you spend needlessly on clothing is, in effect, stolen from God and the poor! How many precious opportunities of doing good you have missed! How often you have prevented yourself from doing good by purchasing what you did not need! For what purpose did you buy these ornaments? To please God? No; only to please yourself, or to gain the approval of those who were no wiser than you. How much good you might have done with that money, and what an irretrievable loss it is, if it is true that "every man shall receive his own reward, according to his own labor!"

I pray that you consider this well. Perhaps you have not seen it in this light before. When you spend that money on expensive clothing which you could have used to help the poor, you deprive them of what God, the owner of all, has put into your hands for them. If so, the clothes which you put on, you are, in effect tearing from the back of the naked; and the expensive and delicate food which you eat, you are snatching from the mouth of the hungry. Out of mercy, out of pity, for Christ's sake, and for the honor of His Gospel, do not throw this money away! Do not spend on that which means nothing, or worse than nothing, that which could clothe your poor, naked, shivering fellow-creature!

Many years ago, when I was at Oxford, on a cold winter's day, one of the young maids who worked at the school visited me. I said, "You seem half-starved. Do you have nothing to cover you but that thin linen gown?" She said, "Sir, this is all I have!" I put my hand in my pocket; but found I had almost no money left, having just spent what I had. It immediately struck me, "Will your Master say, 'Well done, good and faithful steward?' You have decorated your walls with the money which might have sheltered this poor creature from the cold! Are these pictures not the blood of this poor maid?" See your expensive clothing in the same light; your gown, hat, or wig! Everything around you which cost more than Christian duty required you to spend is the blood of the poor! Be wise in the future! Be more merciful! Be more faithful to God and man! Be more richly adorned like men and women who profess godliness with good works!

Perhaps you argue, "But I can afford it." Lay aside that nonsensical word once and for all! No Christian can afford to waste any part of what God has entrusted to him. May you not tomorrow, or even tonight, be called to give an account of this and every one of your talents to the Judge of the living and dead?

Why is it that after so many warnings you persist in the same foolishness? Is it not because there are still some among you that do not benefit from what they hear, and are not willing that others should either? And these, if you become convinced that you should dress as a Christian, argue and ridicule you out of it. You foolish ones, I urge you to stop doing the devil's work! Whatever you yourselves do, do not harden the hearts of others. And you that know better, carefully avoid these tempters.

Then why does not everyone that either loves or fears God, run from it, as from a snake? Why do you still conform to the irrational, sinful customs of a frantic world? Why do you still reject the clear commandment of God? You see the light. Why do you not follow the light of your own mind? Your conscience tells you the truth. Why do you not obey your own conscience?

You answer, "Universal custom is against me, and I do not know how to resist it." I realize that not only the secular but the religious world, runs violently in the opposite direction. Look not only in the theaters, but in the churches, and in the meetings of every denomination (except a few old-fashioned Quakers, or the people called Moravians); look into the congregations, in London or elsewhere, of those that are called "gospel ministers;" look at the people that sit near the pulpit. Are those that can afford it not as fashionably dressed as those of the same class in other places?

This is a sad truth. I am ashamed of it. But I call heaven and earth to witness that it is not my fault! For nearly fifty years, God knows I have given a clear and faithful testimony. In print, in preaching, and in meetings with the believers, I have declared the whole counsel of God. I am therefore innocent of the blood of those who will not hear.

I warn you again, in the name and in the presence of God, that the great number of those that rebel against Him is no excuse for your rebellion. He has told us, "Thou shalt not follow the multitude to do evil." Who among you wants to share in the glorious character of those who are willing to stand against an entire world? If millions condemn you, it will be enough that you are found innocent by God and your own conscience.

Some say, "I am able to endure any contempt except that of my own family, and especially that of the members of my own household. My father, my mother, my brothers and sisters, ridicule me continually." This is a trial, to be sure; one that is hard to understand except by those who have it. But there is strength set aside for you. God's grace is sufficient for you; and He is ready to give it you. In the meantime, remember His declaration regarding those who love man more than God: "He that loves father or mother, brother or sister, husband or wife, more than Me, is not worthy of Me."

I urge all of you who have any regard for me, show me, before I am gone, that I have not labored in vain for nearly half a century. Let me see, before I die, a Methodist congregation as plainly dressed as a Quaker congregation. Only be consistent with yourselves. Let your clothing be inexpensive as well as plain; otherwise, you merely play with God and your own souls. I ask, let there be no expensive silken garments among you, even if they have the appearance of plainness. Be fully consistent, dressed from head to foot as those who profess godliness; professing to do all things, great and small, with the one purpose of pleasing God.

I urge you, every man that is present here before God, every woman, every child that knows good from evil, take this truth to heart. Take the Apostle's advice; or, at the very least, do not prevent others from taking it. I urge you, parents, do not keep your children from following their own convictions, even though you might think they would look prettier if they had such ornaments as other children wear! I urge you, husbands, do not hinder your wives! Wives, do not hinder your husbands, either in words or actions, from doing as they are persuaded in their own minds! In a little while we will not need these meager coverings; for our mortal bodies will be clothed in immortality. In the meantime, let this be our only concern, to "put on, as the elect of God, a heart of mercy, kindness, gentleness, longsuffering." In a word, let us "put on Christ;" that "when He shall appear we may appear with Him in glory."

18

Rules of the Band-Societies

Written Dec. 25, 1738

The purpose of our meeting is to obey that command of God, "Confess your faults one to another, and pray one for another, that ye may be healed."

For this purpose, we intend,

1. To meet at least once a week.
2. To come punctually at the set time, unless unusual circumstances prevent it.
3. To begin exactly on time, with singing or prayer.
4. To each describe plainly and freely the true condition of our souls, as well as the sins we have committed in thought, word, or deed, and the temptations we have felt since our last meeting.
5. To end every meeting with prayer, according to the needs of each person present.
6. To have one person present describe his own condition first, and then to ask the rest, one by one, as

many searching questions as are needed, concerning their spiritual condition, sins, and temptations.

Some of the questions each one is asked before being accepted into our group are as follows:

1. Do you have the forgiveness of your sins?
2. Do you have peace with God through our Lord Jesus Christ?
3. Do you have the witness of God's Spirit with your spirit that you are a child of God?
4. Is the love of God poured out in your heart?
5. Are you free from the dominion of both inward and outward sin?
6. Do you desire to be told your faults?
7. Do you desire to be told all your faults clearly and personally?
8. Do you desire every one of us to tell you, from time to time, whatever is in his heart concerning you?
9. Consider this carefully! Do you desire that we tell you whatever we think, whatever we fear, whatever we hear, concerning you?
10. Do you desire that, in doing this, we should search your heart completely?
11. Is it your desire and intent to remain entirely open, so as to speak everything that is in your heart without exception, without disguise, and without reservation?

Any of the preceding questions may be asked as often as needed; the four following questions should be asked at every meeting:

1. What known sins have you committed since our last meeting?

2. What temptations have you encountered?
3. How were you delivered from those temptations?
4. What have you thought, said, or done, being unsure of whether or not it is sin?

DIRECTIONS GIVEN TO THE BAND-SOCIETIES

Written Dec. 25, 1744

You are supposed to have the faith that "overcometh the world." To you, therefore, it is not burdensome,

I. To keep from doing evil; specifically,

1. Neither to buy nor sell anything on the Lord's Day.
2. To taste no alcoholic drink unless it is prescribed by a physician.
3. To be honest in all that you say, both in buying and selling.
4. To pawn nothing, not even to save your own life.
5. Not to mention anyone's faults behind his back, and to stop those that do.
6. To wear no unnecessary ornaments, such as rings, earrings, necklaces, lace, or ruffles.
7. To avoid needless self-indulgence, such as taking snuff or tobacco, unless it is prescribed by a physician.

II. To continue in good works; specifically,

1. To provide financially for the needs of others to the best of your ability.
2. To correct all who sin in your sight, in love and humility of wisdom.
3. To be an example of diligence and frugality, of self-denial, and taking up the cross daily.

III. To give constant attention to all the ordinances of God; specifically,

1. To be at church and at the Lord's table every week, and at every public meeting of the Bands.
2. To attend the ministry of the word every morning, unless distance, business, or sickness prevent you from doing so.
3. To pray privately every day, and lead family prayer if you are the head of a family.
4. To read the Scriptures and meditate on them whenever you are not otherwise occupied.
5. To observe each Friday as a day of fasting or abstinence.

19

The Origin, Properties, and Use of God's Law

"Wherefore the law is holy, and the commandment holy, and just, and good."
Romans 7:12.

There are few subjects in religion as little understood as this one. The reader of Romans is usually told that by "the law" St. Paul means the Jewish law, and so he considers it irrelevant.

But a careful observer of the Apostle's discourse will not be content with this superficial explanation of it. The more he considers these words, the more convinced he will be that St. Paul does not refer only to the ceremonial law of Moses in this chapter. Consider his theme. He begins the chapter, "Know ye not, brethren (for I speak to them that know the law), that the law hath dominion over a man as long as he liveth?" What! the ceremonial law? Certainly not, rather the moral law. "For," to give an example, "the woman which hath a husband is bound by the law to her husband so long as he liveth; but if the husband be dead, she is loosed from the law of her husband. So then if while her husband liveth, she be married to another man, she shall be called an adulteress: But if her husband be dead, she is free from that law; so that she is no adulteress though she be married to another man." From this example the Apostle concludes: "Wherefore, my brethren, ye also are become dead to the law," the whole Mosaic system, "by the body of Christ, that ye should" without any blame "be married to another, even to Him who is raised from the dead."

The Apostle, proving that the Christian has set aside the Jewish dispensation, and that the moral law, though it can never pass away, now stands on a different foundation, now stops to consider an objection: "What shall we say then? Is the law sin?" Some might infer as much from a misunderstanding of those words, "the motions of sins [sinful passions], which were by the law." "God forbid!" says the Apostle, that we should say so. The law is an enemy to sin, exposing it wherever it is. "I had not known sin, but by the law: For I had not known lust," or evil desire, to be sin, "except the law had said, you shalt not covet" (7:7). After discussing this further in the four following verses, he offers this conclusion, with special regard to the moral law, from which the preceding example was taken: "Wherefore the law is holy, and the commandment holy, and just, and good."

In order to explain these words, I will try to show, first, the origin of this law; second, the nature of it; third, its properties: that it is holy, and just, and good; and, fourth, its uses.

The Origin of the Moral Law

The moral law did not, as some have imagined, originate at the time of Moses. When God made man a living soul, with the power to choose good or evil, He gave the law to this free, intelligent creature; not written on tablets of stone, but engraved on his heart by the finger of God; written in his innermost spirit; intending that it might never be far off, never hard to understand, but always near, and always shining with clear light, even as the sun in the sky.

But man rebelled against God, and by breaking this glorious law, almost erased it from his heart; his understanding being darkened to the same extent that his soul was "alienated from the life of God." Yet God, being reconciled to man through the Son, has, to some degree, re-written the law on the heart of His dark, sinful creature. "He showed you, O man, what is good, even to do justly, and to love mercy, and to walk humbly with your God."

He showed this to our first parents and to all their children, by "that true light which enlightens every man that cometh into the world." But eventually all flesh became corrupt, so He chose a people to whom He gave a more perfect knowledge of His law. He wrote its particulars on two tablets of stone; which he commanded the fathers to teach their children through all following generations.

It is in this way that the law of God is now shown to those who do not know God. They hear the things that were written for our instruction. But this is not enough; God alone reveals this by His Spirit. And He does this for all that truly believe, fulfilling that gracious promise: "Behold, the days come, saith the Lord, that I will make a new covenant with the house of Israel. And this shall be the covenant that I will make; I will put My law in their inward parts, and write it in their hearts, and I will be their God, and they shall be My people" (Jeremiah 31:31, etc.).

The Nature of the Law

Now let us consider the nature of that law which was originally given to man in paradise, and which God has so mercifully promised to write again in the hearts of all true believers. The

Apostle is not speaking of the ceremonial law when he says, "I had not known sin but by the law." This is too obvious to require proof. Neither is it the ceremonial law which says, in the words immediately connected to these, "You shall not covet." Therefore, the ceremonial law has no place in our present discussion.

Neither can the law mentioned in the text be the Mosaic dispensation. It is true that the word is sometimes used in this way; as when the Apostle says to the Galatians, "The covenant that was confirmed before [with Abraham, the father of the faithful], the law cannot disannul" (3:17). But the text we are discussing cannot mean the Mosaic dispensation, for the Apostle never affirms it to be a spiritual law; or that it is holy, just, and good. Neither is it true that God will write that law in the hearts of those He justifies. The law referred to here is none other than the moral law.

This law is an incorruptible picture of the High and Holy One that inhabits eternity. It is God, whom no man has seen in His essence, made visible to men and angels. It is the unveiled face of God; God revealed to His creatures as they are able to bear it; revealed to give life, and not to destroy it, that they may see God and live. It is the heart of God opened to man.

If we look at the law of God from another point of view, it is supreme, unchangeable reason; it is unalterable rightness; it is the everlasting appropriateness of all things. The law of God is a copy of the eternal mind, a transcript of the divine nature. It is the fairest offspring of the everlasting Father, the brightest light of His wisdom, the visible beauty of the Most High. It is the delight and wonder of cherubim and seraphim, and all the company of heaven, and the glory and joy of every wise believer, every well-instructed child of God.

The Properties of the Law

There are three properties of the law mentioned in the text:

It is *holy*, *just*, and *good*.

First, the law is *holy*. With this expression the Apostle does not appear to be speaking of its effects, but instead of its nature. St. James, speaking of the same thing by a different name, says, "The wisdom from above" (which is this law written in our hearts) "is first pure" (3:17). And, consequently, when it is written into our lives, as well as our souls, it is (as St. James terms it in 1:27) "pure religion and undefiled;" the pure, clean, unpolluted worship of God.

It is pure, chaste, clean, and holy in the highest degree. Otherwise it could not be the immediate offspring of God, who is, in essence, holiness. It is pure from all sin, clean and unspotted from any evil. It is a virgin, incapable of being defiled, of being mixted with that which is unclean or unholy. It has no fellowship with sin, for "what communion hath light with darkness?" As sin is by nature opposed to God, so His law is opposed to sin.

Therefore, the Apostle rejects that perverse idea that the law of God is either sin itself, or the cause of sin. God forbid that we should believe it is the cause of sin, simply because it is the discoverer of it; because it detects the hidden things of darkness, and drags them out into the light. It is true that, by this means (as the Apostle observes in Romans 7:13), "sin appears to be sin." All its disguises are torn away, and it appears in its inherent ugliness. It is true, likewise, that "sin, by the commandment, becomes exceeding sinful." Now, pitted against light and knowledge, being stripped even of the plea of ignorance, it loses its excuse, as well as disguise, and becomes far more repulsive both to God and man. Further, it is true that "sin works death by that which is good;" by that which is in itself pure and holy. When it is dragged out into the light, it rages all the more. When it is restrained, it bursts out with great violence. So the Apostle writes (speaking in the role of one who was convicted of sin, but not yet delivered from it), "Sin, taking occasion by the commandment" which detected and tried to restrain it, rejected the restraint, and all the more "wrought in me all manner of concupiscence" (v. 8); all kinds of foolish and harmful desires, which the commandment tried to restrain. Therefore, "when the commandment came, sin revived" (v. 9). But this reveals no impurity in the commandment. Though it is abused, it cannot be defiled. This proves only that "the heart of man is desperately wicked." It remains that "the law is holy".

Second, it is *just*. It prescribes exactly what is right, precisely what we ought to do, say, or think; concerning God, ourselves, and every creature. It is adapted, in every detail, to the nature of things, the nature of the whole universe, and every individual. It is suited to all the circumstances of each, and to all their mutual relations, including those that have existed from the beginning and those that began in any following period. It harmonizes with them perfectly and is never irrelevant to them. If the law is understood in that sense, we see that there is nothing arbitrary in the law of God. And yet all of it is totally dependent on His will; so that, "Thy will be done," is the supreme, universal law, both in earth and heaven.

Some have asked, "But is the will of God the cause of His law? Is His will the origin of right and wrong?" It seems that this difficulty arises from considering God's will to be distinct from God; otherwise, the problem vanishes. Certainly God is the cause of the law of God. But the will of God is God himself willing this or that. Consequently, to say that the will of God, or that God himself, is the cause of the law, is the same thing.

If the law, the rule of right and wrong, depends on the nature and proper state of things, and on their essential relations to each other, then it must come from God, because He designed those things, with all their relations. By His will, "for His pleasure" alone, they all "are and were created." And yet it may be granted that, in every case, God wills this or that (for example, that men should honor their parents), because it is right, agreeable to the proper state of things, and to the relation in which they stand.

The law then is right and just concerning all things. And it is *good* as well. This is obvious because of its source, the goodness of God. What other than tender love caused Him to give man the image of His own nature, and then reveal His will again to fallen man? Was it not love that moved Him to give His law after man's understanding was darkened, and to send His prophets to declare that law to the blind, thoughtless children of men? Certainly it was His goodness that raised up Enoch and Noah to be preachers of righteousness; and caused Abraham, His friend, to bear witness to His truth. It was His goodness which gave a written law to Moses for the nation He had chosen. It was love which explained these living words through David and all the Prophets that followed; until, when the fullness of time had come, He sent His Son, "not to destroy the law, but to fulfill," to confirm every point of it; until, having written it in the hearts of His children, and having put all His enemies under His feet, "He shall deliver up the kingdom to the Father, that God may be all in all."

And this law, given and preserved by the goodness of God, is like the fountain from which it flows, full of goodness. It is gentle and kind; it is, as the Psalmist expresses it, "sweeter than honey and the honey-comb." It includes "whatsoever things are lovely or of good report. If there be any virtue, if there be any praise," they are all contained here; where all the treasures of divine wisdom, knowledge, and love are hidden.

The Uses of the Law

The first use of it is to convict the world of sin. This is the special work of the Holy Spirit, who can work without any means at all, or by whatever means please Him. Therefore, there are some whose hearts have been broken without any visible cause, or by any outward means; and others (very rarely) have been awakened to a sense of the "wrath of God abiding on them," by simply hearing that "God was in Christ, reconciling the world unto himself." But the usual method by which the Spirit of God convicts sinners is by the law. It is this part of the word of God which is especially *quick and powerful*, full of life and energy, "and sharper than any two-edged sword." This, in the hands of God and of those whom He has sent, pierces through a deceitful heart, and "divides asunder even the soul and the spirit." By this a sinner is revealed to himself. The law flashes conviction on every side. He feels he is no more than a sinner. He has nothing to pay. His "mouth is stopped," and he stands "guilty before God."

To kill the sinner is, then, the first use of the law; that is, to destroy the life and strength in which he trusts, and convince him that he is not only under the sentence of death, but actually dead to God, having no spiritual life, "dead in trespasses and sins." The second use of it is to bring him to life, to Christ, so that he may live. It is true that in performing these functions it plays the part of a strict schoolmaster. It drives us by force, rather than drawing us by love. And yet love is the source of it all. It is love by which the law tears away our confidence in the flesh, which leaves us nothing on which to lean, and causes the sinner to cry out in the bitterness of his soul, or groan in the depth of his heart, "I give up every plea beside, 'Lord, I am damned; except that You died.'"

The third use of the law is to keep us alive. It is the means by which the Holy Spirit prepares the believer to receive a larger share of the life of God. I am afraid this great truth is little understood, not only by the world, but even by many who are real children of God by faith. Many of these blindly assume that when we come to Christ, we are done with the law; because, "Christ is the end of the law to every one that believeth." And He is, "for righteousness," that is, justification. The law does not justify men, but rather brings them to Christ. But when it has brought us to Him, it has still another purpose, which is to keep us with Him. For it is continually motivating all believers, the more they see of its height and depth, to urge one another to come closer to Christ and expect grace to do His will.

Agreeing then, that every believer is done with the Jewish ceremonial law; and seeing that the moral law is not a means of justification; for we are "justified freely by His grace, through the redemption that is in Jesus;" in another sense, we are not done with this law, for it is still of great use. First, it convicts us of the sin that yet remains in both our hearts and lives, keeping us close to Christ, so that His blood may continually cleanse us. Second, it leads us to draw strength from Him, by which He empowers us to do what His law commands. Third, it confirms our hope of fulfilling its commands on a level we have not yet attained, the hope of receiving more and more grace until we actually possess the fullness of His promises.

How clearly this agrees with the experience of every true believer! While he cries out, "O what love have I unto your law! All the day long is my study in it;" he sees, in that divine mirror, more of his own sinfulness every day. He sees more and more clearly that he is still a sinner in all things, that neither his heart nor his ways are right before God; and that realization sends him to Christ. For example, the law says, "You shall not kill;" and by this command (as our Lord teaches), prohibits not only outward acts, but every unkind word or thought. Now the more I look into this perfect law, the more I feel how far I fall short of it; and the more I feel this, the more I feel my need for His blood to atone for all of my sin, and for His Spirit to purify my heart and make me "perfect and entire, lacking nothing."

So I cannot do without the law for one moment, any more than I can do without Christ; since I now need it just as much to keep me in Christ as I ever needed it to bring me to Him. Each of these is continually sending me to the other, the law to Christ, and Christ to the law. On the one hand, the height and depth of the law cause me to run to the love of God in Christ; on the other, the love of God in Christ makes the law precious to me, since I know that every part of it is a promise which my Lord will fulfill at the proper time.

Who are you then that "judgest the law, and speakest evil of the law," including it with sin, Satan, and death, and sending them all to hell together? You have set yourself up in the judgment-seat of Christ and done away with the rule by which He will judge the world! Realize what advantage Satan has gained over you; and, in the future, never think or speak lightly of this blessed instrument of the grace of God. Instead, love and value it for the sake of Him from whom it came, and of Him to whom it leads. Let it be your glory and joy, next to the cross of Christ. Declare its praise and make it honorable before all men.

And if you are thoroughly convinced that it is the offspring of God, that it is the copy of His perfection, and that it is "holy, and just, and good," especially to them that believe; then, instead of throwing it away, see that you cling to it more and more. Never let the law of mercy and truth, of love for God and man, of humility, meekness, and purity, leave you. "Bind it about your neck; write it on the table of your heart." Keep close to the law, if you want to keep close to Christ. Let this continually lead you to His atoning blood, continually confirm your hope, until all the "righteousness of the law is fulfilled in you," and you are "filled with all the fullness of God."

And if your Lord has already fulfilled His word, if He has already "written His law in your heart," then "stand fast in the liberty wherewith Christ hath made you free." You are not only free from Jewish ceremonies, from the guilt of sin, and the fear of hell; but, what is infinitely more, from the power of sin, from serving the devil, from offending God. Stand firm in this liberty. Stand firm in loving God with all your heart and serving Him with all your strength! This is perfect freedom; to walk blamelessly in all His commandments. "Be not entangled again with the yoke of bondage." I do not mean Jewish bondage, nor bondage to the fear of hell. These I trust are far from you. But beware of becoming entangled again with the yoke of sin, of any inward or outward transgression of the law. Hate sin far more than death or hell; Hate sin far more than the punishment of it. Beware of the bondage of pride, of desire, or of anger; of every evil temper, or word, or action. "Look unto Jesus;" and, in order to do so, look more and more into the perfect law, "the law of liberty;" and "continue therein." In this way you will, each day, "grow in grace, and in the knowledge of our Lord Jesus Christ."

20

The Law Established by Faith

Discourse I

"Do we then make void the law through faith? God forbid: Yea, we establish the law."
Romans 3:31.

St. Paul, having laid down in the beginning of this epistle his general proposition that "the gospel of Christ is the power of God unto salvation to every one that believeth" (the powerful means, by which God makes every believer a partaker of salvation), goes on to show that there is no other way under heaven by which men can be saved. He speaks particularly of salvation from the guilt of sin, which he calls *justification*. That all men stood in need of this, he proves by various arguments addressed to the Jews as well as the heathens. And so he infers (in 3:13), "that every mouth be stopped" from excusing or justifying himself, "and all the world become guilty before God" (3:19). "Therefore, by the works of the law shall no flesh be justified in His sight." "But now the righteousness of God without the law," without our previous obedience to it, "is manifested;" "even the righteousness of God, which is by faith of Jesus Christ, unto all and upon all that believe:" "For there is no difference," as to their need of justification, or the way they attain it; "for all have sinned, and come short of the glory of God;" the glorious image of God in which they were created. And all (who attain this) "are justified freely by His grace, through the redemption that is in Jesus Christ, whom God hath set forth to be a propitiation through faith in His blood; that He might be just, and yet the justifier of him which believeth in Jesus;" that without compromising His justice, He might show mercy for the sake of that propitiation. "Therefore we conclude that a man is justified by faith, without the works of the law" (3:20–28).

It is easy to foresee an objection which has been raised in every age; that to say we are justified without the works of the law is to abolish the law. The Apostle, without entering into this dispute, simply denies the charge. "Do we then," he says, "make void the law through faith? God forbid! Yea, we establish the law."

Strangely, some imagine that St. Paul, when he says, "A man is justified without the works of the law," means only the ceremonial law. But that is refuted by these words. Did St. Paul establish the ceremonial law? It is evident he did not. He voided that law through faith, and openly said so. It was the moral law only of which he said, in effect, "We do not abolish it, but rather establish it through faith."

But there are many who will not agree to this. Many throughout the history of the Church, even some who called themselves

Christians, have argued that the new covenant was intended to abolish the whole law. They would not allow the moral or the ceremonial law, but say, "If you establish any law, Christ shall profit you nothing; Christ is become of no effect to you; ye are fallen from grace."

But is there any wisdom in the zeal of these men? Do they realize that law and faith are connected and that to destroy one is to destroy both? To abolish the moral law is to leave no proper means of bringing us to faith, or of stirring up that gift of God in our soul.

Therefore, it is wise for all who desire either to come to Christ, or to walk in Him whom they have received, to be careful not to "make void the law through faith." Therefore, let us ask, first, what are the ways in which men usually "void the law through faith?" And, second, how can we follow the Apostle, and "establish the law" by faith?

Common Ways of Making the Law Void through Faith

1. By Not Preaching the Law

What are the most common ways of making the law void through faith? The way for a preacher to make it void is not to preach it at all. This is the same as to erase it from God's Word. This is especially true when it is done intentionally; when it is made a rule not to preach the law; and the very phrase, "a preacher of the law," is used as a term of contempt, as though it meant nothing more than an enemy of the gospel.

All of this comes from the deepest ignorance of the nature, characteristics, and use of the law; and proves that those who act in this way either do not know Christ or are only babes in Christ, and "unskilled in the word of righteousness."

Their grand idea is this: that preaching the gospel, which is, according to their opinion, speaking of nothing but the sufferings and merits of Christ, fulfills all the purposes of the law. We deny this completely. It does not fulfill even the first purpose of the law, which is to convict men of sin; awakening those who are still sleeping on the brink of hell. There may have been some who were awakened simply by hearing the gospel, but God's ordinary method is to convict sinners by the law. The gospel is not the means which God has ordained, or which our Lord himself used, for this purpose. We have no authority in Scripture for applying it in this way, nor any reason to expect this, from the nature of the gospel itself. "They that be whole," as our Lord observes, "need not a physician, but they that are sick." It is absurd, therefore, to offer a physician to those who imagine themselves to be whole. You must first convince them that they are sick; otherwise they will not thank you for your efforts. It is equally absurd to offer Christ to those whose hearts have not yet been broken. It is "casting pearls before swine." "They will trample them under foot," and, more than likely, also "turn again and rend you."

There is no command in Scripture to offer Christ to a careless sinner, nor are there any examples of it in Scripture. This does not appear to have been the practice of any of the Apostles, from any passage in their writings. And though Paul preached Christ as well as the greatest of the Apostles, who preached the law more than he did? It is clear, then, that he did not think that the gospel served the same purpose.

St. Paul's first recorded sermon concludes with these words: "By Him all that believe are justified from all things, from which ye could not be justified by the law of Moses. Beware therefore, lest that come upon you which is spoken of in the Prophets; Behold, ye despisers, and wonder, and perish: For I work a work in your days, a work which you will in no wise believe, though a man declare it unto you" (Acts 13:39, etc.). He first reminds them that they could not be justified by the law of Moses, but only by faith in Christ; and then threatens them with the judgments of God, which is, in the strongest sense, preaching the law.

In his next discourse, to the heathens at Lystra (14:15, etc.), we do not find one mention of the name of Christ. Rather, the whole thrust of it is that they should "turn from those vain idols, unto the living God."

To the jailer, when "he sprang in and came trembling, and fell down before Paul and Silas, and said, Sirs, what must I do to be saved?" Paul immediately said, "Believe on the Lord Jesus Christ" (Acts 16:29, etc.). In the case of one so deeply convicted of sin, who would not have said the same? But you find him speaking in a very different manner to the men of Athens; coming against their superstition, ignorance, and idolatry; and strongly urging them to repent, out of a consideration of future judgment, and the resurrection from the dead (17:24-31). Likewise, when Felix sent for Paul, to "hear him concerning the faith in Christ;" instead of preaching Christ in *your* sense, "he reasoned of righteousness, self-control, and judgment to come," until Felix "trembled" (24:24, 25). Go follow his example. Preach Christ to the careless sinner by reasoning "of righteousness, self-control, and judgment to come!"

Paul's epistles are directed, not to unbelievers, such as those of whom we are now speaking, but to the saints of God in various places. Unquestionably, he would speak more of Christ to these than to the ones who were without God, and he has done so. And yet, every epistle is full of the law, even the epistles to the Romans and the Galatians; in both of which he does what is called "preaching the law."

From this it is clear what it means to preach Christ, in the sense of the Apostle. For it is certain that St. Paul considered himself to be preaching Christ to Felix, and also at Antioch, Lystra, and Athens. From his example every thinking man must conclude, that not only proclaiming the love of Christ to sinners, but also declaring that He will come from heaven in flaming fire, is, in the Apostle's sense, preaching Christ in the full scriptural meaning of the word. To preach Christ is to preach what He has revealed, either in the Old or New Testament; so you are just as truly preaching Christ when you are saying, "The wicked shall be turned into hell, and all the people that forget God," as when you are saying, "Behold the Lamb of God, which taketh away the sin of the world!"

Consider this well; to preach Christ is to preach everything that Christ has spoken; all His promises; all His warnings and commands; all that is written in His book; then you will know how to preach Christ, without making the law void.

When we preach to a congregation of mourners, or of believers, those messages in which we emphasize the merits and sufferings of Christ will probably bring the greatest blessing, because these words fit well with their condition. At the very least, these will usually convey the most comfort. But comfort is not always the greatest blessing. I sometimes receive greater benefit from a discourse that cuts me to the heart, and humbles me to the dust.

2. By Teaching That Faith Makes Holiness Less Necessary

A second way of making the law void through faith is by teaching that faith supersedes the need for holiness. This way divides into a thousand smaller paths, and there are many that walk in them. There are so few who, once being convinced that we are saved by faith, do not sooner or later, to one degree or another, fall into this way of thinking.

Some do not believe that faith in Christ sets aside the necessity of keeping His law entirely; but they assume either that holiness is less necessary now than it was before Christ came or that a lesser degree of it is necessary. They think they can take more liberty in certain situations than they could have before they believed. If they could realize that they are using the term *liberty* to mean liberty from obedience or holiness, it would show at once that their judgment is perverted, and that they are guilty of making the law void through faith, by supposing that faith supersedes holiness.

The first argument of those who teach this is that we are now under the covenant of grace, not works; and therefore we are no longer required to perform the works of the law. But who was ever under the covenant of works? No one but Adam before the fall. He was under that covenant which required perfect obedience as the one condition of acceptance. But no other man was ever under this, neither Jew nor Gentile; neither before Christ nor since. All of Adam's sons were and are under the covenant of grace. The manner of their acceptance is this: the free grace of God, through the merits of Christ, giving pardon to those who believe with that faith which, working by love, produces all obedience and holiness.

The case is not, therefore, that men were at one time more obliged to obey God, or to perform the works of His law, than they are now. All good works, though as necessary as ever, do not come before our acceptance, but result from it. Therefore the nature of the covenant of grace gives you no basis on which you may set aside obedience or holiness.

"But are we not justified by faith, without the works of the law?" Undoubtedly we are; without the works either of the ceremonial or the moral law. And if all men were convinced of this, it would prevent innumerable evils; antinomianism in particular. Usually it is the Pharisees who create the antinomians. Running in a path so obviously contrary to Scripture, they cause others to run in the totally opposite direction. And so, because some desire to be justified by works, others are afraid to allow any place for them.

But the truth lies between these two extremes. We are justified by faith. This is the cornerstone of the whole Christian building. We are justified without the works of the law, as a condition of justification; but rather they are the immediate fruit of justifying faith. So if good works do not follow our faith, both inward and outward holiness, it is clear that our faith is worthless; we are still in our sins. Therefore, that we are justified by faith without works is no basis for making the law void through faith or for imagining that faith is an exemption from holiness.

Some object, "But does St. Paul not say, 'Unto him that worketh not, but believeth on Him that justifieth the ungodly, his faith is counted for righteousness?' Does that not prove that faith replaces righteousness? And if faith replaces righteousness or holiness, what need is there of this too?" This comes to the point, and is the main pillar of antinomianism. But it does not require a long answer. We agree, first, that God justifies him that, until that moment, is totally ungodly; full of evil, and void of good; second, that He justifies the ungodly that, until that moment, can do no good works; third, that He justifies him by faith alone, without any preceding goodness or righteousness; and, fourth, that faith is then credited to him as preceding righteousness; that is, God, through the merits of Christ, accepts him that believes as if he had already fulfilled all the conditions of righteousness. But the Apostle does not say, either here or elsewhere, that this faith is counted to him for *subsequent righteousness*. He teaches that there is no righteousness before faith; but where does he teach that there is none *after* it? He asserts that holiness cannot precede justification; but not that it must not *follow* it. St. Paul, therefore, gives no excuse for making the law void by teaching that faith supersedes the need for holiness.

3. By Living As Though Faith Excuses Us from Holiness

Another way of making the law void through faith is by doing it practically; *living* as though faith excuses us from holiness.

How earnestly the Apostle guards us against this with those well-known words: "What then? Shall we sin, because we are not under the law, but under grace? God forbid" (Romans 6:15). This caution is of the greatest importance.

Being "under the law," could possibly mean, first, being required to observe the ceremonial law; second, being required to conform to the whole Mosaic system; third, being required to keep the whole moral law as the condition of our acceptance by God; and, fourth, being under God's anger and curse; under the sentence of eternal death; under a sense of guilt and condemnation, full of horror and fear.

Although a believer is "not without law to God, but under the law to Christ," from the moment he believes, he is no longer "under the law" in any of the preceding senses. Because he is no longer under the ceremonial law, nor under the Mosaic system; because he is not required to keep even the moral law as the condition of his acceptance; he is delivered from God's anger and curse, from that sense of guilt and condemnation, and from all that horror and fear of death and hell by which he was once enslaved. And he now obeys (which while "under the law" he could not do) willinglly and completely. He does not obey out of fear, but on a nobler principle; that is, the grace of God ruling in his heart, and causing all he does to be done in love.

What then? Will this evangelical principle of action be less powerful than the legal one? Will we be less obedient to God out of love than we were out of fear? Has this practical antinomianism infected you? Examine yourself carefully and honestly. Do you do now what you dared not do when you were "under the law," or (as we commonly call it) under conviction? Do you allow yourself more flexibility now? Do you indulge yourself a little more than you did? Take care that you do not "sin because you are not under the law, but under grace!" Is your conscience as tender now as it was then? Have you gone back to the things you had once given up; the things you could not use at that time without wounding your conscience? And have you learned to say, "I am not so scrupulous now?" I wish to God you were! Then you would not sin in this way, "because you are not under the law, but under grace!" Do not let the mercy of God mean less to you now than His fiery indignation did before. Is love a less powerful motive than fear? If not, let it be your unchanging rule: "I will do nothing now that I am 'under grace,' which I dared not do when 'under the law.'"

Examine yourself, likewise, concerning sins of omission. Are you as innocent of these, now that you "are under grace," as you were when "under the law?" You were diligent then in hearing the word of God! What could have kept you away? A little business? A visitor? A slight illness? A soft bed? A dark or cold morning? Repent! See and feel your terrible loss! Remember how far you have fallen! Now be zealous and do the works that you did at first; or else, if you continue to "make void the law through faith," God may cut you off, and reward you as one of the unbelievers!

21

The Law Established by Faith

Discourse II

"Do we then make void the law through faith? God forbid: Yea, we establish the law."
Romans 3:31.

In the preceding discourse, we saw the most usual ways of making the law void through faith. These are: first, by not preaching it at all; which makes it all void, under the guise of preaching Christ and magnifying the gospel; second, by teaching that faith supersedes the need for holiness; that this is less necessary now, or that a lesser degree of it necessary than before

Christ came; or that it is less necessary for us, because we believe, than it would have been otherwise; which is to say that Christian liberty is a liberty from holiness; or, third, by making the law void in practice, by living as though faith excuses us from holiness; allowing ourselves to remain in sin, "because we are not under the law, but under grace." Now we will consider how we may follow a better pattern, so that we may be able to say with the Apostle, "Yea, we establish the law."

We do not establish the old ceremonial law; we know that is abolished forever. Neither do we establish the whole Mosaic system; we know our Lord has nailed this to His cross. Nor do we establish the moral law, as if keeping all the commandments were the basis of our justification. But, all this being agreed, we still, according to the Apostle's use of the term, "establish the law," the moral law.

I. We Establish the Law by Our Doctrine

We establish the law, first, by our doctrine; by trying to preach it in its entirety, to explain and enforce every part of it, in the same manner as our great Teacher did while on the earth. We establish it by following St. Peter's advice: "If any man speak, let him speak as the oracles of God;" teaching what the holy men of long ago and the apostles, moved by the Holy Spirit, spoke and wrote for our instruction. We establish it when we speak, by holding back nothing from those who hear; by declaring to them, without reservation, the whole counsel of God. And in order to be effective, we use plain language. "We are not as many that corrupt the word of God;" we do not *mix*, *adulterate*, or *soften* it, to make it suit the taste of the hearers.

We establish the law when we declare every commandment, not only regarding the outward action which it either forbids or commands, but also the inward principle; the thoughts, desires, and intents of the heart.

And we do this diligently, not only because the law is so

important; but also because it is little understood. We could say that the law in its full spiritual meaning is "a mystery which was hid from ages and generations since the world began." It was completely hidden from the heathen world. They, with all their supposed wisdom, neither found God, nor His law. "Their foolish hearts were darkened;" while "professing themselves wise, they became fools." And it was almost equally hidden, as to its spiritual meaning, from nearly all of the Jewish people. Our Lord continually scolded them for their misinterpretations of it. For they assumed that they only needed to make the outside of the cup clean; that outward exactness would atone for inward unholiness, for the total neglect of both justice and mercy, of faith and of love for God.

But, alas! The law of God, as to its inward, spiritual meaning, is not hidden from the Jews or heathens only, but also from a vast majority of what is called the Christian world. The spiritual meaning of God's commandments is still a mystery to these as well. Nor is this observable only in those lands which are covered with Romish darkness and ignorance. It is certain that even most Protestants are complete strangers to the law of Christ, to its purity and spirituality.

Therefore, to this day, "the Scribes and Pharisees," those who have the powerless form of religion, and who are wise in their own eyes, and righteous in their own pride, "hearing these things, are offended" when we speak of the religion of the heart; and particularly when we show that without this, even if we were to "give all our goods to feed the poor," it would be of no benefit to us. But they must be offended, for we must speak the truth. It is our responsibility, whether they will hear or not, to rescue our own souls. We are to declare all that is written in God's Word, not to please men, but the Lord. At the same time that we proclaim all the blessings and privileges which God has prepared for His children, we are also to teach all the things He has commanded. And we know that all these are useful; either for waking those that are asleep, instructing the ignorant, or building up and perfecting the saints. We know that "all Scripture, given by inspiration of God, is profitable for doctrine, for reproof, for correction, or for instruction in righteousness;" and that "the man of God," as God works in his soul, needs every part of it, so that he may "be perfect, thoroughly furnished unto all good works."

It is our responsibility to preach Christ by preaching all that He has revealed. Perhaps we may receive a special blessing from God by declaring the love of our Lord Jesus Christ; we may speak especially of "the Lord our righteousness;" we may describe the grace of God in Christ, "reconciling the world unto himself;" and we may declare His praise, as "bearing the iniquities of us all, as wounded for our transgressions, and bruised for our iniquities, that by His stripes we might be healed:" but we would still not be preaching Christ according to His word if we were to limit ourselves to this. We are not innocent before God unless we proclaim Him in all His offices. To preach Christ is to preach him not only as our great High Priest, "reconciling us to God by His blood" and "ever living to make intercession for us;" but also as a King forever, giving laws to all whom He has purchased with His blood; as reigning in all believing hearts until He has "subdued all things to himself," until he has utterly cast out all sin and brought in everlasting righteousness.

II. We Establish It By Preaching That Faith Produces Holiness

Second, we establish the law when we preach faith in Christ so as not to replace, but to produce all holiness, negative and positive, of the heart and of the life. In order to do this, we continually declare that Christian faith is only the servant of love. As glorious as it is, it is not the ultimate goal of the commandment. God has given this honor to love alone; love is the purpose of all the commandments of God. And it will endure when heaven and earth pass away; for "love" alone "never faileth." Faith will be swallowed up in the everlasting vision of God. But even then, love,

Its nature and its work still the same, Lasting its lamp and unconsumed its flame, — In deathless triumph shall forever live, And endless good diffuse, and endless praise receive.

Wonderful things are spoken of faith, and whoever partakes of it may say with the Apostle, "Thanks be to God for His unspeakable gift." But it still loses all its excellence when compared with love. The thing St. Paul observes concerning the glory of the gospel, which is greater than that of the law, may also be said of the glory of love, which is greater than that of faith: "For if that which is done away is glorious, much more does that which remaineth exceed in glory." The glory of faith is that it serves love. It is the great temporary means by which God accomplishes that eternal purpose.

Faith, then, was originally designed by God to re-establish the law of love. By speaking of it in this way, we are not undervaluing it, but showing its real worth, and giving it that place which the wisdom of God gave it from the beginning. It is the glorious means of restoring that holy love in which man was originally created. Therefore, although faith has no value in itself, but because it leads to that purpose, and because it is the only means under heaven for accomplishing it; it is an unspeakable blessing to man, and of unspeakable value before God.

III. We Establish It in Our Hearts and Lives

The most important way to establish the law is to establish it in our own hearts and lives. Without this, what good would all the rest do? If the law we preached were not established in our hearts, our preaching would only increase our damnation.

How can we establish the law in our hearts so that it may

have the greatest influence on our lives? It is faith alone that fulfills this purpose, as we have learned from daily experience. While we look steadily, not at the things which are seen, but at those which are unseen, we are more and more crucified to the world. If our soul's eye is continually fixed, not on the things which are earthly, but on those which are eternal, then our affections are gradually loosened from earth, and set on things above. And so, faith is the means by which all righteousness and true holiness grows; by which the holy and spiritual law is established in the hearts of those who believe.

And by our faith, our confidence in a pardoning God, we establish His law in our own hearts even more effectively. For there is no motive which so powerfully inclines us to love God as our sense of the love of God in Christ. Nothing enables us to give our hearts to Him who was given for us like a piercing conviction of this. And this principle of grateful love for God causes us to love our brother also. As a result, it is, as the Apostle observes, "the fulfilling of the law." "For this, Thou shalt not commit adultery; thou shalt not kill; thou shalt not steal; thou shalt not bear false witness; thou shalt not covet; and if there be any other commandment, it is briefly comprehended in this saying, thou shalt love your neighbor as thyself." Neither is love content with merely not doing evil to our neighbor. It continually motivates us to do as much good as we can to all men, as we have time and opportunity. It is, therefore, the fulfilling of both the positive and the negative law of God.

And faith does not only fulfill the law externally, but it works inwardly by love, purifying of the heart, cleansing it from all evil desires. Everyone that has this faith, "purifieth himself even as He is pure;" purifies himself from every earthly, sensual desire; from all evil and perverse affections; even from that carnal mind which is opposed to God. At the same time, if it completes its work, it fills him with all goodness, righteousness, and truth. It brings heaven into his soul; and causes him to walk in the light, even as God is in the light.

Let us try, in this manner, to establish the law in ourselves; not sinning "because we are under grace," but rather using all the power we receive from it "to fulfill all righteousness." Remembering the light we received from God while His Spirit was convicting us of sin, let us be careful that we do not put out that light. Let nothing influence us to rebuild what we have destroyed; to resume anything, great or small, which we clearly once knew was not for the glory of God, or for the benefit of our own soul. And let us not neglect anything, great or small, which we could not have neglected before with a clear conscience. To increase and perfect the light which we had before, let us now add the light of faith. Walking now with joy, and not with fear, in a clear, steady view of eternal things, we see pleasure, wealth, praise, all the things of earth, as bubbles in the water; considering nothing important, nothing desirable, nothing worth a second thought, except that which is "within the veil," where Jesus "sitteth at the right hand of God."

Can you say, "You are merciful to my unrighteousness; my sins You remember no more?" Then, in the future, see that you run from sin as from a snake! How exceedingly sinful it appears to you now! How hellish beyond all description! On the other hand, in how attractive a light you now see the holy and perfect will of God! Therefore, work that it may be fulfilled, both in you, by you, and upon you! Watch and pray so that you may no longer sin, so that you may see and avoid the least violation of His law! You see the sins which you could not see before, now that the Sun of Righteousness shines in your heart. Then be careful to walk according to the light you have received! Strongly desire to receive more light each day, more of the knowledge and love of God, more of the Spirit of Christ, more of His life, and of the power of His resurrection! Now use all the knowledge, and love, and life, and power you have already attained. In this way you will continue on from faith to faith;

increasing in holy love day by day, until faith is swallowed up in sight, and the law of love is established for all eternity!

22

First Dialogue between an Antinomian and His Friend

Editor's note: The statements by the antinomian that are in quotation marks are quotations that Wesley selected from a writer who defended the antinomian position. The term antinomian *means "one who is against law." An antinomian denies that the law of God has any relevance to a Christian, alleging that grace frees the believer from any requirement whatsoever, except to believe. In this, they imply that all of the commands of Scripture can be ignored. While there are few, if any, who would call themselves antinomians, the term is frequently used by those who debate them.*

ANTINOMIAN. — My friend, I am glad to see you. But I am sorry to hear you have changed your religion.

FRIEND. — Changed my religion! I do not know what you mean.

Ant. — You once believed that we are saved by faith.

Friend. — Yes; and I still do.

Ant. — Do you believe, then, that the "whole work of man's salvation was accomplished by Jesus Christ on the cross?"

Friend. — I believe that by that one offering, He made a full satisfaction for the sins of the whole world.

Ant. — But do you believe that "Christ's blood and our sins went away together?"

Friend. — I do not understand what you mean.

Ant. — Did Christ, "when He was upon the cross, take away, put an end to, blot out, and utterly destroy, all our sins forever?"

Friend. — He did pay the price, so that all who truly believe in Him are now saved from their sins; and, if they endure to the end, will be eternally saved. Is this what you mean?

Ant. — I mean, He did then "heal, take away, put an end to, and utterly destroy, all our sins."

Friend. — Did he heal the wound before it was made, and put an end to our sins before they began? This is so obviously absurd, that I cannot imagine how you can accept it.

Ant. — I thought you would come to your "carnal reasoning." What has faith to do with reasoning?

Friend. — Do you ever read the Bible? Does not God himself say to sinners, "Come now, and let us reason together?" (Isaiah 1:18). Does not our Lord reason continually with the Scribes and Pharisees; St. Peter with the Jews (Acts 2:14, etc.); and St. Paul both with the Jews and Gentiles? Is not a great part of Paul's epistles, both to the Romans and to the Galatians, and the largest part of that letter to the Hebrews, one entire chain of reasoning?

Ant. — You may do what you please. But I do not reason, I believe.

Friend. — I both believe and reason, for they are not inconsistent with each other. And I would be as willing to pluck out my eyes to secure my faith, as to lay aside my reason.

Ant. — But do not men continually abuse their reason? Therefore it is best to have nothing to do with it.

Friend. — Now you are doing the very thing you condemn! You are reasoning against reasoning. And no wonder; for it is impossible, without reasoning, either to prove or disprove anything.

Ant. — But can you deny the fact? Do not men continually abuse their reason?

Friend. — They do. But if we must lay aside whatever men abuse continually, we must lay aside the Bible; and meat and drink too.

Ant. — But come to the point. In what do you trust for justification and salvation?

Friend. — Only in the merits of Christ, which are mine if I truly believe that He loved me, and gave himself for me.

Ant. — If! So you make salvation conditional!

Friend. — And you do not? Otherwise, you make God a liar: for His clear words are, "He that believeth shall be saved; he that believeth not shall be damned." What is this except to say, "If you believe (therefore conditionally), you will be saved?"

Ant. — But I do not like that word, "conditional."

Friend. — Then find a better one, and we will lay it aside.

Ant. — However, I insist that "nothing else beside faith is required" for justification and salvation.

Friend. — What do you mean that nothing else is required?

Ant. — I mean, "There is but one duty, which is that of believing. One must do nothing but quietly attend the voice of the Lord. The gates of heaven are shut upon workers, and open to believers. If we do nothing for heaven, we do as much as God requires."

Friend. — Do you really mean that we are to do nothing in order to have present or final salvation, except "only to believe?"

Ant. — Have I not told you so? "To believe certainly, that Christ suffered death for us, is enough; we need no more. We are justified by submitting to accepting the truth of God's grace in Christ Jesus. It is not necessary that a man do any works, that he may be justified and saved. God does not require you to do anything that you may be saved or justified. The law sets you to work; but the gospel binds you to do nothing at all. Nay, the works are not only not required, but forbidden. God forbids us to work for justification. And when the Apostle Paul presses men to believe, it is as much as if he had bid them not to work."

Friend. — Let Paul be permitted to answer for himself. In the twenty-sixth chapter of the Acts of the Apostles, he tells how our Lord sent him "to open the eyes of the Gentiles, — that they might receive remission of sins" (vv. 17, 18). "Whereupon," he says, "I was not disobedient to the heavenly vision; but showed — to the Gentiles, that they should repent, and turn to God, and do works meet for repentance." Observe: He "obeyed the heavenly vision," by teaching the Gentiles, before they were justified, before they had "received forgiveness of sins," to "repent and do works meet for repentance." So he was hardly "bidding them not to work," though he was "pressing them to believe."

Ant. — You have started your "carnal reasoning" again.

Friend. — "Carnal reasoning" seems to be a term that you use when you do not know what else to say. But did St. Paul preach according to the instructions given to him from heaven, or not?

Ant. — Certainly he did; otherwise he would have been "disobedient unto the heavenly vision."

Friend. — How then can you say that a minister of Christ ought to preach nothing but "Believe, believe?" and that telling men to do anything is "preaching the law?" Do you not condemn, not only the great Apostle, but also Him that sent and commanded him "thus to preach?"

Ant. — Surely you would not want us to be "under the law!"

Friend. — I am afraid you do not know what that expression means. St. Paul uses it three times in his Epistle to the Romans, five times in that to the Galatians, and in one passage of his first Epistle to the Corinthians; where he declares in what sense he was "under the law," and in what sense he was not. "Unto them that are under the law" (that still adhere to the whole Jewish dispensation), "I became as under the law" (I conformed to their ceremonies), "that I might gain them that are under the law: But unto them that are without the law" (the Gentiles or heathens), "as without the law: Being," all the while, "not without law to God, but under the law to Christ" (1 Corinthians 9:20, 21). It is clear that the Apostle was "under the law" of Christ, though he was not "under the law" of ceremonies.

Ant. —But does St. Paul not say to the believers at Rome, "Ye are not under the law, but under grace?"

Friend. — He does; and what he means is, "You are not under the Jewish, but the gracious Christian dispensation." The same also holds in the next verse, where he says, "We are not under the law, but under grace."

Ant. — But what does he mean, when he says to the Galatians, "Before faith came, we were kept under the law?"

Friend. — Undoubtedly he means that we were kept under the Jewish dispensation until we believed in Christ (3:19). And so we read in the next chapter, "When the fullness of time was come, God sent forth His Son, made under the law" (the Jewish dispensation), "to redeem them that were under the law, that we might receive the adoption of sons" (vv. 4, 5); might serve God, without fear, in righteousness and holiness, with a free, loving, child-like spirit.

Ant. — You cannot convince me of this; I know better. The law of works (the "moral law," as you call it) means nothing to me. "From the demand of the law, no man is obliged to go one step, to give away one farthing, to eat, or omit one morsel. For what did our Lord do with the law? He abolished it."

Friend. — However, should we not, after we believe in Him, obey all the commandments of Christ?

Ant. — Obey! Law! Works! Commandments! What "legalness is in your spirit!" So, I suppose, "your comforts vanish away when you are not assured that you obey all Christ's commandments!" On the contrary, "a spiritual man beholds justifying grace in believing, without his obedience to commands for external worship and good works."

Friend. — But how does this agree with countless texts of Scripture, and, specifically, with our Lord's own words? "Think not that I am come to destroy" (or abolish) "the law: I am not come to destroy, but to fulfill. For verily I say unto you, until heaven and earth pass, one jot or one tittle shall in nowise pass from the law. Whosoever, therefore, shall break one of these least commandments, he shall be called the least in the kingdom of heaven" (Matthew 5:17, etc.).

Ant. — I tell you clearly, I will not reason with you.

Friend. — That is as much as to say, "I will not be convinced: I love darkness rather than light."

Ant. — No; it is you that is in darkness. I was until a few weeks ago. But now my eyes have been opened. I see my liberty now. Now I am free. I was in bondage long enough.

Friend. — What are you free from?

Ant. — From sin, and hell, and the devil, and the law.

Friend. — You put the law of God in good company. But how did you become free from the law?

Ant. — Christ made me free from it.

Friend. — What? From His own law? Please, tell me where that is written!

Ant. — Here, in Galatians 3:13: "Christ hath redeemed us from the curse of the law, being made a curse for us."

Friend. — How is this relevant to the question? This tells me that "Christ hath redeemed us" (all believers) "from the curse," or punishment, that our past violations of God's law deserve. But it does not say a word about redeeming us from the law, any more than from love or heaven. But what do you mean by bondage?

Ant. — Why, being bound to keep the law.

Friend. — You have not one Scripture for this. Bondage to fear and bondage to sin are mentioned there; and bondage to the ceremonial law of Moses. Why, according to your sense of the word, all the angels in heaven are in bondage!

Ant. — Well, I am not bound. St. Paul himself says to believers, "Why are ye subject to ordinances?" (Colossians 2:20).

Friend. — True; that is to say, "Why are you Christian believers subject to Jewish ordinances?" He mentions a few of these in the very next verse, "Touch not, taste not, handle not."

Ant. — No, that is not all. I say, "Outward things do nothing avail to salvation." This is clear; for "if love to God, and love to our neighbor, and relieving the poor, are completely unprofitable either for justification or salvation; then these outward works, submitting to outward ordinances, are much less valuable."

Friend. — Are you speaking of the ordinances of Christ?

Ant. — I am. "They bring in the most dangerous kind of Popery, and pervert the pure gospel of Christ, who persuade men, that if they do not submit to the ordinances of the Lord Jesus, He will not confess them before His Father." So I affirm, "It is better not to practice outward ordinances at all, than to practice them on these gospel-destroying principles, to the ruining of our souls."

Friend. — What Scripture do you produce for this?

Ant. — I wish you would not build your case so much upon the letter and rather talk of inherent righteousness.

Friend. — Then do you say that a believer has no inherent righteousness?

Ant. — I do. I say, "God will save us to the utmost, without any righteousness or holiness of our own." To look for inherent righteousness, "is to deny the Spirit, and trample under foot the blood of the covenant. Believers have no inherent righteousness in them. Our righteousness is nothing but the imputation of the righteousness of Christ."

Friend. — I believe that Christ, by His Spirit, works righteousness in all those to whom faith is imputed for righteousness.

Ant. — "By no means; all our righteousness is in Christ. It is wholly imputed, not inherent. We are always righteous in Christ, but never righteous in ourselves."

Friend. — Is not, then, every believer righteous or holy?

Ant. — Undoubtedly; but he is holy in Christ, not in himself.

Friend. — Does he not live a holy life; and is he not holy in heart?

Ant. — Most certainly.

Friend. — Is he not then holy in himself?

Ant. — No, no, in Christ only. He has no holiness in himself at all.

Friend. — Does he not have love for God and for his neighbor in him; even the entire image of God?

Ant. — He has. But this is not gospel holiness.

Friend. — What useless noise this is! You dispute the name, all the while agreeing with the thing I contend for. You agree that a believer is holy both in heart and life. This is all I mean by inherent righteousness or holiness.

Ant. — But I tell you, this is not gospel holiness. Gospel holiness is faith.

Friend. — If you stand for this, you still lose your whole argument. For, based on your supposition, I reason: faith is holiness or righteousness; but faith is in every believer: therefore, holiness or righteousness is in every believer.

Ant. — I pity you. Take my word for it, you are in complete darkness. You know nothing of true faith; nothing at all.

Friend. — Will you then be so kind as to explain it to me?

Ant. — I will make it as clear as the sun. I will show you the heart of that doctrine which "I recommend, with all my heart, to all, as the most wholesome doctrine of Jesus Christ."

"Many think they know it, when they have but crude, carnal, indigested notions of it. And they imagine we rest contented with such a faith as theirs; that Christ has died to ward off the wrath of God, to purchase His favor, and, as an effect of that, to obtain certain inherent qualities and dispositions, to make us fit for the kingdom of heaven. If this were our faith, it would be necessary to seek after this sort of sanctification, and not to be at rest unless we felt something of it. But, on the contrary, we believe that the blood shed upon the cross has put away and blotted out all our sins, and that then there was an everlasting righteousness brought in. By believing this, our hearts and consciences are made as perfectly clean as though we had never sinned. In this consists true purity of soul, and not in habitual qualities. And whoever are thus made pure and perfect are delivered from the dominion of sin. They do also bear forth the fruits of righteousness, not in order to become more holy, but because they are perfectly holy, through faith. It is true, we have still the vile, sinful body, which continually disposes the mind to evil. But the blood of Jesus makes us free from sin."

Friend. — Of all the explanations I have heard, this is the most "crude and indigested." But let us go over it step by step. You first described what you consider a false faith, that is, "A faith that Christ has died, to ward off" (or satisfy) "the wrath of God, and to purchase His favor;" (by example, for me, a lost sinner) "and as an effect of that," (of God's favor purchased with the blood of Christ) "to obtain" for me "certain inherent qualities and dispositions, to make me fit for the kingdom of heaven." Now, how do you prove this is a false faith?

Ant. — Easily enough; for men "are obliged to support it by reasons, feelings, and works."

Friend. — And did not you agree, just now, that whoever has true faith is "holy both in heart and life?" That he has "love for God and for his neighbor; even the entire image of God" in him?

Ant. — I did. What about it?

Friend. — Then you have contradicted yourself: For you have

agreed that true faith cannot be supported, or even exist for a moment, without "certain inherent qualities and dispositions" (love for God and for all mankind), "which make us fit for the kingdom of heaven." You have agreed that true faith cannot exist without a holy heart, a continuance in good works, and a sense of God's love for me, a sinner.

Ant. — I hear you. Go on.

Friend. — You said next, "If this were our faith, it would be necessary to seek after this sort of sanctification." From your own words it appears that this is your faith, if you have any true faith at all. You must then "seek after this sort of sanctification," love for God and for your neighbor. For if you can be "at rest" without it, it is clear that your heart is not clean, but rather hardened.

Ant. — You can say what you please. You do not know any better.

Friend. — You went on: "On the contrary, we believe that the blood shed upon the cross has put away and blotted out all our sins." Who believes otherwise? If you mean only that Christ did away with the punishment of all the sins of those who believe in Him; I ask, who is to be corrected by this line of argument?

Ant. — It corrects you, who deny that "an everlasting righteousness was then brought in."

Friend. — I deny it no more than you understand it. But I ask, in what sense was it "brought in?" What was it brought into? Was it first brought into the world? You cannot say this without saying that all who departed from the world before that time were lost. Or was it brought into the souls of believers? Then believers have an inward or inherent righteousness. You had better, therefore, leave this text alone. It will do nothing to help your cause.

Ant. — I see that you are still as blind as a beetle. I am afraid your head knowledge will destroy you. Did not I tell you, "Our hearts and consciences are made perfectly clean by our believing; and that in this consists true purity of soul, and not in habitual qualities? Thus we are made perfectly holy." And though "the vile, sinful body continually disposes the mind to evil," yet "the blood of Christ makes us free from sin."

Friend. — How can my mind be "continually disposed to evil," and "free from sin, perfectly clean, perfectly holy," all at the same time?"

Ant. — The dullness of some men! I do not mean actually holy, but holy by imputation. I told you clearly, the holiness of which we speak is not in us, but in Christ. "The fruits of the Spirit, (commonly called sanctification) such as love, gentleness, longsuffering, goodness, meekness, self-control, neither make us holy before God, nor in our own consciences."

Friend. — I know that these cannot atone for sin. This is done only by the blood of Christ; for the sake of which, God forgives, and works these qualities in us by faith. Do I understand you now?

Ant. — No, no; I am amazed at your ignorance. I mean, "we are not made good or holy by any inward qualities or dispositions: But being made pure and holy in our consciences, by believing in Christ, we bear forth, inwardly and outwardly, the fruits of holiness." Now, I hope, you understand me.

Friend. — You say, "We are not made good or holy by any inward qualities or dispositions." But are we not made good by inward goodness (remember, we are not speaking of justification, but sanctification); holy, by inward holiness; meek, by inward meekness; gentle, by inward gentleness? And are all of these not "inward qualities or dispositions?"

Ant. — You still do not grasp my meaning. I mean that these inward dispositions "are not our holiness. For we are not more holy, if we have more love to God and man, nor less holy, if we have less."

Friend. — Does a believer not increase in holiness, as he increases in love for God and man?

Ant. — No. "The very moment he is justified, he is wholly sanctified. And he is neither more nor less holy, from that hour, to the day of his death. Entire justification and entire sanctification are in the same instant. And neither of them is thenceforth capable either of increase or decrease."

Friend. — I thought we were to grow in grace!

Ant. — "We are so; but not in holiness. The moment we are justified, we are as pure in heart as ever we shall be. A newborn babe is as pure in heart as a father in Christ. There is no difference."

Friend. — It serves your purpose well to ignore Scripture and reason. For until a man abandons both, he can never swallow this. You are acting as if you had found the most important truths, the likes of which no one ever knew before. All that is truly remarkable in your doctrine is this heap of broad absurdities, in which you almost always contradict yourselves, as well as Scripture and common sense. In the meantime, you boast as if "ye were the men, and wisdom should die with you." I pray that God will "humble you, and examine you, and show you what is in your hearts!"

23

Second Dialogue between an Antinomian and His Friend

Editor's note: The statements by the antinomian that are in quotation marks are quotations that Wesley selected from an antinomian writer. In this essay he cited the source, "Mr Cudworth's Dialogue."

"Do we then make void the law through faith?
God forbid: Yea, we establish the law."
Romans 3:31.

FRIEND. — You have had time to consider. What do think of our last conversation?

ANTINOMIAN. — I think, "The giving of scandalous names has no warrant from Scripture." (*Mr. Cudworth's Dialogue*, p. 2).

Friend. — Scandalous names?

Ant. — Yes; you called me *antinomian*. But "Our Savior bids me not return railing for railing." (Ibid.)

Friend. — St. Peter does, and that is the same. But how is that a scandalous name? I think it is very appropriate, for it means, "one that speaks against the law." And you did this quite freely at that time. But what would you like for me call to you?

Ant. — "A Preacher of God's righteousness." (Ibid., p. 1).

Friend. — What do you call me then?

Ant. — "A Preacher of inherent righteousness." (Ibid.)

Friend. — So you mean that inherent righteousness is opposite to that righteousness of God which is by faith.

Ant. — Yes; for, "I plainly perceive you know but one sort of righteousness, that is, the righteousness of inherent qualities, dispositions, and works." Let me ask you one question. Do you believe that "Christ hath appeared, to put away sin by the sacrifice of himself?"

Friend. — I do.

Ant. — But in what sense?

Friend. — I believe He made, by that one offering of himself, a full, perfect, and sufficient sacrifice for the sins of the whole world. And yet He has not done all that was necessary for the inevitable salvation of the whole world. If He had, the whole world would be saved; but it remains that, "he that believeth not shall be damned."

Ant. — But is it not said, "'He was wounded for our transgressions, and with His stripes we are healed?' And is He not 'the Lamb of God, that taketh away the sins of the world?'" (p. 4).

Friend. — Yes. But this does not prove that He "put an end to our sins before they had a beginning!" (Ibid.)

Ant. — Ignorance! Did our sins not begin in Adam?

Friend. — Original sin did. But Christ will not put an end to this before the end of the world. And, as for actual sin, if I feel anger toward you in my heart, and it comes out in reproachful words; to say that Christ put an end to this sin before it began is absurd.

Ant. — Then you believe that Christ has only redeemed us from the punishment that our past transgressions deserve. "Then who must redeem us from those which are to come, since there remains no more sacrifice for sin?" (*Cudworth's Dialogue*).

Friend. — The same Jesus Christ, by the same merit of that one sacrifice, which is applied to the conscience when we believe, as you yourself have often asserted. But whatever punishment He redeems us from, that punishment assumes that sin has already been committed. After all, it must first exist, before it can be either punished or pardoned.

Ant. — You have a strange way of talking. You say, "We are forgiven for the sake of the blood of Christ." (Ibid.)

Friend. — And do you not?

Ant. — No; I say, "We have forgiveness in His blood, and not merely for the sake of it."

Friend. — You are perfectly welcome to say so.

Ant. — Well, enough of this. Let me ask you another question. Do you believe that salvation is "conditional?" (Ibid.)

Friend. — I believe, "He that believeth shall be saved, and he that believeth not; shall be damned." Can you deny this? If not, why do you fight over a word; especially after I told you, "Find me a better one, and I will lay this aside?"

Ant — "Then this faith leaves you just in the same state it found you; that is, still having the condition to perform." (Ibid.)

Friend. — Not so; for faith itself is that condition.

Ant. — No, "faith is only necessary in order to receive forgiveness or salvation; not to procure it by way of condition." (Ibid.)

Friend. — Enough of this. We are in agreement then. If you

allow that "faith is necessary in order to receive forgiveness or salvation," this is all I mean by calling it a condition. A condition that earns salvation is something entirely different.

Ant. — Will you answer one more question? Is a believer not free from the law?

Friend. — He is free from the Jewish ceremonial law; that is, he does not need to observe it. And he is free from the curse of the moral law; but he is not free from observing it. He still walks according to this rule, and all the more, because God has written it in his heart.

Ant. — But St. Paul says, "Christ is the end of the law for righteousness to every one that believeth." (Ibid.)

Friend. — He is. He put an end to the Mosaic dispensation, and established a better covenant, in which "faith is counted for righteousness to every one that believeth."

Ant. — And yet, "as many as are of the works of the law are under the curse" (Galatians 3:10), are they not?

Friend. — They are; those who still "seek to be justified by the works of the law;" that is, by any works which come before, or are independent of, faith in Christ.

Ant. — "But does not the Apostle also say, 'Ye are become dead to the law?' (Romans 7:4)." (Ibid.)

Friend. — You are, as to its condemning power, if you truly believe in Christ. For "there is no condemnation to them which are in Christ Jesus." But you are not dead as to its directing power; for you "walk not after the flesh, but after the Spirit." You "love Him, and keep His commandments."

Ant. — But I maintain, "a believer is entirely free from the law." (Ibid.)

Friend. — By what Scripture do you prove that?

Ant. — By Galatians 4:4, 5: "God sent forth His Son, made under the law, to redeem them that were under the law."

Friend. — I mentioned the clear meaning of this before: "'God sent forth His Son, made under the law' (the Jewish dispensation), 'to redeem them that were under the law, that we might receive the adoption of sons;' might 'serve God without fear, in righteousness and holiness,' with a free, loving, child-like spirit.'" Do you mean only that he obeys the law of Christ by free choice, and not by force? That he keeps the commandments of God out of love, not fear? If so, no one will oppose you. But if you mean he is free from obeying that law, then your liberty is a liberty to disobey God.

Ant. — God forbid. It is "a liberty to walk in the Spirit, and not fulfill the lust (or desire) of the flesh." (Ibid., p. 8).

Friend. — Why, this is the very thing I am contending for. The thing I continually assert is this, that Christian liberty is a liberty to obey God, and not to commit sin.

Ant. — Then you must consider these words of our Lord to exclude the moral law: "Think not that I am come to destroy the Law or the Prophets: I am not come to destroy, but to fulfill. For verily I say unto you, until heaven and earth pass, one jot or one tittle shall in nowise pass from the law, until all be fulfilled" (Matthew 5:17, 18). But I say that our Lord has fulfilled the moral law too.

Friend. — I agree that He has. But do you infer from that, "therefore He has destroyed the law?" Our Lord's argument is the opposite of yours. He mentions His coming to "fulfill the law," as a proof that He did not come to "destroy" or "take it away." But suppose you could get past the first verse, what can you do with the next one? "Verily I say unto you, One jot or one tittle shall in nowise pass from the law, until heaven and earth pass;" or, which is to say the same thing, "until all be fulfilled." Here, the word "all" does not refer to the law, but to heaven and earth and "all things" therein.

I cannot, in good conscience, speak in the way that you do because it is an unscriptural way of speaking. Both the Old and New Testament speak of holiness, of good works, of the law and the commandments of God, as clearly and frequently as they speak of believing in Jesus Christ.

I also find, by experience, that it is a dangerous way of speaking, both to the speaker and to the hearers. As for the speaker, it has a tendency to make him exalt himself (under the pretense of exalting the grace of God) and despise others. As for the hearers, it keeps many from ever waking from the sleep of spiritual death; it lulls others back into that fatal slumber, who were just beginning to awaken; it stops many in their Christian walk, and turns others completely out of the way; and even plunges many into unclean living. Considering this, I earnestly desire to "speak as the oracles of God;" that is, to express scriptural meanings in scriptural words; to keep as close as I can to "the law and the testimony;" being convinced that there are no words so fit to express the deep things of God, as those which "holy men of old spake" when "they were moved by the Spirit of God."

24

A Dialogue between a Predestinarian and His Friend

Out of your own mouth!

TO ALL PREDESTINARIANS:

Some of you have said that the following quotations are false; that these words were not spoken by these authors; others say that the words were not spoken in this sense; and others say that neither you, nor any true predestinarian ever did, or ever would, speak in such a way.

My friends, the authors quoted here are well-known. You may read their words with your own eyes. And you who have read them know in your conscience that they were spoken in this sense, and no other; that this sense of them is openly defended throughout the writings from which they are taken.

But do you say, "No true predestinarian ever did or would speak in this way?" Why, every true predestinarian must speak in this way, and you must also, if you dare to speak out, unless, of course, you renounce your fundamental principle.

Your fundamental principle is this: "God from eternity ordained whatever should come to pass." But from this single position undeniably follows every assertion I will mention here. It remains only for you to respond in one of these three ways: either,

(1) To evade the question and continue deceiving your hearers; or,
(2) To swallow all these assertions, and honestly claim them; or,
(3) To renounce them altogether, and believe in Christ, the Savior of all.

FRIEND. — Sir, I have heard that you make God the author of all sin, and the merciless destroyer of most of mankind.

PREDESTINARIAN. — I deny it; I only say, "God did from all eternity unchangeably ordain whatever comes to pass" (*Assembly's Catechism*, ch. 3).

Friend. — Do you make no exceptions?

Pred. — No; for "nothing is more absurd than to think anything at all is done but by the ordination of God" (*Calvin's Institutes*, bk. 1, ch. 16, sect. 3).

Friend. — Does this include the actions of men?

Pred. — Without a doubt. "Every action and motion of every creature is so governed by the hidden counsel of God, that nothing can come to pass, but what was ordained by him" (Ibid., sect. 3).

Friend. — What then becomes of men's wills?

Pred. — "The wills of men are so governed by the will of God, that they are carried on straight to the mark which He has fore-ordained" (Ibid., sect. 8).

Friend. — I suppose you mean the permissive will of God?

Pred. — No; I mean, "all things come to pass by the efficacious and irresistible will of God" (*Twissi Vindiciae Gratiae Potestatis & Providentiae Dei. Editio Jensoniana*, par. 3, p. 19).

Friend. — Why, then all men must do exactly what they do?

Pred. — True. "It is impossible that anything should ever be done, but that to which God impels the will of man" (Ibid., p. 19).

Friend. — But does this not imply the necessity of all events?

Pred. — "I will not scruple to own that the will of God lays a necessity on all things, and that everything he wills necessarily comes to pass" (*Calvin's Institutes*, bk. 3, ch. 24, sect. 8).

Friend. — Then does sin necessarily come to pass?

Pred. — Undoubtedly, for "the almighty power of God extends itself to the first fall, and all other sins of angels and men" (*Assembly's Catechism*, ch. 5).

Friend. — I agree that God foresaw that the first man would fall.

Pred. — No, "God not only foresaw that Adam would fall, but also ordained that he should" (*Calvin's Institutes*, bk. 3, ch. 23, sect. 7).

Friend. — I know God permitted Adam's fall.

Pred. — I tell you, "he fell not only by the permission, but also by the appointment, of God" (Calvin *Responsio ad Calumnias Nebulonis cujusdam ad Articulum primum*). "He sinned because God so ordained, because the Lord saw good" (*Calvin's Institutes*, bk. 3, ch. 24, sect. 8).

Friend. — But do those who differ from you not object to this?

Pred. — They do. "Those poisonous dogs vomit out many things against God" (Ibid., bk. 3, ch. 23, sect. 2). "They deny that the Scripture says God decreed Adam's fall. They say he might have chosen either to fall or not; and that God fore-ordained only to treat him according to his desert: As if God had created the noblest of all His creatures, without fore-ordaining what should become of him!" (Ibid., sect. 7).

Friend. — Then did God make Adam so that he might fall?

Pred. — Undoubtedly. "God made Adam and Eve to this very purpose, that they might be tempted and led into sin. And by force of His decree, it could not otherwise be but they must sin" (*Piscatoris Dispute*. Praedest., Praef., p. 6).

Friend. — But do you not base God's decree on God's foreknowledge rather than His will?

Pred. — No. "God foresees nothing but what He has decreed, and His decree precedes His knowledge" (*Piscat. Disput.* Praedest).

Friend. — Well, this decree may truly be called horrible.

Pred. — "I confess it is a horrible decree; yet no one can deny but God foreknew Adam's fall, and foreknew it because He had ordained it so by His own decree" (*Calvin's Institutes*, bk. 3, ch. 23, sect. 7).

Friend. — Do you believe that God has, by His own positive decree, not only elected some men to life, but also reprobated the rest?

Pred. — Yes, for if I believe one, I believe the other. "Many indeed (thinking to excuse God) accept election, and yet deny reprobation; but this is quite silly and childish. For without reprobation, election itself cannot stand; whom God passes by, those He reprobates" (*Calvin's Institutes*, bk. 3, ch. 23, sect. 1).

Friend. — Please explain what you mean by election and reprobation.

Pred. — "All men are not created for the same end; but some are fore-ordained to eternal life; others to eternal damnation. So according as every man was created for the one end or the other, we say he was elected or predestinated to life, or reprobated, that is, predestinated to destruction" (Ibid., ch. 21, sect. 1).

Friend. — Please say again what you mean.

Pred. — "God has once for all appointed, by an eternal and unchangeable decree, to whom He would give salvation, and whom He would devote to destruction." (Ibid., sect. 7).

Friend. — Did God make any man simply for the purpose that he might be damned?

Pred. — Did I not tell you before? "God's first constitution was that some should be destined to eternal ruin; and to this end their sins were ordained, and denial of grace in order to their sins" (*Zanchius de Natura Dei*, pp. 553, 554).

Friend. — But is God's predestining men to life or death not based on His foreknowledge?

Pred. — "So the vulgar think; that God, as He foresees every man will deserve, elects them to life, or devotes them to death and damnation" (*Calvin's Institutes*, bk. 3, ch. 22, sect. 1).

Friend. — And do you not think that reprobation, at least, is based on God's foreknowing men's sins?

Pred. — No. "God of His own good pleasure ordains that many should be born, who are from the womb devoted to inevitable damnation. If any man pretend that God's foreknowledge lays them under no necessity of being damned, but rather that He decreed their damnation because He foreknew their wickedness, I grant that God's foreknowledge alone lays no necessity on the creature; but eternal life and death depend on the will rather than the foreknowledge of God. If God only foreknew all things that relate to all men, and did not decree and ordain them also, then it might be inquired whether or not His foreknowledge necessitates the thing foreknown. But seeing He therefore foreknows all things that will come to pass, because He has decreed they shall come to pass, it is vain to contend about foreknowledge, since it so plain all things come to pass by God's positive decree" (Ibid., ch. 23, sect. 6).

Friend. — But if God has positively decreed to damn the majority of mankind, why does He call them to repent and be saved?

Pred. — "As God has His effectual call, whereby He gives the elect the salvation to which He ordained them, so He has His judgments towards the reprobates, whereby He executes His decree concerning them. As many, therefore, as He created to live miserably, and then perish everlastingly; these, that they may be brought to the end for which they were created, He sometimes deprives of the possibility of hearing the word, and at other times, by the preaching thereof, blinds and stupefies them the more" (Ibid., ch. 24, sect. 12).

Friend. — How is this? If God has created them for never-ending death, why does He call to them to turn and live?

Pred. — "He calls to them, that they may be more deaf; He kindles a light, that they may be the more blind; He brings His doctrine to them, that they may be more ignorant; and applies the remedy to them, that they may not be healed" (Ibid., bk. 3, ch. 24, sect. 13).

Friend. — Enough, enough. And yet you do not make God the author of sin?

Pred. — No. "God cannot be termed the author of sin, though He is the cause of those actions which are sins" (Petri Martyris Vermillii *Commentary on Romans*, p. 413).

Friend. — Then how is He the cause of them?

Pred. — In two ways: first, by His eternal, unchangeable decree; and second, by His present irresistible power.

Friend. — Did God foreordain the sins of any man?

Pred. — "Both the reprobates and the elect were foreordained to sin, as sin, that the glory of God might be declared thereby" (*Zanchius de Nat. Dei*, p. 555). "The reprobates," more especially, "who were predestinated to damnation, and the causes of damnation, and created to that end, that they may live wickedly, and be vessels full of the dregs of sin" (*Piscator contra Tauffium*, p. 47).

Friend. — But surely the sins of the elect were not foreordained?

Pred. — Yes, they were; "For we neither can do more good than we do, nor less evil than we do; because God from eternity has precisely decreed that both the good and the evil should be so done" (*Piscatoris Responsio ad Amicam Duplicationem Conradi Vorstii*, p. 176).

Friend. — So that is how you believe that God decrees sin. But how is His irresistible power involved in the sins of men?

Pred. — "God is the author of that action which is sinful, by His irresistible will" (Dr. Twisse, par. 3, p. 21).

Friend. — How do you mean?

Pred. — "God procures adultery, cursings, lyings" (*Piscatoris Responsio ad Apologiam Bertii*). "He supplies wicked men with opportunities of sinning, and inclines their hearts thereto. He blinds, deceives, and seduces them. He, by His working on their hearts, bends and stirs them up to do evil" (Petri Martyr. Vermilli, pp. 36, 413). And thus "thieves, murderers, and other malefactors are God's instruments, which He uses to execute what He hath decreed in himself" (*Calvin's Institutes*, bk. 1, ch. 17, sect. 5).

Friend. — Do you not then charge God with sin?

Pred. — No. "God necessitates them only to the act of sin, not to the deformity of sin" (*Twissi Vindiciae*, par. 3, p. 22). Besides, "when God makes angels or men sin, He does not sin himself, because He does not break any law. For God is under no law, and therefore cannot sin" (Zwingli in "Sermon on Providence," ch. 5, 6).

Friend. — But how does God make angels or men sin?

Pred. — "The devil and wicked men are so held in on every side with the hand of God, that they cannot conceive, or contrive, or execute any mischief, any farther than God himself doth not permit only, but command. Nor are they only held in fetters, but compelled also, as with a bridle, to perform obedience to those commands" (*Calvin's Institutes*, bk. 1, ch. 17, sect. 11).

Friend. — This is true Turkish [Muslim] doctrine, and ought

so to be refuted as such, as in these words:

"I do anathematize the blasphemy of Mahomet [Mohammed], which says that God deceives whom He will, and whom He will He leads to that which is good. Himself does what He wills, and is himself the cause of all good and all evil. Fate and destiny govern all things" (Nicetus Saracenita).

Pred. — Our doctrine is older than Mahomet. It was held by St. Augustine.

Friend. — Augustine speaks sometimes for it, and sometimes against it. But all the tradition of the first four centuries is against you, as is the whole Eastern [Orthodox] Church to this day; and the Church of England, both in her catechism, articles, and homilies. And so are many of our most holy martyrs, Bishop Hooper and Bishop Latimer in particular.

Pred. — But does tradition not say that Judas was predestined to damnation?

Friend. — Quite the contrary. St. Chrysostom's words are, "Judas, my beloved, was at first a child of the kingdom, and heard it said to him with the disciples, 'Ye shall sit on twelve thrones;' but afterwards he became a child of hell."

Pred. — However, you will admit that Esau was predestined to destruction.

Friend. — I will not. Some of your own writers believe he was ultimately saved, which was the general opinion of the ancient church fathers. And that Scripture, "Jacob have I loved, and Esau have I hated," clearly refers not to their persons but their descendants. But, supposing Esau or Judas was damned, what was he damned for?

Pred. — For unbelief. For as we are saved by faith alone, so unbelief is the only damning sin.

Friend. — By what faith are you saved?

Pred. — By faith in Christ, who gave himself for me.

Friend. — But did He give himself for Esau and Judas? If not, you say they are damned for not believing a lie. It was this consideration that forced Archbishop Usher to cry out, "What would not a man fly unto, rather than yield, that Christ did not die for the reprobates; and that none but the elect had any kind of title to Him; and yet many thousands should be bound in conscience to believe that He died for them, and tied to accept Him for their Redeemer and Savior? Whereby they should have believed that which in itself is most untrue, and laid hold of that in which they had no kind of interest."

Pred. — Then what do *you* mean by the words, election and reprobation?

Friend. — I mean that, first, God decreed from the beginning to elect or choose, in Christ, all that should believe and be saved. This decree proceeds from His own goodness, and is not based on any goodness in the creature. Second, God decreed from the beginning to reprobate all who continue to the end in stubborn unbelief.

Pred. — What do you think, then, of absolute, unconditional election and reprobation?

Friend. — I think it cannot be found in Scripture, and that it is a plant which bears dismal fruit. We find evidence of this in Calvin himself; who confesses that he ordered the burning to death of Michael Servetus, only for differing from him in opinion on matters of religion.

25

Predestination Calmly Considered

That to the height of this great argument,
I may assert eternal Providence,
And justify the ways of God with man.
— MILTON.

I believe that many who now have the "faith which works by love" may remember a time when the power of the Highest worked within them in a remarkable way; when the voice of the Lord brought the mountains low, broke all the rocks into pieces, and powerfully spread His love in their hearts by the Holy Spirit given to them. At that time they had no power to resist the grace of God. They were no more able to stop the course of that flood than to stop the waves of the sea with their hand, or stop the sun in the sky.

And the children of God can see how His love leads them from faith to faith; how tenderly He watches over their souls; how carefully He brings them back if they wander, and then upholds them as they walk in His path, so that they do not slip and fall. They see how unwilling He is to let them go from serving Him; and how, against the stubbornness of their wills, and the wildness of their passions, He goes on doing His work, conquering until He has put all His enemies under His feet.

The longer this work continues in their hearts, the more earnestly they cry out, "Not unto us, O Lord, but unto Thy name give the praise, for Thy mercy and for Thy truth's sake!" For they are more deeply convinced that "by grace we are saved, not of works, lest any man should boast;" that we are not pardoned and accepted by God for the sake of anything we have done, but completely and only for the sake of Christ, of what He has done and suffered for us; the more surely they know that the only condition of this acceptance is faith; which, before it is given, no good work can be done that does not have the nature of sin in it.

How easily may a believer conclude, from what he has experienced in his own soul, that the true grace of God always works irresistibly in every believer! That God will finish wherever He has begun this work, so that it is impossible for any believer to fall from grace! And, last, that the reason God gives this to some and not to others is because of His own will. Without regard either to their faith or their works, He has absolutely, unconditionally, predestined them to life, before the foundation of the world!

Agreeing with this is "The Protestant Confession of faith," drawn up at Paris, in 1559, with these words:

"We believe, that out of the general corruption and condemnation

in which all men are plunged, God draws those whom, in His eternal and unalterable counsel, He has elected by His own goodness and mercy, through our Lord Jesus Christ, without considering their works, leaving the others in the same corruption and condemnation" (Article 12).

The Dutch theologians speak to the same effect, assembled at Dort in 1618. Their words are:

> *"Whereas, in process of time, God bestowed faith on some, and not on others, — this proceeds from His eternal decree; according to which, He softens the hearts of the elect, and leaves them that are not elect in their wickedness and hardness.*
>
> *"And herein is discovered the difference put between men equally lost; that is to say, the decree of election and reprobation. Election is the unchangeable decree of God, by which, before the foundation of the world, He has chosen in Christ unto salvation a set number of men. This election is one and the same of all which are to be saved.*
>
> *"Not all men are elected, but some not elected; whom God, in His unchangeable good pleasure, has decreed to leave in the common misery, and not to bestow saving faith upon them; but leaving them in their own ways, at last to condemn and punish them everlastingly, for their unbelief, and also for their other sins. And this is the decree of reprobation"* (Article 6, et seq).

Likewise, in "The Confession of Faith" set forth by the Assembly of English and Scotch theologians, in 1646, are these words:

> *"God from all eternity did unchangeably ordain whatsoever comes to pass . . . By the decree of God, for the manifestation of his glory, some men and angels are predestined unto everlasting life, and others fore-ordained to everlasting death.*

> *"These angels and men thus predestined and fore-ordained are particularly and unchangeably designed, and their number so certain and definite that it cannot be either increased or diminished.*
>
> *"Those of mankind that are predestined unto life, God, before the foundation of the world, has chosen in Christ unto everlasting glory, without any foresight of faith or good works.*
>
> *"The rest of mankind God was pleased, for the glory of His sovereign power over His creatures, to pass by, and to ordain them to dishonor and wrath"* (Ch. 3).

Equally clear are Mr. Calvin's words, in his "Christian Institutes:"

> *"All men are not created for the same end; but some are foreordained to eternal life, others to eternal damnation. So according as every man was created for the one end or the other, we say, he was elected, that is, predestined to life, or reprobated, that is, predestined to damnation"* (Ch. 21, Sect. 1).

Now let us look carefully at this doctrine. It states that before the foundations of the world were laid, God, out of His own will and pleasure, set a decree concerning all the children of men who would be born. This decree was unchangeable by God, and irresistible to man. And it was ordained that one part of mankind should be saved from sin and hell, and all the rest left to perish forever, without help, without hope. God decreed that not one of these should have that grace which could prevent their burning with everlasting fire, for this cause alone: "because it was His good pleasure;" and for this purpose: "to show His glorious power, and His sovereignty over all the earth."

Do the Scriptures speak of election? They say that St. Paul was "an elected or chosen vessel;" and speak of great numbers of men as "elect according to the foreknowledge of God." Election commonly means one of two things: first, a divine appointment of particular men, to do some particular work in the world. And so, Cyrus was elected to rebuild the temple, and St. Paul, along with the Twelve, to preach the gospel. But I do not find this to have any necessary connection with eternal happiness, for one who is elected in this sense may still be eternally lost. "Have I not chosen" (elected) "you twelve?" said our Lord; "yet one of you hath a devil." Judas was elected just as the rest; and yet is punished with the devil and his angels.

Second, I believe election means a divine appointment of some men to eternal happiness. But I believe this election is conditional, as well as the reprobation which is opposite to it. I believe that the eternal decree concerning both is expressed in those words: "He that believeth shall be saved; he that believeth not shall be damned." God will not change this decree, and man cannot resist it. According to this, all true believers are called elect in Scripture, as all who continue in unbelief are termed *reprobates*, that is, unapproved of God, and without discernment of the things of the Spirit.

Now, God, who sees all eternity at once, "calls the things that are not as though they were;" the things that are not yet as though they were now already existing. So He calls Abraham the "father of many nations," even before Isaac was born. And so Christ is called "the Lamb slain from the foundation of the world," even though He was not slain at that time. Likewise, God calls true believers, "elect from the foundation of the world;" although they were not actually elect, or believers, until many ages afterward. It was only then that they were actually elected, when they were made the "sons of God by faith." They were then actually "chosen and taken out of the world; elect," says St. Paul, "through belief of the truth;" or, as St. Peter expresses it, "elect according to the foreknowledge of God, through sanctification of the Spirit."

I believe this election as firmly as I believe the Scripture to be of God. But unconditional election I cannot believe; not only because I cannot find it in Scripture, but also because it necessarily implies unconditional reprobation. Find any election which does not imply reprobation, and I will gladly agree to it. But reprobation I can never agree to while I believe the Scripture to be of God; for it cannot be reconciled to the message of both the Old and New Testament. Impartially consider how it is possible to reconcile reprobation with the following Scriptures:

"Because thou hast eaten of the tree of which I commanded thee, saying, Thou shalt not eat of it; in the sweat of thy face shalt thou eat bread" (Genesis 3:17). That is, "The curse will not come because of any of My absolute decrees, but because of your sin."

"If thou doest well, shalt thou not be accepted? And if thou doest not well, sin lieth at the door" (Genesis 4:7). Only sin, not the decree of reprobation, keeps you from being accepted.

"Know that the Lord thy God, He is the faithful God, which keepeth covenant and mercy with them that love Him and keep His commandments to a thousand generations; and repayeth them that hate Him to their face, to destroy them. Wherefore, if ye hearken to these judgments, and keep, and do them, the Lord thy God shall keep unto thee the covenant which He sware unto thy fathers" (Deuteronomy 7:9, 12). "Behold, I set before you this day a blessing and a curse; a blessing, if you obey the commandments of the Lord your God; and a curse, if you will not obey" (11:26, 27, 28). "See, I have set before thee this day life and good, and death and evil; in that I command thee this day to love the Lord thy God to walk in His ways, and to keep His commandments, and the Lord thy God shall bless thee. But if thou wilt not hear, I denounce unto you this day, that ye shall surely perish. I call heaven and earth to record this day, that I have set before you life and death, blessing and cursing.

Therefore, choose life, that both thou and thy seed may live" (30:15, etc).

"And the Spirit of God came upon Azariah, and he said, The Lord is with you while ye be with Him; and if ye seek Him, He will be found of you; but if ye forsake Him He will forsake you" (2 Chronicles 15:1, 2). "After all that is come upon us, for our evil deeds, and for our great trespass; should we again break Thy commandments, wouldest Thou not be angry with us, until Thou hadst consumed us? "(Ezra 9:13, 14).

"Behold, God is mighty, and despiseth not any" (Job 36:5). How could He then reprobate any? "The Lord is good to all: And His tender mercies are over all His works" (Psalm 145:9).

"Turn you at my reproof: Behold, I will pour out My Spirit unto you. Because I have called, and ye refused; I have stretched out My hand, and no man regarded: I also will laugh at your calamity, I will mock when your fear cometh. Then shall they call upon Me, but I will not answer; they shall seek Me early, but they shall not find Me" (Proverbs 1:23, etc.). Why? Because of His decree? No; but "because they hated knowledge, and did not choose the fear of the Lord."

"I have spread out My hands all the day unto a rebellious people; a people that provoked Me to anger continually to My face. Therefore will I measure their former work into their bosom. Ye shall all bow down to the slaughter; because when I called, ye did not answer. Therefore, ye shall leave your name for a curse unto My chosen; for the Lord God shall slay thee, and call His servants by another name" (Isaiah 65:2, etc.).

"The soul that sinneth, it shall die. The son shall not bear" (eternally) "the iniquity of the father, neither shall the father bear the iniquity of the son. Have I any pleasure at all that the wicked should die? saith the Lord; and not that he should return from his ways, and live?" (Ezekiel 18:20, 23).

"Then began He to upbraid the cities wherein most of His mighty works were done, because they repented not. Woe unto thee, Chorazin! Woe unto thee, Bethsaida! For if the mighty works which were done in you had been done in Tyre and Sidon, they would have repented long ago in sackcloth and ashes." (What, even if they were not elected? And if those in Bethsaida had been elected, would they not have repented too?) "Therefore I say unto you, It shall be more tolerable for Tyre and Sidon in the day of judgment than for you. And thou, Capernaum, which art exalted unto heaven, shalt be brought down to hell. For if the mighty works which have been done in thee, had been done in Sodom, it would have remained until this day. But I say unto you, It shall be more tolerable for the land of Sodom in the day of judgment than for thee" (Matthew 11:20, etc.).

"The men of Nineveh shall rise in judgment with this generation, and shall condemn it: Because they repented at the preaching of Jonas; and, behold, a greater than Jonas is here" (12:41). But what point would there be to this, if the men of Nineveh were elected, and this generation of men were not?

"They which were called were not worthy" (22:8). They were shut out from the marriage of the Lamb. Why? Because "they would not come" (v. 3). "This is the condemnation, that light is come into the world, and men love" (or choose) "darkness rather than light" (John 3:19).

"Thy money perish with thee! Thou hast neither part nor lot in this matter; for thy heart is not right in the sight of God. Repent therefore of this thy wickedness, and pray God, if perhaps the thought of thine heart may be forgiven thee" (Acts 8:20, etc.). St. Peter had no thought of any absolute reprobation even in the case of Simon Magus.

"They are without excuse; because when they knew God, they glorified Him not as God — wherefore God also gave them up to uncleanness — who changed the truth of God into a lie. — For this cause God gave them up to vile affections. — As they did not like to retain God in their knowledge, God gave them over to a reprobate mind, to do those things which are not convenient" (Romans 1:20, etc.).

"Them that perish, because they received not the love of the truth, that they might be saved. And for this cause God shall send them strong delusion, to believe a lie; that they all might be damned who believed not the truth, but had pleasure in unrighteousness" (2 Thessolonians 2:10, etc.).

How will you reconcile reprobation with the following Scriptures, which declare God's willingness that all should be saved? "As many as ye shall find, bid" (invite) "to the marriage" (Matthew 22:9). "Go ye into all the world, and preach the gospel to every creature" (Mark 16:15).

"And when He came near, He beheld the city, and wept over it, saying, If thou hadst known, at least in this thy day, the things which belong unto thy peace!" (Luke 19:41, etc.) "These things I say, that ye may be saved" (John 5:34), to those who persecuted Him, and "sought to slay Him" (v. 16), and of whom He says, "Ye will not come unto Me, that ye may have life" (v. 40).

"God that made the world and all things therein — giveth to all life, and breath, and all things, and hath made of one blood all nations of men, for to dwell on all the face of the earth — That they should seek the Lord" (Acts 17:24). Observe that this was God's purpose in creating all nations on the earth.

"As by the offense of one, judgment came upon all men to condemnation; so by the righteousness of one the free gift came upon all men unto justification of life" (Romans 5:18). "The same Lord over all is rich" (in mercy) "unto all that call upon Him" (10:12).

"This is good and acceptable in the sight of God our Savior; who willeth all men to be saved" (1 Timothy 2:3, 4). "Who is the Savior of all men, especially of those that believe;" (6:10). That is, *intending* to save all, and *actually* saving believers. "If any man lack wisdom, let him ask of God, who giveth to all men liberally, and upbraideth not" (James 1:5). "The Lord is longsuffering toward us, not willing that any should perish, but that all should come to repentance" (2 Peter 3:9). "We have seen and do testify that the Father sent the Son to be the Savior of the world" (1 John 4:14).

How will you reconcile reprobation with the following Scriptures, which declare that Christ came to save all men; that He died for all; that He atoned for all, even for those that are ultimately lost?

"The Son of man is come to save that which is lost" (Matthew 18:11), without any limitation mentioned. "Behold the Lamb of God, which taketh away the sin of the world" (John 1:29). "God sent His Son into the world, that the world through Him might be saved" (3:17). "I came not" (now) "to judge the world, but to save the world" (12:47).

"Destroy not him with thy meat, for whom Christ died" (Romans 14:15). "Through thy knowledge shall thy weak brother perish, for whom Christ died" (1 Corinthians 8:11).

"We thus judge, that if one died for all, then were all dead; and that He died for all, that those who live should live unto Him which died for them" (2 Corinthians 5:14, etc.). Here you not only see that Christ died for all men, but also the purpose of His dying for them.

"Christ Jesus, who gave himself a ransom for all" (1 Timothy 2:6). "We see Jesus made lower than the angels, that He might taste death for every man" (Hebrews 2:9).

"There shall be false teachers among you, who shall privately bring in damnable heresies, even denying the Lord that bought them, and bring upon themselves swift destruction" (2 Peter 2:1). Here you see that He bought or redeemed even those that are lost, that bring swift destruction on themselves.

"If any man sin, we have an Advocate with the Father, Jesus Christ the righteous; and He is the propitiation for our sins and not for ours only, but also for the sins of the whole world" (1 John 2:1, 2).

You realize that these are only a few of the Scriptures which could be cited. But they are enough; and they require no comment. Taken in their clear, easy, and obvious sense, they prove that there cannot be any such thing as unconditional reprobation.

Do you think it will cut the knot to say, "If God could have justly refused all men" (which is to say, "If God could have justly reprobated all men"), "then He can justly refuse some." But could God have justly refused all men? I cannot find it in the Word of God. Therefore I reject it as an assertion completely unsupported by Holy Scripture.

In supposing what God might have done justly, you think of His justice separate from His other attributes, from His mercy in particular. But all His attributes are inseparably joined. They cannot be divided even for a moment. Therefore this whole argument stands on an unscriptural and impossible supposition.

But some object, "Hath not the potter power over his own clay?" Let us consider the context of these words. They are found in the ninth chapter of the Epistle to the Romans. The general intent of this epistle is to declare the eternal, unchangeable purpose or decree of God, which is, "He that believeth shall be saved: He that believeth not shall be damned." The Apostle proves, in the first three chapters, God's justice in condemning those that did not believe and the necessity of believing in order to have salvation, which he then confirms in the fourth by Abraham's example. In the first part of the fifth and in the sixth chapter, he describes the happiness and holiness of true believers. (The latter part of the fifth is a digression, concerning the extent of the benefits flowing from the death of Christ.) In the seventh, he shows in what sense believers in Christ are delivered from the law; and describes the bondage of those who are still under the law; that is, those who are convicted of sin, but not able to conquer it. In the eighth he again describes the joy-filled freedom of those who truly believe in Christ; and encourages them to suffer for the faith, for, "We know that all things work together for good to them that love God, to them that are called" (by the preaching of His word) "according to His purpose" (v. 28), or decree, which is unchanged from eternity, "He that believeth shall be saved." "For whom He did foreknow" as believing, "He also did predestinate to be conformed to the image of His Son. Moreover, whom He did predestinate, them He also called," by His word (so that term is usually intended in St. Paul's epistles); "and whom He called, them He also justified; and whom He justified, them He glorified." From there to the end of the chapter, he strongly encourages all those who had the love of God poured out in their hearts, to have a good hope that no sufferings would ever "be able to separate them from the love of God which is in Christ Jesus."

But the Apostle was aware of how deeply the Jews were offended by the whole theme of his doctrine, especially by his assertion that many Gentiles already partake of the great salvation, while many Jews fall short of it. Why? Because they would not receive it by faith. And whoever believes not cannot be saved; but, "whosoever believeth in Christ," whether Jew or Gentile, "shall not be ashamed" (vv. 30-33).

Those words, "Hath not the potter power over his own clay?" are part of St. Paul's answer to the objection that it was unjust for God to show mercy to the Gentiles while He withheld it from His own people. First, he simply denies this, saying, "God forbid!" Then he observes that, according to God's own words to Moses, God has a right to set the terms by which He will show mercy, which neither the will nor the power of man can alter (vv. 15, 16); and to withdraw His mercy from those who, like Pharaoh, will not comply with those terms (v. 17). And that accordingly, "He hath mercy on whom He will have mercy," those that truly believe; "and whom He will," obstinate unbelievers, He allows to be "hardened."

He adds, "Shall the thing formed say unto him that formed

it, Why hast thou made me thus?" Why have You made me capable of salvation only on those terms? But "Hath not" the great "Potter power over His own clay to make," or appoint, one kind of "vessels," that is, believers, "to honor, and" the others "to dishonor?" Does He not have a right to bestow eternal honor and dishonor on whatever terms He pleases? Especially, considering that He "endures, with much longsuffering," those "vessels of wrath," who had earlier "fitted" themselves "to destruction." There is then no more room to speak against God, for making His vengeance known on those vessels of wrath, than for "making known" His glorious love "on the vessels of mercy whom He had before," by their faith, "prepared for glory."

Neither our Lord, in the parable, nor St. Paul, in these words, saw God's sovereign power as the basis of unconditional reprobation. Beware that you go no further than you are authorized by them. Take care whenever you speak of these things to "speak as the oracles of God." If you do, you will never speak of the sovereignty of God except along with His other attributes. For the Scripture nowhere speaks of this one attribute as separate from the rest. Much less does it speak of the sovereignty of God alone deciding the eternal states of men. God acts according to the known rules of His justice and mercy; but never assigns His sovereignty as the reason why any man is punished with everlasting destruction.

Imagine yourself in this situation! Here you are, a sinner, convinced that you deserve the damnation of hell. Sorrow and fear have filled your heart. How will you be comforted? By the promises of God? But perhaps you have no share in them; for they belong only to the elect. By considering His love and tender mercy? But what are these to you if you are a reprobate? What basis can you have for even the least bit of hope? Only that it is possible that God's sovereign will may be on your side. God may possibly save you, simply because He chooses! What little encouragement this is to despairing sinners! I am afraid that "faith" rarely "cometh by hearing" this!

The sovereignty of God is never to be seen to supersede His justice. And unconditional reprobation (the clear consequence of unconditional election) flatly contradicts the scriptural account of God's justice. The Scripture describes God as the Judge of the earth. But how will God judge the world in justice if there is any decree of reprobation? What should those on His left hand be condemned for? For having done evil? They could not help it. God, you say, "of old ordained them to this condemnation." He "sold" them, you say, "to work wickedness," even from their mother's womb. Will He then condemn them for what they could not help? Will the Just, the Holy One of Israel, condemn millions of men to everlasting pain, only because their blood moved in their veins? They could not have escaped from sin without that grace which you say God had determined never to give them. And yet you suppose He will send them into eternal fire for not escaping from sin! That is, for not having that grace which God had decreed they should never have! What strange justice! What a picture you draw of the Judge of all the earth!

Rather, are they not condemned for not doing good, according to those solemn words of the great Judge, "Depart, ye cursed; for I was an hungered, and ye gave Me no meat; I was thirsty, and ye gave Me no drink; a stranger, and ye took Me not in; I was naked, and ye clothed Me not; sick, and in prison, and ye visited Me not. Then shall they answer." But how much better an answer you put into their mouths! Based on your supposition, they could say, "O Lord; still let us plead with You. Why do You condemn us for not doing good? Was it possible for us to do anything well? Did we ever abuse the power of doing good? We never received it, and You know that. Will You, the Holy One, the Just, condemn us for not doing what we never had the power to do? Will You condemn us for not casting down the stars from heaven? For not holding the winds in our fist? Why, it was as possible for us to do this, as to do any work acceptable in Your sight! O Lord, before You plunge us into everlasting fire, let us know how it was ever possible for us to escape the damnation of hell."

Or, how could they have escaped from inward sin, from evil desires, from unholy tempers and affections? Were they ever able to save their own souls, to rescue themselves from this inward hell? If so, they might be rightly blamed for their inaction, and would be left without excuse. But this was not the case; they never had the power to rescue themselves from the enemies within. Who is able to purify a corrupt heart; to bring a clean thing out of an unclean thing? Is mere man sufficient for this? Certainly not. Only God is. But what if He answers, "I will not, because I will not: Be thou unclean still?" Will God doom that man to the bottomless pit because of that uncleanness which he could not save himself from, and which God could have saved him from, but would not? If an earthly King were to execute justice such as this on his helpless subjects, one might expect the vengeance of the Lord to soon sweep him from the face of the earth.

Perhaps you will say, "They are not condemned for actual but for original sin." What do you mean by this? The inward corruption of our nature? If so, it has already been spoken of. Or do you mean the sin which Adam committed in paradise? That this is imputed to all men, I agree; even that it is the reason that "the whole creation groaneth and travaileth in pain together until now." But that any will be damned for this alone, I deny, until you show me where it is written.

Instead, should you not say that unbelief is the damning sin, and that those who are condemned in that day will be condemned, "because they believed not on the name of the only-begotten Son of God?" But could they believe? Was this faith not both the gift and the work of God in their souls? And was it not a gift which He had eternally decreed never to give them?

Was it not a work which He was determined never to work in their souls? Will these men be condemned because God would not work; because they did not receive what God would not give?

There is also a special difficulty here. You say that Christ did not die for these men. But if so, it was impossible for them to ever believe and be saved. For what is saving faith, but "a confidence in God through Christ, that loved me, and gave himself for me?" But did He love the reprobate, who was damned before he was born! There never was any object for his faith; there never was anything for him to believe. God himself could not make him believe that Christ atoned for his sins, without making him believe a lie.

And how will you reconcile reprobation with these clear passages: "Have I any pleasure at all that the wicked should die, saith the Lord God; and not that he should return from his ways and live? Cast away from you all your transgressions whereby ye have transgressed: For why will ye die, O house of Israel? For I have no pleasure in the death of him that dieth, saith the Lord: Wherefore, turn yourselves, and live ye" (Ezekiel 18:23, etc.). "As I live, saith the Lord God, I have no pleasure in the death of the wicked; but that the wicked turn from his way and live. Turn ye, turn ye from your evil ways: For why will ye die, O house of Israel?" (Ezekiel 33:11).

But perhaps you will say, "These ought to be balanced with other passages of Scripture, where this doctrine is as clearly affirmed as it is denied in these." I must answer very clearly: if this were true, we must give up the Scriptures altogether; nor would the infidels so readily call the Bible a "cunningly-devised fable." But it is not true. To uproot reprobation, and all of its connected doctrines, God explicitly declares these three things in His word:

(1) "Christ died for all," (2 Corinthians 5:14);

(2) "He is the propitiation for the sins of the whole world" (1 John 2:2), which is the *consequence* of His dying for all; and,

(3) "He died for all, that they should not live unto themselves, but unto Him which died for them" (2 Corinthians 5:15); that they might be saved from their sins, which is the *purpose* of His dying for them.

Now show me Scripture where God declares in equally clear terms that Christ did not die "for all," but only for some, and that Christ is not "the propitiation for the sins of the whole world." There are none. Nor is it possible to evade the force of those mentioned above, except by supplying in sheer number that which is lacking in weight; by heaping many texts together, by which (though none of them speak directly to the point) the proponents of that opinion dazzle the eyes of the unwary.

What a portrayal of the sincerity of God this doctrine gives in a thousand declarations like these: "O that there were such an heart in them, that they would fear Me, and keep My commandments always, that it might be well with them, and with their children forever!" (Deuteronomy 5:29). "My people would not hear My voice, and Israel would not obey Me. So I gave them up unto their own hearts' lusts, and let them follow their own imaginations. O that My people would have hearkened unto Me! For if Israel had walked in My ways, I should soon have put down their enemies, and turned My hand against their adversaries" (Psalm 81:11, etc.). And all this time you suppose God had unchangeably ordained that there never should be "such a heart in them!" That it should never be possible for the people He seemingly lamented over, to obey Him!

How clear the reasoning of Dr. Watts is on this subject: "It is very hard indeed, to vindicate the sincerity of God or of His Son, in Their universal offers of grace and salvation to men, and Their sending ministers with such messages and invitations to accept mercy, if there is not at least a conditional pardon and salvation provided for them. His ministers, since they do not know the outcome of things, may be sincere in offering salvation to all persons, according to their general commission, 'Go ye into all the world, and preach the gospel to every creature.' But how can God or Christ be sincere in sending them with this commission, to offer His grace to all men, if God has not provided such grace for all men, even conditionally?"

Our blessed Lord commands and invites "all men everywhere to repent." He calls everyone. He sends His ambassadors to "preach the gospel to every creature." He himself "preached deliverance to the captives," without limitation. But is He standing at the prison doors, with keys in His hands, continually inviting the prisoners to come out, commanding them to accept that invitation, appealing to every motive which can possibly influence them; adding the most precious promises if they obey, and the most dreadful threats if they do not; and all this time is He absolutely determined never to open the doors for them? Even while He is crying, "Come ye, come ye, from that evil place: For why will ye die, O house of Israel!" "Why?" one of them might reply, "Because we cannot help ourselves; and You will not help us. It is not in our power to break the gates of brass, and it is not Your pleasure to open them. We must die because it is not Your will to save us." Alas! my brothers, what kind of sincerity is this which you ascribe to God our Savior?

So we see that election and reprobation have little agreement with the truth and sincerity of God! But they agree least of all with the scriptural account of His love and goodness. His love extends even to those who neither love nor fear Him. He is good even to the evil and the unthankful. For "the Lord is loving to every man, and His mercy is over all His works." But how is God good or loving to a reprobate, or one that is not elected? You cannot say that he is an object of the love or goodness of God, regarding his eternal state. After all, this is one whom He created, says Mr. Calvin clearly, "to live a reproach, and die everlastingly." Surely no one can imagine that the goodness of God is even remotely concerned with this man's eternal state. But it is said, "God is good to him in this world." What? When because of God's unchangeable decree, it would have been better for this man never to have been born? Even the gifts of God, such as food, clothing, and other comforts are not blessings to him. At the price he will pay for them, every one of them is a curse. For every moment's pleasure which he now enjoys, he will suffer more than a thousand years of torment, for the smoke of that pit ascends forever. God knew this would be the result of whatever he would enjoy. It was His very purpose in giving him those enjoyments. So that, by all of these, He is only fattening the ox for slaughter. And the common grace that he has was not given for the purpose of saving his soul; or for doing him any good at all; but only for restraining him from hurting the elect. Far from doing him good, this grace only increases his damnation. "And God knows this," you say, "and designed it should; it was one great end for which He gave it!" It may properly be termed, "damning grace;" since it is not only damning in its results, but also in its intention. He received it from God for that very purpose, that he would receive a greater damnation. So I ask, how is God good or loving to this man, regarding either life or eternity?

Does this love not make your blood run cold? Does it not cause the ears of him that hears of it to tingle? Can you fathom that the loving, merciful God ever dealt this way with any soul which He made? But you must believe this if you believe unconditional election.

But you are afraid that if you do not allow election, you must allow free will, and rob God of His glory in man's salvation. I answer:

(1) Many of the greatest proponents of election deny the

logical consequence of it, the impossibility of free will, and do not agree that even man's natural free will is contrary to God's glory. They assert that every man has a measure of natural free will. So, the Assembly of Divines (representing the Calvinists both in England and Scotland) writes, "God hath endued the will of man with that natural liberty that is neither forced, nor, by an absolute necessity of nature, determined to do good or evil" (Chap. 9). And they affirm this of man in his fallen state even before he receives the grace of God.

(2) But I do not defend this kind of free will. Natural free will, in mankind's fallen state, I do not understand. I only assert that there is a measure of free will that is supernaturally restored to every man, together with that supernatural light which "enlightens every man that cometh into the world." But as to whether this free will is natural or not, some object, saying, "If man has any free will, God cannot have the whole glory of his salvation;" or, "It is more for the glory of God to save man by an irresistible power, than to save him as a free agent, with an ability to either accept or resist His grace."

But although God does not do the entire work without man's working together with Him, God may still have all the glory. The very power to "work together with Him" was from God. Therefore He receives all the glory. Has experience not taught you this? Have you not often felt power either to resist or yield to the grace of God when facing a particular temptation? And when you have yielded to "work together with Him," did you not find it still possible to give Him all the glory? So both experience and Scripture make it clear to every impartial mind that, although man has the freedom to work or not "work together with God," God may still have the whole glory of his salvation.

And if you say, "We ascribe to God alone the whole glory of our salvation;" I answer, so do we. If you add, "But we affirm that God alone does the whole work, without man's working at all;" in one sense, we allow this as well. We agree that it is the work of God alone to justify, to sanctify, and to glorify; which, taken together, make up the whole of salvation. But we cannot agree that man is totally unable to "work together with God;" or that God is the sole worker of our salvation, in a sense that excludes man's working entirely. This I dare not say; for it is so obviously contrary to Scripture; for the Scripture is clear, that (once having received power from God) we are to "work out our own salvation;" and that (after the work of God is begun in our souls) we are "workers together with Him."

Your objection, proposed in another form, is this: "It is not so much for the glory of God, to save man as a free agent, having received a capacity of either concurring with, or resisting, His grace; as to save him by a power which he cannot possibly resist." But how is it more for the glory of God to save man irresistibly, than to save him as a free agent, by grace which he may either concur with or resist? I am afraid this is a confused, unscriptural idea of "the glory of God." The Scripture frequently speaks of the glory of God as the visible display of His essential glory, of His eternal power and godhead, and of His glorious attributes, especially His justice, mercy, and truth. And it is in this sense alone that the glory of God is said to be advanced by man. Now this is the point which you must prove: "That it more clearly shows the glorious attributes of God, especially His justice, mercy, and truth, to save man irresistibly, than to save him by grace which he may either concur with, or resist."

Let us see then whether the plan of free will or the plan of reprobation is more for the glory of God, for the display of His glorious attributes, for the manifestation of His wisdom, justice, and mercy, to the sons of men.

First, His wisdom. If man is to some extent free; if, by that light which "lighteneth every man that comes into the world," there is "set before him life and death, good and evil;" then how gloriously does the wisdom of God appear in the whole system of man's salvation! Being willing that all men should be saved, yet not willing to force them into it; willing that men should be saved, yet not as trees or stones, but as men, as rational creatures, endued with understanding to discern what is good, and freedom either to accept or refuse it. How marvelously He tailors His operations to His plan, "the counsel of His will!" His first step is to enlighten the understanding to distinguish between good and evil. He adds many inward convictions to this, which every man on earth has often felt. At other times He gently nudges their wills, He draws and woos them, as it were, to walk in the light. He places good desires into their hearts, even though they may know not the source. He does this even with those who do not have His written word. But what wisdom is displayed in this, if man is to some degree a free agent! To save man, as man; to set life and death before him, and then persuade (not force) him to choose life. According to this grand purpose of God, a perfect rule is first set before him, to serve as a "lantern to his feet, and a light in all his paths." This is offered to him in the form of a law, with the most glorious rewards for them that obey, and the severest penalties for them that break it. To reclaim these violators, God tries every avenue of their souls. Sometimes He appeals to their understanding, showing them the foolishness of their sins; sometimes to their affections, tenderly scolding them for their ingratitude, and even bending low to ask, "What could I have done for" you (consistent with My eternal purpose, not to force you) "which I have not done?" He sometimes threatens, "Except ye repent, ye shall all likewise perish;" sometimes promises, "Your sins and your iniquities will I remember no more." What wisdom there is in all of this, if man can indeed choose life or death! But if every man is eternally assigned to either heaven or hell before his birth, where is the wisdom in this; of dealing with him as if he were free, when he is not? How can this dispensation of God help a reprobate? What are promises or threats, or scoldings or reprimands to the citizen of hell? Only an empty farce, fake scowls, and noisy words that mean nothing? Where is the wisdom in this? What purpose does this system serve? If you say, "To ensure his damnation;" why was that needed, since this was ensured before the foundation of the world? Let all of mankind judge which of these plans is more for the glory of God's wisdom!

In the same way it displays His love, if it is given to one out of every hundred of His creatures, with no regard for the rest. Let the ninety-nine reprobates perish without mercy. It is enough for Him to love and save that one elect. But why will He have mercy on this one alone, and leave the rest to inevitable destruction? "He will, because He will!" I ask, what would the universal voice of mankind say of a man that would act in this way? That he, being able to deliver millions of men from death with a single breath of his mouth, should refuse to save more than one in a hundred, and say, "I will not, because I will not!" How then do you exalt the mercy of God in this? What a strange commentary this is on His own word, that "His mercy is over all His works!" I appeal to every impartial mind to consider how the mercy of God would be most gloriously displayed: in saving a few by His irresistible power, and leaving all the rest without help, to perish eternally; or, in offering salvation to every creature, actually saving all that accept it, and doing for the rest all that infinite wisdom, almighty power, and boundless love can do, without forcing them to be saved. I appeal to every mind unblinded by prejudice to consider which of these plans most glorifies the mercy of God.

I do not deny the other attributes of God, such as His sovereignty, unchangeableness, and faithfulness. But in deciding the eternal states of men, it is clear that not sovereignty alone, but also justice, mercy, and truth hold the reins. In this, the Governor of heaven and earth acts only as these direct. This is His eternal and irresistible will, as He has revealed it to us, declaring in the strongest terms, adding His oath to His word, and, because He could swear by none greater, swearing by himself, "As I live, saith the Lord God, I have no pleasure in the death of him that dieth." The death of him that dies can never be resolved into God's pleasure or sovereign will. There is no scriptural proof that God ever acted merely as sovereign in eternally condemning any soul.

What about the case of Pharoah? We read, "When Pharaoh saw that there was respite" (after he was delivered from the plague of frogs), "he hardened his heart, and hearkened not unto them" (Exodus 8:15). Also after the plague of flies, "Pharaoh hardened his heart at this time also, neither would he let the people go" (v. 32). Again, "When Pharaoh saw that the rain and the hail were ceased, he sinned yet more, and hardened his heart, he and his servants" (9:34). After God had given him all this space to repent, and had rebuked him for his stubborn refusal to repent, in those solemn words, "How long wilt thou refuse to humble thyself before Me?" (10:3), is it any surprise that God then "hardened his heart," that is, permitted Satan to harden it? What if He ultimately withdrew his softening grace completely, and "gave him up to a reprobate mind?"

Esau's case is different. We have an account of how he despised and sold his birthright, then how he was wronged by his brother Jacob at the time of Isaac's blessing. Realizing this, "Esau cried with a great and exceeding bitter cry, and said unto his father, Bless me, even me also, O my father!" (v. 34). But "he found no place," says the Apostle, "for repentance," for recovering the blessing, "though he sought it carefully with tears." "Thy brother," said Isaac, "hath taken away thy blessing: I have blessed him, yea, and he shall be blessed." So all Esau's sorrow and tears could not recover his birthright and the blessing connected to it. Yet there is great reason to hope that Esau (as well as Jacob) is now in Abraham's bosom. Although for a time "he hated Jacob," and afterward came against him "with four hundred men," probably intending to take revenge for his injuries, when they met, "Esau ran and embraced him, and fell on his neck and kissed him." God had changed his heart so thoroughly! And why should we doubt that this change continued?

You can base no solid objection to this on St. Paul's words in the Epistle to the Romans: "It was said unto her, The elder shall serve the younger. As it is written, Jacob have I loved, but Esau have I hated" (9:12, 13). It is clear that both of these verses relate, not to Jacob and Esau individually, but to their descendants; the Israelites arising from Jacob, and the Edomites arising from Esau. Only in this sense did "the elder" (Esau) "serve the younger;" not personally (for Esau never served Jacob), but in his posterity. The descendants of the elder brother served the descendants of the younger. This, then, is no instance of a man being condemned by the sovereign will of God alone.

We also affirm the unchangeableness of God. "In Him is no variableness, neither shadow of turning."

(1) The Scripture teaches that God is unchangeable with regard to His decrees. But what decrees? The same ones that He has commanded to be preached to every creature: "He that believeth shall be saved; he that believeth not shall be damned."

(2) The Scripture teaches that God is unchangeable with regard to His love and hatred. But how? God unchangeably loves righteousness, and hates sin. He unchangeably loves faith, and unchangeably hates unbelief. Therefore He unchangeably loves the righteous, and hates those who walk in sin. He unchangeably loves those who believe, and hates obstinate unbelievers. So the scriptural account of God's

> unchangeableness with regard to His decrees is this: He has unchangeably decreed to save holy believers, and to condemn obstinate, unrepentant unbelievers. And, according to Scripture, His unchangeableness of affection pertains to tempers; and to persons only as those tempers are found in them. Let the Scripture be allowed to establish the objects of the unchangeableness of God.

The faithfulness of God is that He will do what He has promised. But let us find in the Word of God, to whom the promises of life and immortality are made. It is, "To Abraham and his seed;" that is, to those who "walk in the steps of that faith of their father Abraham." The gospel promises are made to those who believe, as believers. To these the faithful God has made a guarantee that He will do what He has spoken. "He will fulfill His covenant and promise which He hath made to a thousand generations;" which means that, "The Lord will give grace and glory; and no good thing will He withhold from them that live a godly life."

To examine thoroughly whether this covenant between God and man is unconditional or conditional, let us go back as far as Abraham, the father of the faithful; to see what kind of covenant it was which God made with him; and whether any reason is given for God's unique blessing of Abraham and all the nations of the earth in him. The first mention of the covenant between God and him occurs in Genesis 15:18: "The same day the Lord made a covenant with Abram, saying, Unto thy seed will I give this land." But this is more explicitly related in chapter 17: "The Lord appeared unto Abram, and said unto him, I am the almighty God; walk before Me, and be thou perfect. And I will make My covenant between Me and thee, and will multiply thee exceedingly. And Abram fell on his face: And God talked with him, saying, As for Me, behold, My covenant is with thee, and thou shalt be a father of many nations. Neither shall thy name any more be called Abram, but thy name shall be Abraham; for a father of many nations have I made thee. And I will establish My covenant between Me and thee, and thy seed after thee, for an everlasting covenant, to be a God unto thee, and to thy seed after thee. Every man-child among you shall be circumcised; — it shall be a token of the covenant betwixt Me and you. The uncircumcised man-child shall be cut off; he hath broken my covenant" (17:1, etc.). So we see that this original covenant, though everlasting, was conditional, and man's failure to meet the condition cleared God.

We have St. Paul's account of this covenant of God with Abraham, in the fourth chapter of Romans: "Abraham," he said, "believed God, and it was counted to him for righteousness." (This was shortly before God established His covenant with him, and is related in Genesis 15:6.) "And he received the sign of circumcision, a seal of the righteousness of the faith which he had yet being uncircumcised, that he might as the father of all them that believe, though they be not circumcised, that righteousness might be imputed unto them also; and the father of circumcision" (that is, of those who are circumcised) "to them who are not of the circumcision only, but also walk in the steps of that faith of our father Abraham, which he had being yet uncircumcised" (Romans 4:3, etc.) Now, if these words do not express a conditional covenant, none can.

The nature and basis of this covenant of God with Abraham is further explained: "And the Lord said, Shall I hide from Abraham that thing which I do, seeing all the nations of the earth shall be blessed in him? For I know him, that he will command his children and his household after him: And they shall keep the way of the Lord, to do justice and judgment; that the Lord may bring unto Abraham that which He hath spoken of him" (Genesis 18:17, etc.). Does God say here, "I will do it, because I will"? Not at all. The reason is clearly stated: "All nations shall be blessed in him; for he will command his children, and they shall keep the way of the Lord." The reason is stated again (22:16, etc.): "By myself have I sworn, saith the Lord, because thou hast done this thing, and hast not withheld thy son, thine only son: That in blessing I will bless thee; — And in thy seed shall all the nations of the earth be blessed;" that is, the Messiah will arise from you, "because thou hast obeyed my voice." This is declared again: "And the Lord appeared unto Isaac, and said, — Sojourn in this land, and I will be with thee, and bless thee: For unto thee, and unto thy seed, — I will perform the oath which I sware unto Abraham thy father, — in thy seed shall all nations of the earth be blessed: Because that Abraham obeyed My voice, and kept My charge, My commandments, My statutes, and My laws" (Genesis 26:2, etc.).

This covenant, made to Abraham and his seed, is mentioned again: "And the Lord called unto Moses, saying, Thus shalt thou say to the house of Jacob, and tell the children of Israel: Ye have seen what I did to the Egyptians, and how I bare you on eagles' wings, and brought you unto myself. Now therefore, if ye will obey My voice indeed, and keep My covenant, then ye shall be a peculiar treasure unto Me above all people" (Exodus 19:3, etc.).

According to the spirit of this covenant, made to Abraham and his seed, God afterward declares, "If ye walk in My statutes, and keep My commandments, and do them; then I will establish My covenant with you, and I will be your God, and ye shall be My people. But if ye will not hearken unto Me, so that ye will not do all My commandments, but that ye break My covenant; I will set My face against you, and I will avenge the quarrel of My covenant. Yet if they shall confess their iniquity, and if their uncircumcised hearts be humbled; then will I remember My covenant with Jacob, and also My covenant with Isaac, and also My covenant with Abraham will I remember" (Leviticus 26:3, etc.). Therefore, the covenant with Abraham was conditional, as were those God made with his descendants.

And I find no promise in Scripture, "that none who once believes shall ultimately fall." Yet this opinion is so pleasing, so agreeable to flesh and blood, so suitable to whatever part of the natural mind that remains in those who have tasted the grace of God, that I see nothing short of the mighty power of God which can keep anyone who hears it from accepting it. But it still lacks one thing: clear, scriptural proof.

Arguments from experience alone will never settle this issue. They can only prove that our Lord is exceedingly patient; that He is unwilling that any believer should be lost; that He bears very long with all their foolishness, waiting to be gracious and to heal their backsliding; and that He does actually bring back many lost sheep who seemed irrecoverable. Still, none of this is proof that no believer can fall from grace.

If we produce many examples of those who were once strong in their faith and are now more unbelieving than ever, some will say, "But they will be brought back; they will not die in their sins," or, "They were only hypocrites; they never had true faith." Therefore, Scripture alone can determine this question; and Scripture does determine it, so that we only need to look at a few texts, with some short reflections upon them.

First, evidence that one who has the faith which produces a good conscience may ultimately fall appears from the words of St. Paul to Timothy: "War a good warfare; holding faith and a good conscience; which some having put away concerning faith have made shipwreck" (1 Timothy 1:18, 19). Consider that,

(1) These men once had the faith that produces "a good conscience;" which they must have had, or else they could not have "put it away."
(2) They made shipwreck of their faith, which implies the total and final loss of it.

But one may object: "Men may have a good conscience, in some sense, without true faith." I allow it, in a restrained, limited sense; but not a good conscience, simply speaking. But that is what the Apostle speaks of here, and that which he urges Timothy to "hold fast." Therefore, one who has the faith that produces a good conscience may ultimately fall.

Second, those who are grafted into the good olive tree, the spiritual, invisible church, may ultimately fall. For the Apostle said: "Some of the branches are broken off, and thou art grafted in among them, and with them partakest of the root and fatness of the olive tree. Be not high-minded, but fear: If God spared not the natural branches, take heed lest He spare not thee. Behold the goodness and severity of God! On them which fell, severity; but toward thee, goodness, if thou continue in His goodness: Otherwise thou shalt be cut off" (Romans 11:17, etc.). We can see here that,

(1) The persons spoken to were actually ingrafted into the olive tree.
(2) This olive tree is not merely the outward, visible church, but the invisible one, consisting of holy believers. For the text says, "If the root be holy, so are the branches." And "because of unbelief they were broken off, and thou standest by faith."
(3) Those holy believers were still liable to be cut off from the invisible church into which they were grafted. It remains, then, that those who are grafted into the spiritual, invisible church, may ultimately fall.

Third, those who are branches of Christ, the true vine, may ultimately fall from grace. For our blessed Lord himself said: "I am the true vine, and My Father is the husbandman. Every branch in Me that beareth not fruit, He taketh away. I am the vine, ye are the branches. If a man abide not in Me, he is cast forth as a branch, and is withered; and men gather them, and cast them into the fire, and they are burned" (John 15:1, etc.). Here we may observe that,

(1) The persons spoken of were in Christ, branches of the true vine.
(2) Some of these branches "abide not" in Christ, but "the Father taketh them away."
(3) The branches which "abide not" are "cast forth," cast out from Christ and His church.
(4) They are not only "cast forth and withered," but also "cast into the fire," and, "They are burned." It is not possible for words to declare more strongly that those who are branches of the true vine may ultimately fall. It remains then, that true believers, who are branches of the true vine, may still ultimately fall.

Fourth, those who know Christ, and by that knowledge have escaped the pollutions of the world, may fall back into those pollutions, and be lost eternally. For the Apostle Peter says, "If, after they have escaped the pollutions of the world, through the knowledge of the Lord and Savior Jesus Christ" (the only possible way of escaping them), "they are entangled again therein and overcome, the latter end is worse with them than the beginning" (2 Peter 2:20). Therefore, those who, by the inward knowledge of Christ, have escaped the pollutions of the world, may fall back into those pollutions, and be lost eternally.

Fifth, those who see the light of the glory of God in the face of Jesus Christ, and who have been made partakers of the Holy Spirit, of the witness and the fruits of the Spirit, may so fall away from God as to be lost eternally. For the writer to the Hebrews says: "It is impossible for those who were once enlightened, and have tasted of the heavenly gift, and were made partakers of the Holy Spirit, if they fall away, to renew them again to repentance; seeing they crucify to themselves the Son of God afresh, and put Him to an open shame" (6:4-6). Must not every unprejudiced person see that the expressions used here are so clear that they cannot, without obvious twisting, be understood to mean anything other than true believers?

Sixth, those who live by faith may fall away from God, and be lost eternally. For the Apostle says: "The just shall live by faith: But if any man draw back, My soul shall have no pleasure in him" (Hebrews 10:38). "The just" (the justified person, the only one of whom this can be said) "shall live by faith;" will live the life which is hidden with Christ in God; and if he endures to the end, will live with God forever. "But if any man draw back," says the Lord, "My soul shall have no pleasure in him;" that is, "I will utterly cast him off." And accordingly, the drawing back spoken of here is rendered in the verse immediately following, "drawing back to perdition." Can any man draw back from faith who never came to it in the first place? It remains, then, that those who live by faith may fall away from God, and be lost eternally.

Seventh, those who are sanctified by the blood of the covenant may fall, so as to be lost eternally. For again the Apostle says: "If we sin willfully, after we have received the knowledge of the truth, there remaineth no more sacrifice for sin; but a certain fearful looking for of judgment and fiery indignation, which shall devour the adversaries. He that despised Moses' law died without mercy under two or three witnesses. Of how much sorer punishment shall he be thought worthy, who hath trodden under foot the Son of God, and hath counted the blood of the covenant, wherewith he was sanctified, an unholy thing?" (Heb. 10:26-29).

It is undeniably clear that,

(1) The person mentioned here was once sanctified by the blood of the covenant.

(2) Sometime afterward, he trod under foot the Son of God by known, willful sin. And,

(3) He, in doing this, incurred a sorer punishment than death; that is, everlasting death. Therefore, those who are sanctified by the blood of the covenant may be lost eternally.

If you imagine these texts are not sufficient to prove that a true believer may ultimately fall, I will offer a few more for your consideration:

"Ye are the salt of the earth. But if the salt have lost its savor, wherewith shall it be salted? It is thenceforth good for nothing, but to be cast out, and trodden under foot of men" (Matthew 5:13). "And then shall many be offended; and the love of many shall wax cold. But he that shall endure to the end, the same shall be saved" (24:10, etc.).

"Take heed to yourselves," you that believe, "lest at any time your heart be overcharged with the cares of this life, and so that day come upon you unawares:" (Luke 21:34). This clearly implies that otherwise they would not be "accounted worthy to stand before the Son of man." "If ye continue in My word, then are ye My disciples indeed; and ye shall know the truth, and the truth shall make you free" (John 8:31, 32). "I keep my body under; lest by any means, when I have preached to others, I myself should be a castaway" (1 Corinthians 9:27). "Our fathers did all eat the same spiritual meat, and did all drink the same spiritual drink: For they drank of that spiritual rock that followed them: And that rock was Christ. But with many of them God was not well pleased: For they were overthrown in the wilderness. Now, these things were for our examples: Wherefore let him that thinketh he standeth take heed lest he fall" (10:3, etc.).

"Ye are fallen from grace" (Galatians 5:4). "We are made partakers of Christ, if we hold the beginning of our confidence steadfast unto the end" (Hebrews 3:14). "Beware lest ye also, being led away with the error of the wicked, fall from your own steadfastness" (2 Peter 3:17). "Look to yourselves, that we lose not the things which we have wrought" (2 John 8). "Hold that fast which thou hast, that no man take thy crown" (Revelation 3:11). And, to conclude: "So likewise shall My heavenly Father do also unto you, if ye from your hearts forgive not every one his brother their trespasses" (Matthew 18:35). That is, He will take back the pardon He had given, and give you over to the tormentors.

I declare simply what I find in the Bible, neither more nor less; that salvation is purchased for every child of man, and actually given to everyone that believes. If you call this conditional salvation, God made it so from the beginning of the world; and He has declared it to be so, at many times and in many ways; long ago by Moses and the Prophets, and in later times by Christ and His Apostles.

Do you object, "Then I never can be saved; for I can meet none of the conditions; for I can do nothing"? Neither can I, nor can any man under heaven, without the grace of God. "But I can do all things through Christ strengthening me." And He has strengthened, and will continue to strengthen you more and more, if you do not willfully resist until you quench His Spirit.

Do you object, "But all saving grace is irresistible." But this doctrine is not only unsupported by Scripture, it is clearly contrary to it. How will you reconcile it with the following texts:

"He sent to call them, and they would not come" (Matthew 23:3, etc). "He could do no mighty works there, because of their unbelief" (Mark 6:5, 6). "The Pharisees and lawyers made void the counsel of God against themselves" (Luke 7:30). "O Jerusalem, Jerusalem, how often would I have gathered thy children, and ye would not!" (13:34). "Ye do always resist the Holy Spirit: As your fathers did, so do ye" (Acts 7:51). "Ye put it from you, and judge yourselves unworthy of eternal life" (13:46). "While it is called today, harden not your heart. Take heed lest there be in any of you an evil heart of unbelief, departing from the living God" (Hebrews 3:8, 12). "See that ye refuse not Him that speaketh" (12:25).

I only offer here a sampling of the countless verses of Scripture that could be produced on this subject. Why will you cling to an opinion not only unsupported by, but contrary to both reason and Scripture? Also remember that you must consider the doctrine of irresistible grace only as it stands in connection to unconditional reprobation. That millstone hangs around the neck of your whole hypothesis.

This is my greatest objection to the doctrine of reprobation, or unconditional election (which is the same thing). I know that it is an error; because, if it were true, the Scriptures must be false. But it is not only for this reason that I oppose it so earnestly. I reject it because it is an error of such terrible consequence to men's souls. By its nature, it tends to thwart the inward work of God in every stage of its progress.

For example, is a man careless and unconcerned, completely dead in trespasses and sins? Then urge him to be concerned for his soul. "Why should I have concern?" he says. "Whatever must be, must be. If I am elect, I must be saved; and if I am not, I must be damned." The reasoning is so obvious and natural. It accomplishes nothing to say, "But men can abuse any doctrine." Of course they can. But this is not abusing yours. It is the obvious, natural use of it. The result is clear and undeniable. Is a man a little serious and thoughtful now and then, though generally cold or lukewarm? Then urge him to stir up the gift that is in him; to work out his salvation with fear and trembling. "Alas!" he says, "what can I do? You know that man can do nothing." If you reply, "But your problem is that you are not willing to be saved;" he will say, "This may be true, but God will make me willing in the day of His power." So, waiting for irresistible grace, he falls into an even deeper sleep. Now see him some time later, when he is thoroughly awakened; when fear and trembling have taken hold of him. How will you comfort him then? If you are able to at all, it is by applying the promises of God. But there is a fence on every side of these promises, keeping him out. "These," he says, "belong to the elect only. And I am not one of them. I can never be; for His decree is unchangeable. Therefore, God's promises mean nothing to me."

Suppose one has already had a taste of God's good word, and the powers of the world to come. Being justified by faith, he has peace with God. Sin has no authority over him. But eventually, thinking he can fall into sin without being ultimately lost, he grows more and more careless, until he falls again into the sin from which he had once escaped. As soon as you see that he is entangled again and overcome, you urge him not to harden his heart any more, lest his final condition be worse than the first. "How can that be?" he says, "Once in grace, always in grace; and I am sure I was in grace at one time." So he sins on, and sleeps on, until he wakes up in hell.

Seeing these sad examples day after day, this dreadful havoc which the devil makes of souls, especially of those who had begun well, by means of this anti-scriptural doctrine, forces me to oppose it. The doctrine of absolute predestination naturally leads to the chambers of death.

Brothers, would you lie for the cause of God? I am persuaded you would not. Know then that in this we are the same. I speak truthfully, particularly of those who were recently converted to your opinion. I have known many of these; but I have not known one in ten in whom it did not quickly work some of the effects I have just described. And I have known of only one among them all who, after the closest and most impartial observation, did not show, within one year, that his heart was changed for the worse.

I know that you cannot easily believe this. But whether you believe it or not, you believe as I do that without holiness no man will see the Lord. Let us then, at the very least, join in this, in declaring the nature of inward holiness, and testifying to the need for it. Let us all join in tearing away the broken reeds in which so many rest, without either inward or outward holiness, which they idly trust will take its place. As far as it is possible, let us join in destroying the works of the devil, and in setting up the kingdom of God on the earth, in promoting righteousness, peace, and joy in the Holy Spirit. Of whatever opinion or denomination we are, we must serve either God or the devil. If we serve God, our agreement is far greater than our difference. Therefore, as far as we can, setting aside that difference, let us unite in destroying the works of the devil, in bringing as many as we can from the power of darkness into the kingdom of God's dear Son. And let us help each other to value more and more the glorious grace by which we stand, and to grow day by day in that grace and in the knowledge of our Lord Jesus Christ.

The Editor

Stephen Gibson served for five years as professor and academic dean at Kiev Wesley Bible College, six years at Union Bible College, and several years at various Christian schools.

He is adjunct professor at God's Bible School and College and at Allegheny Wesleyan Bible College

He graduated from Union Bible College with a Th.B., from Wesley Biblical Seminary with an M.A. in Theology, from Louisiana Baptist University with an M.A. in Biblical Studies, and from Grace Theological Seminary with a D.Min.

Books written include *The Prosperity Prophets* (English & Russian) and *Steps of Grace* (Russian).

Books edited include *I Believe: Fundamentals of the Christian Faith* and *Wesley for the 21st Century*.

The editor may be contacted at globalseminary@cs.com.

This book is available in the Russian language. For information, contact the editor at globalseminary@cs.com.